Just *Imagine*:

A New Life on an Old Boat

by

Michelle Caffrey

Just *Imagine*:
A New Life on an Old Boat
All rights reserved.
Copyright © 2006 by Michelle L. Caffrey

A Barge & Breakfast Imprint

On demand manufacturing and distribution is by Lulu.com and their affiliate Ingram Industries and its retail bookstore customers.

ISBN
10 digit: 1-4116-7141-4
13 digit: 978-1-4116-7141-6

For Paul: my partner, my best friend and my life's inspiration.

Acknowledgements

I'm grateful for the help of the Internet Writer's Workshop members especially Gary Presley, Dawn Goldsmith, Carol Moore, and my book's midwife, Peggy Vincent. Thanks for all the "crits."

I wish to thank Roger Van Dyken for his support of both my boating and my writing; thanks to Richard Goodwin whose wonderful series, *Barging through Europe*, provided us with the original inspiration for this adventure.

I wish to acknowledge Sandy King for her diligent offsite backups of this book for years, taking my Word files from wherever I was on the globe.

I'm indebted to my family and friends who've supported me over the years, both in my chosen barging career and my writing: our daughter Sue for her understanding of our wanderlust, and Paul III, without whom we could have never done what we've done.

I'd like to thank Bourgogne Marine, and our port buddies there, Jim Marett for his chartering advice, and Rosie Weidner, who read and reread my work as we sat on *Imagine*'s deck. Keep on writing, Petal.

I wish to acknowledge all of our guests and friends from the early years. Without their support, we couldn't have made our new life work, especially Suzanne Sanders, Margaret Dempster, Renee Freireich, Marsha Olian, Holly and Doug Bruce, Greg and Julie Hillenbrand, Masha and Svetlana Alexander, Joel and Ngam Chapman. Thank you Jo Ann Hay and Richard Whitman for honoring us with your wedding on board, and Debbie Visner for your support all these years.

Most of all, I wish to thank all of our guests over the years who've made us one of the most successful chartering businesses in France. As one of you wrote in our guest book, "We arrived as guests and left as friends."

Contents

Map of the first half of our maiden voyage

Grave to Chalons en Champagne

Map of the second half of the voyage

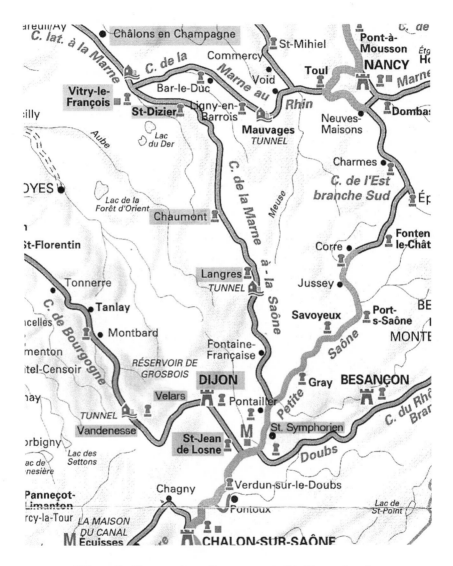

Vitry-le-Francois to homeport, St. Symphorien

"Imagine" was the epitome of our partnership and our love. John and I made the most beautiful music together.

-Yoko Ono

1 - Learning Curve

September 1999

A key to a vital life is an eagerness to learn and a willingness to change.

-Maryanne N. Hershey '97

The day before my forty-ninth birthday I stood at the helm of a 60-ton barge, about to enter my first lock on the Canal de Briare. My husband, Paul, rode on the front deck, ready to work the lines for me. Appearing oh so casual, he pretended to study the landscape. Roger Van Dyken, my instructor, hovered just off my left shoulder. He was an owner of this boat, *Vertrouwen*, Dutch for "trustworthy." I squeezed the eighty-year-old wheel and prayed the boat would live up to her name. I had two locks to navigate, the first just ten minutes ahead. I stared down the seventy-foot deck, which seemed as long as an aircraft carrier.

Roger moved behind me, centering his gaze on my line of approach. That he could also grab the wheel reassured me – a little. Ahead, water poured over the back lock door like a waterfall. My navigation chart showed it to be a lock nine feet deep. We'd been in a dozen or more locks already this trip so I knew from experience how narrow these granite chambers were. I also knew what it felt like to have rushing water fill the compartment to lift the boat up to the next section of the canal. It could be a wild ride, depending on the lockkeeper's whim. The difference this time, however, was profound.

I was the pilot.

"Is the lock open?" Roger asked.

"I....think so." Even though I was wearing my glasses, all I saw a few hundred feet ahead of me was a black hole with rushing water.

He peered through his field glasses. "It is."

Good, I wouldn't have to wait for the lockkeeper to crank the doors open with those big metal levers.

"Keep your eyes on the lock doors, though," Roger said. "If a boat on the other side of the lock is closer, the lockkeeper may shut the doors, especially if it's a *péniche.*"

Commercial barges, *péniches,* had the right of way over pleasure boats like ours. As sweat from my palms made the varnished amber wheel glisten I wasn't sure "pleasure" applied at the moment.

"Is there anyone behind us?" he asked.

I checked. "No," and I heard relief in my voice. No smaller pleasure boats to contend with, thank God.

"Now slow her down." I felt his touch on my arm. He didn't need to tell me twice. Breathing diesel fumes, I throttled to a crawl but remained in gear. Only eighty or so feet remained before we were in – or would hit the sides of the lock if I misjudged.

"Relax. You're doing okay. Which lock wall do you see more of?" How could he sound so calm when I might scrape the barge, take out a lock door…and put a big dent in his boat? Just the tiniest miscalculation on my part could create disaster.

I grabbed the field glasses and checked. "The right." My God, so much to remember.

"And that means…?"

Which was it, left or right? "Um, I need to steer more to the right so both walls seem even." Everything moved in slow motion, even my brain. I turned the wheel back and forth; we glided right, and then straightened out.

He patted my shoulder. "Good. You're steering much better now."

This meant a lot. Until that day, I'd had trouble piloting. I'd turned the wheel right when I wanted to go left and vice versa. We'd owned boats before, but this barge intimidated me.

"The walls are even now." I set the glasses down.

"I agree," he said. "Remember what I told you about lining up on your approach?"

I nodded, pictured a white line from the middle of the lock and aimed the front flag of the barge at it. I saw the lockkeeper in his bright blue serge pants leaning on the huge lever ready to close the steel doors behind us. The lock was only a few feet away now. Only a foot of churning water separated each side of the boat and granite lock walls. From my angle it seemed like an inch. Believe, I told myself.

The water poured into the lock and carried with it the scent of fish and decaying plants. On tiptoe, I checked left, then right. Confident at last, I shifted to neutral. Almost in, I thought.

"Don't stop steering," Roger said.

This was it. I would hit the corner of the lock or nudge us in. *Vertrouwen* veered toward the left wall shoved over by the strong currents. I turned the wheel hand-over-hand to the right, spinning it so hard its spokes blurred. Then back left. The bow was in, then the stern.

I'd made it. I wiped my sweaty palms on the legs of my bib overalls.

"Check aft. Make sure we're in far enough so he can close the back door."

The boat glided forward caught in the currents of the lock. I twisted, peered over my shoulder. The stern was clear. Now I needed to stop this baby – without brakes – before 60 tons of barge crashed into the front steel doors, only a few feet away.

"Get ready to reverse," Roger said.

The boat inched forward like a lumbering elephant. I held my breath. Paul stood up, ready to throw his line to a nearby bollard. Now, I thought, and shifted into reverse.

"Leave it, leave it, now neutral," Roger said.

Vertrouwen shuddered, burped a cobalt blue puff of diesel smoke, and stopped.

"Good job, Michelle. I think you have a knack for this." Roger gave me a quick hug and headed out to work the back lines.

My shaking hands rested on top of the wheel and I took a deep breath.

Paul smiled and gave me a thumbs-up. He took his line, tossed it like a cowboy and looped it over a mushroom-shaped bollard ten feet over his head. Then he wrapped the loose end under one ear of *Vertrouwen*'s bollard and held fast.

The lockkeeper put all his body weight behind the huge lever, pushed with all his might, and one massive back door clunked shut. He walked around the front of the lock, and came back to repeat the maneuver to shut the other door. Then he ambled back to the front, cranked a handle, and a torrent of water rushed into the lock through the front gates.

I grinned and savored Roger's compliment. A knack for this. Could he be right?

Emerging from the corner of the pilothouse where they'd watched my performance, Fred and Shirley hugged me. Retirees who lived in the Caribbean on a sailboat, they were considering the barging life on European waterways. This week was a test for all four of us. We were paying Roger for a week's stay on his boat and lessons in handling barges to see if we could take the plunge and own one of these behemoths. Would we translate "considering" into "doing"?

"Great job, Sweetie," Shirley said. "And you didn't hurt the paint job one bit."

I gazed down the long deck of the 1908 steel barge-turned-houseboat, painted in forest green with brown and white trim. Jaunty, handsome, even graceful came to mind. Before this week, when I thought about barges, I remembered the big, ugly black utilitarian things on the rivers in the States. In Europe, barges have style and class, the older the better.

In the sixties, someone with an eye for old barges had the vision to turn *Vertrouwen* into a houseboat with most of the modern comforts. The first day aboard, as we followed Roger like obedient school children, we had learned its quirks as part of our orientation.

"This is how you operate a marine toilet." He yanked on a nothing in it, however."

"Nothing? Not even toilet paper?" I'd asked.

"Well, you could, but then if it jams up, you'll be the one to Roto-rooter it out, not me."

I'm not a plumber. Used toilet paper went into plastic bags for disposal.

The electrical system wasn't set up for gadgets like bathroom hairdryers. I had to ask Roger to run the generator while I blew my hair dry, hunched over in a corner of the living room. When I complained to Paul, he reminded me we could fix our boat the way we wanted it.

Our boat?

Fred trudged up the steep stairway, carrying a cup of steaming coffee in one hand and a chocolate-filled croissant – a *pain au chocolat* – in the other.

"For *Madame capitaine*," he said.

I nibbled the rich pastry and sipped the French roast. Then Roger nodded and pointed at the fully retracted lock doors.   I shifted into forward and *Vertrouwen* crept ahead. The only trick now was to steer her away from the wall where she'd been tied and then keep her straight.

The lockkeeper leaned on the door handle. A dark Gauloise jutted from the corner of his full mouth, interrupting his bored expression.

"*Merci, monsieur. Au revoir*," I called out. I even dared to take one hand off the wheel and wave at him.

A shadow of a smile passed over his weathered face. He gave me the barest of nods, as if to acknowledge my status as captain, and I treasured it as if it were a French Legion of Honor medal.

"*Bon voyage, Madame.*"

*

There are times in our lives when we get "a cosmic kick in the butt." Challenge and opportunity demonstrate they are two sides of the same coin. Our kick came when the small software company where Paul and I worked was sold in June of 1999. Paul's job was now obsolete. At 56, he had a choice: take a demotion to become a salesman or....

He quit. Just like that.

"I can't give one more sales demo – I'm sick of the computer industry," he said. "How about you? Do you love consulting?"

"No. You know I like to teach and mentor, but the rest...leaving you for days, even weeks at a time, is terrible. But what are we going to do for money?"

"Don't worry. We'll think of something."

I clung to my software-consulting job and waited for Paul to come up with an idea for a new career. We could make ends meet on my salary alone, at least for a while. We'd "retired" once already and had run a video and computer store for a couple of years and we'd taken software sales and support employment in Penang, Malaysia. We'd been adventurous, but always with the safety net of our computer software backgrounds ready to catch us.

In August 1999, Paul announced, "I think I've found something we'll both like."

"What now?" So far, we'd considered and dismissed owning a winery (too expensive), living on a sailboat (I get seasick), and several other ideas.

"How about buying a barge? You know, like the one we saw on the PBS show *Barging Through France*?"

I remembered the charming series by Richard Goodwin. But buy a barge? "How could we do it?"

"If we sell our house, the cars, and the furniture, we'll have enough to buy a decent barge and have money left over to refit it. We could even charter to help pay for everything." He waved a spreadsheet printout at me.

I imagined all of what I called "home" gone. My stomach dropped as I glanced out our window at the city of Boulder below us, nestled against the foothills. There was the red tile roof of the University of Colorado where I took evening writing classes. We often hiked a nearby hill to glory in the view of the plains and the Continental Divide. To leave a career after 25 years, a house in Boulder, everything we'd worked so hard to acquire....for a big old boat in Europe?

"What if we hate it?" I asked.

"Believe it or not, there's an American guy who teaches people how to handle these boats. We could take a hands-on training class and see if we like it."

"You're kidding. Where?"

"France."

I raised my eyebrows. "France?"

He nodded. He knew how to get to me. France, gorgeous France.

"Well? Want to try it?"

"Sure, why not?" After all, I told myself, we won't like it enough to go through with this... idea. Besides, I couldn't pass up a trip to the country where we'd celebrated our tenth anniversary, four years earlier. I imagined sitting on deck gazing at the bucolic countryside as I nibbled Brie and sipped crisp Pouilly-Fuissé.

Paul is adventurous, and I'm not. But I AM romantic.

*

I was heady with success the evening of my first piloting, but we had a new problem to solve – no food on board. Grocery stores are closed on Sunday in France, and Dordives near Montargis was as quiet as a small town in the Midwest after midnight. Roger, Paul and I volunteered to find a restaurant. On the rear deck sat a black Austin Mini Cooper, a tiny shoebox-shaped English car, one of my favorites. It looked small enough for three of us to lift it and place it on the grassy canal bank. Instead, Paul and Roger put down two metal planks, Roger twisted his six-foot-three-inch frame into the Mini and putt-putted to shore. Paul crawled into the tiny backseat and I rode shotgun.

We stopped at an ivy-covered hotel. A buxom woman in a white lace apron told me in French the empty restaurant was for guests only. Another café had people crowded around its smoky bar, but the patron told me the restaurant was *fermé*. Closed. I was thrilled my high school French still worked.

As we bumped over cobblestone streets, one restaurant kept reappearing, but we vetoed it because of its pulsing neon lights and flashing sign advertising Le Ranchville Grill. We asked for a recommendation at a gas station, and the attendant pointed at the neon sign.

"Good food," he said.

The three of us looked at one another and with a shrug, Paul said, "Le Ranchville Grill it is."

Inside the door, we flinched as a French interpretation of the American West assaulted us – crudely painted cowboy murals, wagon wheel chandeliers and blaring American country music. It wasn't what I'd expected for my first dinner out in France, but the tantalizing aroma of frying steaks helped me make the decision. While Roger went back to the ship for Fred and Shirley, Paul and I studied the salad bar with its odd mixture of American-style salads and French pâtés. We ordered steaks with fries from a waitress who spoke no English. Too bad. I was dying to find out the story behind this place.

The waitress, no more resembling a cowgirl than I, placed hot, crisp *frites* and steaks done to perfection in front of us. Even in a modest place like this, each bite was a delight. Wasn't there any bad French food? I thought. We poured Côtes du Rhône from a carafe and after a few glasses, I said to Shirley, "Why fight it?" She giggled and we all started to sing along with Johnny Cash, "And it burns, burns, burns, the ring of fire. The ring of fire."

That night, a flash of lightning and a percussive clap of thunder woke me from sound sleep. I peered out the porthole of our back cabin. Sycamore leaves scattered in gusts of wind. I held my breath and waited for the boat to shake. When I was little, I used to lie awake trembling whenever there were storm warnings, trying to distinguish between the sounds of freight trains rumbling by on the tracks behind my house and tornadoes. *Vertrouwen* didn't budge. I cocooned myself in my down comforter and listened to the rat-a-tat-tat of rain on steel. Trustworthy, I thought, and fell back to sleep.

The next morning Roger warned us a commercial barge, a *péniche,* would be passing by; he'd heard their transmissions on our radio. No big deal I figured; we'd been passed before.

First we heard the throbbing engines of the large boat and then felt it sucking *Vertrouwen* off the bank. We all ran up top. The lines at the bow held, but the ones at the stern pulled out our stakes as if they were toothpicks in a club sandwich. The car ramps still stretched to shore, but we were about to lose them into the canal as the stern continued swinging out. Paul grabbed those first, while Roger stood ready to fend off the larger boat with his boathook. I doubted it would be effective against a barge three times our size. As it rumbled by at full speed, I gaped at the barge captain who smiled and waved. Did he really expect a wave back?

After it passed, Roger pointed out a lesson for us.

"Do you know what happened?" he asked.

I raised my hand. "Yeah. We were sucked off the bank by a maniacal, sadistic barge captain who waved and smiled at us."

"I missed the wave and smile, but why were we pulled off our mooring?" Roger asked. When I shrugged, he explained: The stakes pulled from the rain-softened ground and couldn't hold us. The fully loaded *péniche* sucked us off the bank because its propeller pushed all of the water from the narrow canal.

Paul nodded and said, "So, if we were underway, a *péniche* could run us aground."

Roger nodded.

"What should I do? I mean it's bound to happen, isn't it?" Paul asked.

"Stay under power, but sometimes you'll run aground, especially if the commercial barge is in a hurry. You just have to figure out how to get your boat off the bank."

Paul raised his eyebrows. "That's a sobering thought."

I would remember the smiling captain every time one of those big dark barges bore down at us.

On my forty-ninth birthday, we shopped at the tiny village of Châtillon Coligny, its ancient grey stone buildings clinging to the sides of the canal. It was market day, a once-a-week event. The flower stalls brimmed with ruby, ginger and gold: asters, chrysanthemums, dahlias, yarrow and strawflowers. Underneath the tents were housedresses for *Mesdames*, jeans for kids, lacy underwear for young women and sturdy cotton panties and bras for the more mature figure. Other stalls offered more utilitarian items: vacuum cleaner bags, kitchenware, American music cassettes, mattresses, pillows and linens.

But we were on a provisioning mission to get food. One truck sold whole fresh fish, and another neatly tied roasts and dried sausages. A rotisserie spun with golden chickens, and next to it, a bread truck displayed *baguettes* and round country loaves with dark, thick crusts. I smelled roasted nuts and vowed to find the source.

We'd all been given an essential food-group to procure: meat, bread, pastries, produce and wine. I'd volunteered to roundup cheeses since that form of calcium had always been a favorite with me. When it was my turn in the cheese truck line, the young woman *fromagère* smiled encouragingly when I wished her, "*Bonjour, Madame.*"

"You are English, *non?*" she said.

Jeez, two words out of my mouth and I couldn't fool anyone. Ah well. I told her I was an American, traveling on a *bateau*, a boat.

I recognized some of the cheeses, artfully arranged on grape leaves: wheels of Brie, wedges of Bresse Bleu, circles of Camembert, and molded goat cheese, chèvre. The soft ones oozed in the sun, some had ferns pressed onto their powdery white rinds, while others had veins of indigo running like road maps through the center. When I pointed at a cheese, she cut a slice and I caught the scent of goat, grass, the cellar where it had aged. I let each sliver dissolve in my mouth and tasted the balance of saltiness and sourness, the pleasant tang of mold.

She weighed my purchases, and then cut a large chunk of the local sausage. The hand lettered sign next to it read "*rosette du porc.*"

"It is a gift for you," she said as she handed me the carefully wrapped package. "Welcome to France, *Madame.*"

I thanked her, touched by her generosity to me, a foreigner. This, I thought, was a genuine birthday present.

We dined on the feast from the market: a cheese and sausage course, fresh crunchy *baguettes, poulet en rôti,* juicy roasted chicken, boiled new potatoes and the meatiest artichokes I'd ever tasted. Roger gave me a bouquet of golden mums while my shipmates sang Happy Birthday. We devoured chocolate cake, *gateau au chocolat,* each morsel melting on my tongue.

Later, Paul and I went on deck, surveying the canal bordered by peaceful farmland on both sides. In the twilight, a paper lantern moon rose over the fields. The breeze rustled the leaves of the sycamores that lined the banks, trees as timeless as the landscape. Most of them were planted by Napoleon's men and will be standing long after I'm gone. I studied the nearest sycamore, its bark a pattern of camouflage, standing like a sentinel. Just at the top of a rolling hill, a stone farmhouse's chimney sent out puffs of wood smoke into the air while cattle grazed in the meadow below it. It could have been any century.

We stood with our arms around each other, and I yawned. All of the fresh air and exercise had contributed to my sleeping well since we'd arrived on *Vertrouwen.* I wore my birthday present, a necklace of gray-blue pearls Paul brought from the States, and fingered them like rosary beads.

He said, "You know how on almost every trip there's a pleasant surprise?"

I nodded.

"Sometimes it's the food, or the people you meet. Sometimes it's the country itself. This time, it's you."

I knew what he meant. I'd taken to the routine more than I'd ever imagined. I was proud of my developing prowess working the lines and piloting the boat. I'm usually an observer; instead, I'd enjoyed being in the middle of the action. I had surprised myself.

Over the next few days, we all made mistakes – bumped the sides of the boat against the lock, touched the rudder on the shallow sides of the canal while commercial barges passed us, and banged around when mooring. But by the end of the week, the four of us could go through locks without Roger's constant coaching. When he gave us a comprehensive written test, we all passed.

"As the Dutch say, 'To water in the blood,'" Roger said as he toasted us with his finest brandy. "You are now part of an elite group – barge pilots."

"What now?" I asked Fred and Shirley.

"Not for us," Shirley said. "At least not till my hip improves."

I tried to imagine doing something this physical with the pain Shirley had and realized the window of opportunity for barging was limited. The previous night, Paul and I had weighed the pros and cons of barging. It would be a completely different existence for us. Part of this life would be better, but much of it was unknown. I grabbed Paul's hand and squeezed.

"We've decided to find our own barge," Paul said.

"Fantastic," Roger said. "You two are naturals. May barging cruise into your heart and stay forever, like it did mine." He raised his glass.

The brandy warmed the back of my throat. It occurred to me that Roger was being kind to include me in the compliment. Paul was a natural all right. From the first day on board, it was clear who the best student was. He'd handled the lines, the mechanics and the helm better than any of us. I'd expected it of him – he'd been a boater all his life. I had always considered myself more cerebral than physical, one of the last girls to be picked for a team. None of the physical side of boating came naturally to me.

Another sip of brandy warmed my limbs. I watched Paul's animated gestures as he described our ideal barge with three cabins and three baths to set up for chartering. He was charged with the adventure.

"I think I've found a market niche no one's filled," Paul said. "Instead of five-star service like the hotel boats, we'll try a more casual style, welcoming people into our home just like a bed and breakfast. So, I'm thinking of calling it "Barge and Breakfast."

Roger nodded. "That's a catchy name. There're plenty of hotel barges out there, but most of them I call "hand-and-foot cruises" because that's how they wait on you."

For almost 30 years in business, I'd been too busy to hear my soul. My life had been filled with voicemails, emails, demos, sales quota pressure, delayed flights, hotels, budget constraints, irate customers, hiring and firing. I craved peace. I wanted the energy back that my jobs had leeched from me. I needed the time to create, to think, and to just "be." I'd had a tantalizing glimpse at tranquility on a boat gliding through France at an *escargot*'s pace.

"To our future as *bargées*," I said, clinking my glass against Paul's.

This week I'd discovered that if I wanted something I could do it, even if it didn't come naturally.

I could learn.

But, could I learn it quickly enough to make this venture work?

2 - Barge Shopping

March 2000

> *Not all who wander are lost.*
>
> *-Anonymous*

I sighed. "Three down, four to go."

With seven barges on our to-view list, we were back in Europe shopping for our own boat. In France, we'd found one barge under contract and another a rusty ruin. A third barge advertised "a bathroom" which consisted of a urinal. Period.

Paul maneuvered our rental Peugeot along the asphalt streets of Nijmegen in the Netherlands. Unlike the small French towns where we'd been looking at boats for the last two days, this outsized city bustled. The cacophony of car horns plus the sulphuric emissions of cars assailed our senses. I longed for peaceful French villages where rock-solid Romanesque churches hovered over stucco cottages like bishops giving benedictions. I missed men in wool suit coats, baggy trousers and berets who chatted in front of *boulangeries* and stabbed the air with *baguettes* as if they were jousting sticks.

Employed until the end of March, I used all of my remaining vacation time for this trip. In Holland we expected to find the most promising three barges ranked by our criteria of price, technical specifics, layout, size and looks. My stomach churned when I realized we were three days into our journey. Our self-imposed budget demanded we find a boat in a week.

And we had to find the right boat, one that either had the layout we wanted for chartering or could be converted with minimal time and expenditure. After we'd returned from our training, Paul had built a website for Bargeandbreakfast.com, and we already had several people interested in cruising, so our tight timeline had us cruising the summer of 2000.

As I stared out the window at umber brick facades reflected in the canals that crisscrossed the city, I reflected on the six busy months that had followed my first experience of piloting a 60-ton barge into a lock. We'd put our house on the market in January and in just a few weeks it was under contract with a closing scheduled for April. I'd jokingly suggested to Paul we should name our barge *Our Home Equity*. We'd started to sell or donate most of the things we'd accumulated during our lives and especially the last fifteen years of marriage. We'd visited our accountant and lawyer, printed business cards, and done all the paperwork necessary to start Barge and Breakfast, LLC. What we needed now was a barge.

Just three days before, we'd been in sleek, modern Boulder, Colorado. After our 12-hour flight landed in Paris, an immaculate taxi perfumed with pine air deodorizer deposited us at the Gare de Lyon. There a bullet train whisked us to Dijon at 180 miles an hour, so fast that peering out the windows reminded me of spinning on the Tilt-A-Whirl at Riverview in my hometown of Chicago. While jet lag interrupted my body rhythms and made me sluggish, the ticking clock troubled me even more. A minute is a minute whether on a European bell tower or the digital alarm clock on our nightstand in Boulder.

Having quickly rejected those three French barges, we found ourselves motoring through the loden green forests of the French Ardennes, past the limestone cliffs of Belgium and the well-tended fields of Holland. With a handful of maps, handwritten directions, and guidebooks, I navigated us to Nijmegen on the Waal River near the German border. Although this was described in our guidebook as "the oldest city in Holland," we'd found a modern skyscraper of a hotel in the middle of the big city like a bull's eye. The stoop-shouldered clerk behind the desk fought back a grin when I asked, "How do you say the name of this city anyway?"

We flinched at the sound he made as if he were trying to clear his throat to spit. The closest we could mimic was "Nī-mā-gen," minus all the guttural nuances.

The next day, we drove to our appointment to view our third-ranked candidate moored in Nijmegen Harbor. As we crossed an arched stone bridge spanning a grass-lined canal, Paul said, "Where's the harbor from here?"

I juggled two maps, Fodor's and Rick Steves' guidebooks, and Paul's Book – a three-ring binder with Internet printouts of pictures and statistics about barges for sale. I shuffled my maps and mumbled, "Umm, umm.."

Shaking his head, Paul squealed into an abrupt left turn saying, "I'm going to follow the water." I squirmed. Since I was directionally-challenged, we often joked that the right way to get somewhere was to reverse whatever way I suggested.

We rounded the corner and spied the ochre Waal River, wide as Lake Geneva, Wisconsin, where we'd lived for a dozen years. I gaped as mammoth commercial barges lumbered past, throwing bow waves the size of Malibu surf. In France, I'd been intimidated by the commercial barges, *péniches*. These behemoths were at least four times the size of their Gallic cousins, a city block on water, complete with full sized cars and cranes to lift them on and off. If we bought a barge here we'd have to travel on the same waterways as these big boys. I watched as they barreled downstream and wondered if they gave a thought to us, their smaller and more humble relatives.

Chemical smoke belched from the modern factories ringing the harbor and hung in the cool spring air. Not my kind of location, I thought. Too much like Franklin Park where I grew up, an industrial town next to O'Hare Airport, with busy railroad tracks in our backyard. I much preferred tiny St. Symphorien set among the Burgundy farm fields of winter wheat, rapeseed and white Charolais cattle the size of Renault panel trucks. We'd decided to moor our barge over the winter at the harbor there – a homeport. Assuming, that is, we ever found a barge to buy.

Ahead, we spotted a cluster of barges tied to the concrete-walled bank. One electric blue barge glowed like a neon sign against the gray sky and leaden water. We parked; I jumped out of the car.

"That's 'Blue Boat,'" I said. On closer look, it reminded me of a sapphire set in platinum. The barge's name was *Pallieter,* but when we'd seen its picture on the Internet, we'd nicknamed it for its noticeable color scheme.

While I posed grinning next to the bow, Paul snapped a photo with our digital camera. I looked at the boat and compared it to the picture we'd downloaded from the Internet. Almost a match, but something was different. Then Paul pointed to a large blue plywood box on the deck. "That wasn't in the picture, was it?" he asked. We scrutinized the slightly blurry photograph from the web site and agreed it was a new addition.

We paced up and down the concrete wall studying Blue Boat's 80-foot exterior. She rode low in the water and swooped up gracefully in the bow and stern. A Reubenesque craft, she was twenty feet longer and ten tons heavier than our training barge. But her bow looked different from other barges.

"Ah ha!" I said. "She's actually busty, isn't she? No wonder they call boats 'she.'"

"You're right. She curves out more in the front than most *klippers.*"

I liked her elegant lines, but the entire exterior needed painting. Someone had started the job but left it unfinished so the side decks were an artist's palette of rusty red and various shades of blue. We climbed aboard and knocked on the pilothouse. A young Dutch woman answered and introduced herself as Desirée, the owner. The name fit the tall, slim woman, with her stylishly cut hair and high-voltage smile.

"How do you say the name of the boat?" I asked after we introduced ourselves.

She pronounced it "pal-ē-ā'-tor." "He is a Flemish character from a quite famous book who represents everything happy."

I liked the notion, but after growing up with the surname Amelianovich, easy appellations that don't need to be spelled out for everyone appeal to me. I made a mental note to find out if boats are commonly renamed in Europe.

Inside the pilothouse, I could imagine a Navy jet coming in for a landing on the deck. I tried to picture shoehorning this barge into one of the French locks. I could envision this barge banging from side to side with only a few inches of roiling water separating us from algae-covered granite walls.

"Will this fit?" I whispered to Paul.

"Oh sure." I wish I were half as confident.

Down a few steps, we checked out the rear stateroom. I gave Paul a look of alarm as we stood in the dark, dingy room. Half of the cabin contained a bathtub, a sink, a toilet and a washing machine. The remaining section was a grubby storage area where some laundry hung from a gray rope. This might become our cabin and bath. I tried hard to see past the grime and weird toilet sitting high on a pedestal like a throne.

"This," Desirée said, "I would like to keep this."

She pointed at a common wooden toilet seat. I raised my eyebrows, shrugged and said, "Sure." Why would I want to separate a woman from her favorite toilet seat?

We returned to the pilothouse and then backed down a steep set of seven steps, more ladder than stairway. Seriously considering whether I could handle this contorted climb on a regular basis, I spun around and viewed the kitchen and huge salon.

I stopped breathing. I'd fallen in love.

Desirée's gigantic dragon plants blocked the view, but peeking through the jungle, I spied a wide-planked, honey pine floor. Soft light filtered through two large hatches like skylights, bright even on this cloudy spring day. The kitchen had tall wooden cabinets painted in pea green and indigo. An orange counter topped them as if custom-built for my 5'7" frame. I stared around and edited out the clown figures, abstract paintings reminiscent of internal organs, bongo drums, and gigantic stereo speakers topped with more plants. I clicked the camera from different angles.

Two staterooms nestled inside the voluptuous bow with enough room to add two bathrooms – our ideal layout. We could set up these cabins as guest rooms. The owners used the starboard cabin, painted orange and marine blue, as the master bedroom. A painting resembling a badly infected small intestine dominated the room.

The port cabin, a studio, brimmed with brushes, acrylics and canvases. A Cerulean blue and viridian green painting of a fanciful artichoke decorated the wall, and candles perched on radiators and shelves. Christmas lights draped over greenery, ceiling hooks, and windows. The décor reminded me of my sixties Hippie period. I was younger than Paul; He'd been into Folk music, I'd been a Beatles fan.

The teakettle whistled and Desirée offered us freshly brewed coffee. We sipped the dark roast at an oak table. Overhead, kudzu-like ivy wrapped around the wrought iron chandelier of votive candles.

"I see you are an artist," I said, automatically eliminating contractions as I'd been taught whenever speaking to someone for whom English was a second language.

"Yes. I paint pictures. Those are not included with the boat, of course."

"Of course not." Thank God.

"I also paint faces at fairs."

"And your husband?"

"He is an actor, no…" she struggled for the word. Then she pantomimed for me.

"A mime?"

"Yes, that is how you say it in English, a mime."

She led Paul on a tour of the engine room and the utility room. I stood under the skylight and dreamed. The cook top was a perfect place to cook a *coq au vin*, or *bœuf Bourgogne*, while our guests sipped a velvety Burgundy wine, like a Savigny les Beaune. Paul liked to sauté the meat course. Perhaps he'd make an *escalope de veau*. I'd steam tiny green beans and fingerling potatoes. I envisioned the ceiling in wood instead of the acoustic tiles. Leather sofas and chairs would line the walls. I'd sip wine in those chairs and read. In my mind, brass replaced the plastic, cabinets and walls were repainted, and my books – Colette's *Cheri* and *My Mother's House*, Mayle's *A Year in Provence*, Julia Child's *Mastering the Art of French Cooking* – lined the shelves.

I took a few more photographs.

I wanted this barge.

"Oh my God," I said as I crawled into the tiny rental car. I twisted as much as I could, grabbed both of Paul's hands, and looked into his eyes. "I'm in love. Of course I'm in love with you, too, but I love it, love it, LOVE it."

"I think you've fallen in love with two skylights and a floor." He shot me a smile and squeezed my knee, squashed against the dash.

"Maybe so, but you have to admit that part of the boat is gorgeous." I cast him a pleading look.

He nodded, but frowned. "But the engine's old – remember, it's a 1959 Volvo. It might need to go right away."

"Yeah, it's old. But we're older. We still work." I squeezed his hand.

Paul's cheeks dimpled, and I felt like I was beginning to make progress.

The mysterious blue box on the deck, a recent addition by the owners, concealed a big, cheap, noisy generator that would have to be replaced. Without one, a microwave, hairdryer, washer or dryer wouldn't run unless we were connected to shore power. And without these conveniences, I wouldn't consider life on any kind of boat, even *Pallieter*.

"I'd have to start that crummy generator like a lawnmower. It's a broken arm waiting to happen."

"You're the engineer. You know I trust your judgment on systems. Well, how much do you think it would it cost to replace the engine and generator?"

"A new generator would probably be anywhere between five and nine thousand dollars installed. The engine – a rebuilt one, not a new one mind you– maybe ten to twenty thousand."

I flinched. "Whoa. There goes half of our remodeling budget."

He nodded. "And the aft cabin bathroom needs work."

"'Needs work' – that's an understatement. It's a nightmare. And I'm definitely *not* going to crawl eighty feet in the middle of the night to use the toilet."

He cast a glance over his glasses. "And all this costs money, lots of money, maybe more than we have."

"What about the mood in there? Didn't you feel it?" I asked. I could still see the light filtering in from above, steam on the windows while the kettle on the stove sang, the soft amber patina of the worn pine floor.

He raised his eyebrows, scratched his cheek. "I admit it's as close as we've seen to our ideal. The layout could work for our chartering. But, please, please try to keep an open mind about the rest of the boats we're going to see."

I said, "Yeah, yeah, I promise I'll keep an open mind," all the while thinking, No way. My mind was made up. Long ago, I'd learned to trust my first impressions.

We drove an hour east to Geertruidenberg. As we zoomed in and out of traffic on bustling highways, I thought about the money we would need if we were to buy *Pallieter.* I reexamined the spreadsheet printouts from his scenarios neatly organized in Paul's Book.

"Figures lie and liars figure," he'd said. "But here're the spreadsheets anyway. The first one shows how much money we'd have if the Dow and NASDAQ stay at their current growth rate." All of our money was in our 401Ks and IRAs, the majority in the stock market.

"Wow. That's fantastic. We won't ever need to work again if this continues." The Dow was at 10000, the NASDAQ at 5000. MSNBC showed stock tickers with charts a mountain climber could scale, especially technology and the latest "dot coms."

We'd studied Paul's other spreadsheets, including a conservative 10 percent growth scenario where chartering covered most expenses. Then, a "Doomsday scenario" with a stock market crash and no charter income where we'd be better off financially living in France full time. I'd hoped it wouldn't come to that. I needed my friends and family in the States.

"Let's get a barge big enough to charter just in case. It doesn't have to cost that much more and it'd be good insurance. We could charter six nights and seven days, include some food on board, and take our guests sightseeing.

There're a few independent barges doing similar cruising in France, especially in Burgundy."

I'd nodded. I was all for "just in case." Although the bulls ruled the stock market in March 2000, who knew what the future held?

The next barge on our candidate list was a floating three-bedroom ranch house similar to the one in which I grew up; beige sculpted-wall-to-wall carpeting, three bedrooms jammed together, one dated bathroom and a tired kitchen done in earth tones off by itself. It would require as much work as *Pallieter* and had an asking price $40,000 higher.

We stood outside with Mr. de Haan, the broker for this boat and *Pallieter*. Like most Dutch men, he was blonde and leggy. "This barge isn't for us," Paul said nodding at the boat tied to the bank. "But, we thought your other barge listing, *Pallieter*, was perhaps a potential."

Perhaps? I thought. When Mr. de Haan looked at me, I nodded, trying to look marginally interested. It's difficult to negotiate when a salesman knows you're "gut-hooked." I looked into his Nordic blue eyes. They gave away nothing.

He said, "A German also liked *Pallieter* and is coming back for a second visit. You may wish to make an offer quickly." He reached down and brushed an invisible piece of lint off his immaculate khaki jacket.

My 'coolness' evaporated and panic wrenched my stomach. Paul and I exchanged glances. One of the oldest buyer manipulations is the Mysterious Other Party who may come along and snatch something you want away from you. There's a reason "As seen on TV" ads command you to "Act NOW!" Did the Dutch barge brokers use the same trick? I didn't know, but it planted a doubt in my mind. So now, in addition to our self-imposed deadline, we started to worry that "the German" would steal *Pallieter* from us.

Our final appointment was with a broker in the east of Holland near Rotterdam, in Vlaardingen. On our short drive from Geertruidenberg, I tried to count the windmills, old ones made of brick and wood and modern ones like tall white metal fans, but there were too many, I lost track. I caught a scent of salt from the North Sea. Too early for the famous tulips, we drove past fields patchworked with early spring bulbs – hyacinth, jonquils and crocus – ranging from deepest royal purple, through lighter lavender, bright yellow, cream and finally white. I tried to enjoy the scenery, but couldn't stop wondering about what we'd find next. Could other boats possibly compare to *Pallieter*?

We arrived at our appointment with another boat broker, Mr. Doeve. A couple had lived aboard the barge he had for sale for seventeen years. Now, in their eighties, they'd decided to buy a house ashore.

Mr. Doeve's son took us over to the barge. When he threw open the door to the only head, we stared. Just a small sink and toilet. I searched for a bathtub, a shower, even a hand-held shower nozzle, a hose, anything.

Nothing.

"They lived aboard for seventeen years with no tub or shower?" I whispered to Paul. "What is with these people? First the urinal-only room, then *Pallieter* with its only bathroom eighty feet away, Desirée's attachment to her toilet seat, and now this." I took a picture of the head, a difficult task with hands shaking from a bad case of the giggles.

To be courteous, we spent time looking the whole thing over, but it wasn't ever really a candidate. *Pallieter* looked better and better.

We'd started barge shopping on Monday. On Friday morning, we drove to meet with Mr. de Haan in his office two hours north in Harlingen. Along the North Sea the gray water merged with the sky. Traveling for miles along one immense dyke, I realized how much water this small country bordered. No wonder barges and boats were an integral part of Dutch life. I hoped the grim gray weather wasn't an omen of things to come.

Mr. de Haan shook our hands and had his secretary brew up some coffee. As cool as the blustery weather outside, he described the purchasing procedure, which was not unlike purchasing a house or boat in the United

States. The entire contract was in Dutch. The boat broker explained each paragraph to us, and promised us a translated version in just a few days. I hoped he was *vertrouwen*, trustworthy. My hand shook when I held the pen. I looked at Paul's signature scrawled at the bottom of the completely indecipherable document.

Once I signed my name, our house would have to close in order to pay for this boat. We'd have no other source of income other than our charter business. I'd turned down a promotion and would be out of a job in two weeks. I thought of my career suicide and realized that it would be tricky to find another software job. All my adult life, I'd been able to support myself and had done so through marriage and divorce. This marriage of fifteen years was a record for me, but I prided myself on our full partnership, including financially.

We were risking more than our careers. Our marriage would have to stand this test. Would Paul and I be able to handle being together everyday, all day, without a nearby support system of friends? We thought we had a good foundation – we'd met at work, respected each other and were good friends. But it still was an unknown as to whether or not we could stand the isolation and the stress of doing something this challenging.

I thought about Paul's two kids, Paul III and Sue, who were in their thirties. We'd spent their teen years and twenties nearby and seen them through college. Sue had just married a great guy, Jeff, and their lives were going well. The kids and their friends were taking bets as to what we might try next. Although barging was a new idea for them, they seemed to take our announcement with aplomb. "Too bad," Paul III had said. "My money was on your moving to Alaska."

I held my breath. I wondered what my parents, if they were still alive, would think of my living on a barge in Europe. I thought my dad would have joined us. An inveterate amateur radio enthusiast, a ham, he'd always wanted to be a ship's radio operator and travel. My mom lived her seventy-seven years within a 60-mile radius of Chicago. Crippled with rheumatoid arthritis since the age of nineteen, she'd vicariously traveled through me. She'd swelled with pride when I returned from China and delivered a slide show to the residents of her convalescent center. Whenever I asked her for her advice, even if the venture would take me away from her, she'd say, "Do it. Do it. You may never get another chance."

I carefully signed my name.

"This is unreal," I said to Paul in the car. "Do you realize we've committed ourselves to a boat we looked at for only one hour and can't even read the contract we just signed?"

"Hey, you were the one who wanted to 'trust her first impressions.'"

To reassure ourselves, all through the two hour drive to our hotel we talked about how beautiful the boat could be (she had great bones), what would stay the same (not much), what would change (virtually everything cosmetic) and speculated on whether An Interested German existed. If we got the boat, I vowed to ask Desirée that very question.

We checked into a creaky hotel in Haarlem and waited. As we sat on the frothy orange and lemon yellow duvet cover, Paul clicked the remote attempting to find some television in English. He found "The Simpsons" subtitled in Dutch, clicked by a sitcom all in Dutch, and finally settled on "Night Rider," the 1980's series with the talking Pontiac Firebird. Whatever it takes to distract us, I thought.

When the phone shrilled, he jumped up, grabbed the receiver and held it away from his ear so I could hear too. Mr. de Haan's deep voice was matter-of-fact. The owners had countered with a price that was only slightly lower than the original asking one.

"It is early in the season and they have already had a great deal of interest," he said.

"The German," I whispered to Paul.

Paul raised his eyebrows and asked the silent question.

I nodded. He nodded.

"Tell the owners we accept their counter offer," Paul said.

As soon as he hung up, I let my breath out, jumped up and hugged him.

"Can you believe it, can you believe it?" I squealed.

"No, I can't," he said shaking his head. We kissed. "Yes, yes I can," he said with a smile. "I could believe anything right now." We held on to each other while the room spun.

On Saturday, with one day to spare in our deadline, we drove to Paris. The cool March wind carried a meager hint of spring. Even in the chilly rain, couples of all ages were out strolling hand in hand under the pruned plane trees along the Seine. We looped our arms around each other and kissed, blending in.

"Let's just walk a little further," Paul said. "There're more boats ahead." As we ambled up and down the river promenade, Paul pointed out barges he knew from the Internet. He called out their names as if they were old friends, recited their statistics, and studied them for a long time. We compared paint schemes and window treatments, decided what we liked best and what we might do with our barge.

Our barge.

3 - Dutch Treat

May and June 2000

Stop worrying about the potholes in the road and enjoy the journey.
--Babs Hoffman

My stomach clenched as Paul and I trotted through the shipyard in Grave, Holland, following our project manager Ben. A thin, nervous-looking man, he said over his shoulder, "Many problems. Many problems." He'd promised us our boat would be completed by the end of May when we planned to move to Europe for six months and cruise to our homeport in France. During the last six weeks while we were back in the States, Paul had been suspicious. His emails to the shipyard about progress on the boat remodel had gone unanswered. Ever the optimist, I'd taken the tack it was all due to the language barrier.

Dwarfed by a massive pier, our 80-foot boat, *Pallieter*, looked like a toy floating in a bathtub. In a work shed above a dry-dock, men in bright blue jumpsuits swarmed over a private mega-yacht the size of a cruise ship. Sparks flew and the acrid odor of welding filled my lungs. We circumvented rusty filings covering the ground, jumped crane rails and stepped over a mound of corroded pipes.

A six-inch wide wooden board balanced across our boat's superstructure, linking it to the pier. Ben disregarded the plank and leapt the three feet aboard while Paul walked across the makeshift gangplank, ignoring the several foot drop to the water. I took a deep breath and tiptoed across the wood as if it were a balance beam, wincing as it bounced beneath my weight. Don't look down, I thought.

I crept down the "stairway" – really a ladder – and spun around to look at my beloved salon with its beautiful pine floors. Like volcanic ash after an eruption, a layer of concrete dust covered everything. We gaped at the one big hole in the floor outlining where the new bathrooms should have been.

After a long minute, Paul asked Ben, "What is the problem?" I could hear him trying to keep his voice casual.

Ben explained they'd had to jackhammer through the concrete ballast below the floors. Since our barge no longer carried cargo, concrete had been poured to keep it from floating too high in the water and skating across the Zuider Zee like Hans Brinker.

"So," Ben said. "We haven't been able to get the plumbing laid yet. And there are no carpenters right now."

We said nothing. If I opened my mouth, I might cry. With our house sold, we'd pared our possessions to essentials. I thought of what was stored in a nearby hotel – all we'd deemed important enough to keep and carry over: clothes, my jewelry, our new Sony VAIO laptop, guidebooks, every book we owned about the European waterways, Colette's novels *Sido* and *My Mother's House*, a paperback copy of *Mastering the Art of French Cooking*. And my two cats, Bear and Sundae, who'd been with us as long as we'd been married.

Optimistically, I'd envisioned moving on board as early as today and setting up our living quarters in the aft cabin, our planned home for the next six months. What had I been thinking? Sure, the shipyard had promised the refit would be completed before our return. We'd remodeled houses before, even built one from scratch, and when had work ever been completed on time? Why had I supposed this time would be any different? And besides, as I ought to have remembered, European time operated on a different clock from American time.

"Do we at least have electricity or water yet?" Paul asked. His face reddened with the effort of containing himself. I thought I might suggest a double dose of his hypertension medication this evening.

"Or a toilet?" I added hopefully.

"Oh no, no, no. But, we have done this." He pointed to a meager bit of wiring. So much completed, I wanted to ask, after only two months of work? But I wasn't sure sarcasm would help. Or even be understood.

But we understood one thing.

We wouldn't be able to live on board for a long, long time.

That night at our hotel restaurant Paul stared down at his plate. "I should've known something was wrong when they didn't answer my emails." He toyed with his overcooked green beans.

I knew he felt responsible for choosing this particular shipyard. In an effort to save money on travel, he'd gone alone to the boat survey to meet both owners, Teuce and Desirée. They'd chosen this yard to have the boat surveyed, hauled out of the water and the bottom inspected, which was required by Dutch law to sell a boat. Paul decided to get a quote for the refit work: new bathrooms, wiring and a generator. The cost was within our budget. And the yard had told him "no problem" with our target date for completion.

No problem? Right.

I chewed on my *schnitzel.* It was a far cry from *veal cordon bleu,* but it was hearty. A heap of crispy fried potatoes was served family-style just like my mom used to make. In fact, the entire meal was the kind she cooked. My mom's grandparents, my great-grandparents, had owned a hotel on the Rhine, just a few miles from here. She would've approved of the neatness and cleanliness of the Dutch just as much as the food. I felt more at home than I would've guessed weeks before.

I grabbed his hand. "Our boat is still the best barge for us, better than any of the others we saw. True, right now, well..." I struggled to find a good analogy. "She looks like an older woman who had a bad makeover at Penney's cosmetic counter. Underneath it all, she really has good bones."

Paul nodded, gave me a weak smile and a quick squeeze of my hand. One pep talk couldn't change the facts. My support was good, but the disappointment he felt was palpable. The food sat in my stomach heavy as a wooden shoe.

The next day we ferreted through the mess on board and puzzled why Teuce and Desirée had left things they'd specifically excluded from the sale, even her precious wooden toilet. We'd paid for the boat in full, we owned *Pallieter* now…why was all this crap of theirs still lying around? I started to say, "In the States…" then stopped. Who knew what the rules in Holland were for possessions left behind?

I stared at the dragon plants tied to the ceiling tiles with string. Covered in concrete dust, they were uglier than ever.

"How are we going to get rid of these?" I pointed at the jungle.

Paul smirked, went into the utility room and came out brandishing a hacksaw. "A machete would be better…but this'll have to do. Once we chop it up, it'll fit up through the hatch."

With evil grins, we prepared for attack. It would be a relief to take some positive action and vent our frustration at the same time.

Just as Paul grabbed the first branch, we heard, "Hello? Hello *Pallieter*?"

I ran to the window. "Oh God – it's Desirée."

Paul threw the hacksaw into the utility room. I tossed in the garbage bags, crawled up the ladder, and invited her into the salon. She gave me a wan smile, and I noticed dark circles beneath her eyes. I pointed out the piles of her things, including her wooden toilet seat, which had taken Paul a half an hour of knuckle-grazing work to remove from rusted bolts.

But even the sight of her beloved possessions didn't seem to rouse her. She said dispiritedly, "I will come back with a trailer to haul our things away, including the plants if you do not want them."

I eyed the scraggly vegetation. "No, you take the plants," I said. "The cats would eat them." Or perhaps use them as an alternative to their litter box.

She patted the long variegated leaves. Little clouds of concrete dust rose in the air.

I hated to interrogate her but I didn't know if we'd ever speak again. We chatted a bit about the progress – and lack of progress – on our boat.

"So, was a German looking at this boat when we were?"

She frowned slightly and nodded. "Yes. A German man was interested, but then you came by and bought our boat."

So it hadn't been a sales ploy. I gulped.

And there was another question. Whenever someone sold me a house – or a boat in this case – I needed to know why he or she was selling. I'd heard conflicting stories from the boat broker Mr. de Haan – Teuce and Desirée wanted a smaller boat or they were moving into a bigger house on land.

"Where will you and Teuce live?"

"Um. We will not be together. We have – how do you say this – broken up?" Her eyes filled with tears. "That is why we sold this boat."

I thought of all the clichés: Better now than later, you're still young, and my mother's favorite comment on any heartbreak, There're more fish in the sea, but said nothing. What can you really say? So instead of speaking, my eyes filled with tears too. It explained why no one had come to clean out the remnants of a dream that didn't work.

We hugged. "You are so sweet," she said. I winced as I thought about the hacksaw in the utility room. Not so sweet.

She wiped her eyes and said, "You know, the couple we bought *Pallieter* from told us they'd never had an argument on board, it is a blessed boat." She swallowed hard and blinked. "But Teuce and I weren't so lucky. I hope you and Paul will be."

As she drove off to get her trailer, I just shook my head and thanked God she hadn't been greeted by her dragon plants in dismembered piles on the floor.

The next day, we arrived at the shipyard, looking forward to speaking with our project leader. Now that we were here, surely progress would begin in earnest. His immaculate office was dark.

"Where's Ben?" Paul asked the boatyard secretary, a tall middle-aged blonde who might have been a supermodel in her previous career.

"He is...how do you say.. on vacation. To move to his new house. He will not be here for a month." I snorted. Oh this makes sense, I thought. The infamous long European vacations are bad enough, but for a boatyard to give a manager a month off in the summer was outrageous. My face flushed, and I wondered about *my* blood pressure, which up till then had always been low.

"Who will be in charge of our work?" Paul clenched and unclenched his hands at his side.

"Oh, Ben will be calling in," she said. "Or you can call him in an emergency."

I wanted to say this *was* an emergency, nothing was happening with our project. But I was trying very hard not to be an Ugly American.

We visited the yard daily to check progress. Or, more accurately, the lack of it. One lone electrician fiddled with wiring. The bathrooms remained ghostly holes in the floor. After a few days, I envisioned Ben entombed in one of the holes. Or at least captured and chained to an exposed pipe.

"I can't stand it anymore," I said to Paul after a week. "We've got to do something. This is driving me crazy. Nothing's happening on our boat."

"Calm down, calm down. Yelling might only make things worse."

I stomped into Ben's secretary's office with Paul reluctantly following.

"Does anyone else manage jobs besides Ben?" I asked. She looked especially good today, in her black leather miniskirt and a see-through white lacy blouse. I could hate her if she weren't such a nice person. She'd even taught me how to say "Grave." The rolling "gr" growl, deep in the throat, the sound that just isn't part of the English language, followed by a soft "a." Then another syllable "va." "Grrrava" I'd rumbled, till she'd nodded approval of my pronunciation.

She frowned and said, "Wim, perhaps, yes, Wim might be able to help. He is not on vacation." Wonder of wonders, I thought. The shipyard hasn't let all management take off for the summer. Hell, why not let the whole work force take a vacation until the snow flies and everything's frozen so work's impossible?

"Where can I find him?" She pointed and I marched off.

We hunted him down in the immaculate employee cafeteria. A short, gray haired man with "Wim" stitched on the pocket of his blue overalls sipped coffee at one of the long, white Formica tables. He looked as if his retirement was just around the bend and the last thing he needed was a trouble-making customer.

We introduced ourselves as the owners of *Pallieter* and he nodded as if he already knew who we were. After all, there weren't any other American couples hanging around the yard. "Can you help us?" I asked, giving him my very best pleading look.

"I will try." He set his cup down and motioned for us to sit.

"When will carpenters come and work on our boat, *Pallieter*?" I asked.

"No one wants to be a carpenter anymore," Wim said shaking his head. "The economy, *ja, ja*, it is too good. No one in the country wants to work in the trades." He sighed. "They all want to be in those computers." He spat the last word out.

"But how long for our job?" I asked, much less concerned with the macro economic situation than with our micro project.

He frowned and scratched his whiskered chin. "Oh four weeks, maybe six. Perhaps longer."

I gasped and stared at Paul.

Paul took a deep breath. "We are already two weeks over the time schedule we agreed to in March. The hotel bills are costing us a fortune." We worried the workers at the yard figured we were rich Americans.

"I think about it." He stood up and walked away, and I wondered what good thinking about it could do. It wouldn't get our toilet installed.

At the shipyard the next morning we picked our way across the debris from other ship work – cables, lines, abandoned gears. A warm breeze carried a tangy hint of the North Sea reminded me summer was here and our cruising time was limited. White gulls circled and screeched overhead. Wim ran up to us, a broad smile brightening his weathered face.

"Come, come." He grabbed my arm, led us past the work shed, down two flights of stairs to a small door I'd assumed was a basement storage area. He used an ancient rusted skeleton key that looked as if it might open the creaky door of a medieval church. Paul and I bent our heads and entered a miniscule apartment. The monastic cell had two single beds, a couch, a table and chairs and a small kitchen area. A bathroom with a shower huddled in one low-ceilinged corner. It smelled as musty as my Grandma Mary's basement.

"No charge!" he said. Clearly, he felt he found a solution.

"I need to think about it," I said.

At least there was a toilet. I walked over, looked in at the three inches of rusty water, and pushed down the handle. It worked. I looked at Paul, tried to smile, and shrugged.

On the boat, Paul and I cleared a spot and sat on the sofa we'd bought from Desirée. The plastic cover was coated in concrete dust.

"Well," I said, trying to catch my breath. "Things aren't so good."

"That's an understatement."

I bit my lip to keep back the tears. Paul rubbed his forehead with this thumb and forefinger. I dared to put my fear into words. "There's a good chance we won't make it out of Grave this season, let alone get to France, isn't there?"

Paul nodded. I felt my throat constrict. Holland was nice, but not what we'd planned. All I could think about was homeport in St. Symphorien amid Charolais-studded fields – not this industrial shipyard.

That night, I tossed and turned in our king-sized bed at the hotel, unsettling my cats curled at my feet. I wanted to get Ben on the phone and yell. Finally, I got up to drink some water. I glanced at the bedside alarm digital clock – 3:00 a.m., the Witching Hour. The generous room was bathed in the glow of the clock and the nightlight in the bathroom.

I sat in the desk chair and looked through the gap in the heavy drapes at the moonlit flat landscape. At this time of year, it stayed light out until 11 p.m.

I felt taunted by long days in which little had been accomplished. What good would it do to be stubborn and not take the apartment? The thought of dwelling in a dank basement was unnerving at best, depressing at worst. Darkness day and night, living right below an office, no privacy. But, it would save money on both a hotel and meals out. We'd already outspent our budget for this part of the refit. And, it might help if we lived fulltime under their noses.

I took some deep breaths and tried to fight off panic. I felt like I'd gone on my first skydive, pulled the cord, then realized my parachute was still being stitched up. This witching hour fretting was becoming a habit lately. In my journal, I'd written:

Close to the edge,
I'm teetering
on the brink.
Ready to sail
into the air,
Or fall
into the abyss.
Which is more likely?

My life had been spent working, meeting deadlines, and ironically, managing large software projects. Would they know a Gant chart at the shipyard if they saw one? I stifled a snort so as not to wake up Paul. Obviously, what mattered more here in Europe was entitlement to a vacation, not a deadline for a boat remodel. They saw nothing whatsoever wrong with what they were doing. My sense of urgency puzzled them.

Bear yawned and jumped down from the bed. He rubbed against my leg until I picked him up and set him purring in my lap. I stroked his black velvet fur. After all, what was time to the people of Grave? Most of them lived in centuries old ancestral dwellings. I'd come from a place where a house a hundred years old was considered historic. One summer probably seemed a miniscule moment against the continuum of their eras.

Why was I undertaking this adventure? I realized I wanted the experience of a different culture, a chance to live in a new environment and to be close to the local people. So what if I was in Holland instead of France? Grave was a beautiful, friendly town. I might lose everything that could be gained if I had a miserable attitude. I inhaled the haunting scent of the blooming linden trees, reminding me of the flowering catalpa tree outside my childhood bedroom. Bear jumped down and I crawled back into bed.

The more I fought the situation, the worse it would be.

I'd thought about it. I'd tell Wim we'd take the apartment.

I slept.

The next morning at the yard we spotted Ben, still supposedly on vacation, walking alongside an Indiana Jones look-alike. Ben smiled. "This is Harry, your carpenter." My carpenter. I liked the sound of that. I didn't know if we'd done something right or if this turn of events was pure luck. Or was it some cosmic response to my acceptance of the situation early that morning? I didn't care why. We had a carpenter.

"Oh my God, I love you, Harry," I said. It took all of my Midwestern restraint not to grab him and plant a big kiss on his smooth-shaven cheek. Harry smiled, but didn't say anything. Ah...he doesn't speak English, I thought. He must have wondered why this middle-aged foreign woman was fawning over him.

"Perhaps I will work on your boat if you'll love me too," Ben said with a smile.

"Only if you're a carpenter." I linked my arm through Harry's and led him to our barge.

I left our new "apartment" to do some grocery shopping one morning and as I climbed our steps, it occurred to me that I'd never lived inside so many walls. The thick concrete walls of our basement apartment entombed us. Two flights up the steep stairway outside, past the shed, a modern brick wall encircled the shipyard. After hours and on weekends, the enormous metal gate clanged shut. We'd been given a key with instructions to lock up. Just a few blocks down ankle-turning cobblestone streets, a crumbling moss-covered limestone wall surrounded Grave itself. I could have felt trapped, but chose to view the walls as they'd been intended. After only two weeks, I'd found a safe home.

I walked past the small neat houses on Koninginnedjik, waved at the young man with aluminum crutches who sat on his stoop every day, down two streets to Hoofdwagt and turned towards my destination. As I passed the church of St. Elizabeth, I glanced at the time. Oh good, it was almost ten o'clock. I waited and was rewarded as the church bells chimed the hour and then played, "Oh! Susannah." I sang, "won't you cry for me?" How on earth did this church ever end up with that tune?

Of the two food shops in Grave I preferred the closer smaller one on Hoofschestraat, part of something called the C100 chain. Our first trip to the store had been an adventure. Not only were we unprepared for the language, we'd stood stupidly staring at the grocery carts chained together wondering how to get one. We'd watched other shoppers and realized a Dutch Guilder would release the cart. Our money would be returned to us after we clinked the cart back in place at the end of our shopping spree. Clever. No one had to run around retrieving the shopping carts. We purchased and paid for food and watched the other people doing their own bagging. Okay, we could do that. But, where were the bags? The cashier motioned to a vending machine. You either brought your own, or you paid for them. A smart way to encourage recycling.

I greeted my kind butcher, who noticed one day I could only point to the meats. He'd run into the back and come out with a photocopied sheet translating Dutch cuts of meat to English. I'd used the little Dutch I'd learned. "*Dank u wel.*" Thank you.

Outside, old women sat astride one-speed bicycles with coaster brakes, market baskets on the handlebars and shopping bags tied to rear fenders. Maple-outlined bike paths stretched along every major road with benches for resting or picnicking. There was always a constant flow of bicyclers: children in school dress, solitary riders carrying goods from markets, young couples and couples who'd spent a lifetime together, riding over the land their ancestors had claimed from the sea, gliding effortlessly across the verdant landscape as gracefully as if they were waltzing.

Over the next few weeks we settled into a routine. A bell's loud clang announced the beginning of the workday at 7:30 a.m., followed by fifty worker's boots clomping above us in the shipyard apartment as most of them headed to work on the other boats. As soon as the evening bell rang at 4:30 p.m., Paul and I ran over to the boat to do our own work – cleaning up after the workmen and painting the interior walls.

Days were spent shopping for the furniture, bedding, kitchenware, appliances and marine supplies we would need. Some things, like art and decoration were in my "need" category. In a bookstore specializing in antique lithographs, I spotted a poster board covered in seed packets. The charming drawings displayed the vegetables the seeds would become: *chou*, cabbage, *céleri tubéreux*, celeriac, *laitue pomme*, head lettuce, *carotte*, carrot, *chou de Savoy*, Savoy cabbage, *rave*, radish, *poireau*, leeks and rutabaga. The board had "1950" written on the corner. I took both the French and my birth year as a sign and bought the display with an eye toward getting it framed for my kitchen.

"Didn't we just get rid of everything?" I asked Paul one day. And now…we were collecting again. In Boulder, we'd disassembled the exterior of our lives. Everything had been examined and categorized: sold, given to someone, donated, thrown away, recycled, brought to France, placed in storage, or put in the motor home.

At our a massive garage sale, a couple had bought our pine hand-hewn log master bedroom suite for their mountain home in Estes Park, Colorado. They'd wanted everything – the mattress, the bedding, even our pillows. We had to schedule the removal at the last minute since we needed the bed to sleep on. I winced when another couple carried out our antique icebox. Paul's darkroom equipment went next. People test-drove his reliable Jeep Cherokee and my "mid-life crisis" SAAB convertible. Both cars sold immediately. We took to driving our 1969 VW Bug instead.

I was delighted to be rid of other things like our home office furniture and boxes of paper records, anything reminiscent of our computer careers. People wanted to know why we were moving, where we were going, how we could leave such a "lovely house."

"We're going to be living six months out of the year in our motor home, and the rest of the time on our boat in Europe," I told one woman as she started to carry out our stereo system.

She set her booty down and looked at me for a few seconds with a raised eyebrow and said, "Your husband is a romantic."

I didn't often label my practical engineer husband with that tag, but the plan was romantic. "I…I guess so," I'd said.

We spent hours at Quantum, a discount store filled with burka and sari-clad immigrants. Like archeologists analyzing hieroglyphics, we scrutinized the Dutch words on paint cans. Did this word mean "exterior"? And what was Dutch for "texture"? Once we bought a can of paint we knew was the right color, but a word or two was different on the label. When we opened the can, it was thicker than what we'd had before. More like concrete. After hours of sweating and grunting, Paul managed to paint one cabin. We figured we'd inadvertently added a half-inch to its walls using paint designed to texture ceilings.

Our cats adjusted to the Dutch food and they particularly liked Purina Gourmet Gold "*Fijne Mousee met kip, met niertjes, met zalm* and *met konijn,*" which translated to expensive little cans of chicken, kidney, salmon, and rabbit. At the pet store in town, the owner, a round-faced, jolly-looking lady, spoke English and deciphered for us. When we told her we were Americans, she became a one-woman tourist information center, and directed us to the tall brick church that housed the tourist information office.

"And don't miss our festival, *Pinksteren,*" she said with a wink. "There will be many beautiful mens there." I suppressed a grin at her plural and promised we wouldn't miss it.

Dutifully, we walked to St. Elizabeth's. I grabbed the one English pamphlet available. Outside stood a life-size plywood horse, its body a large triangle with the point along its back. It must have some significance, it looked impossible to sit on – in fact, the back was razor sharp – but the pamphlet told us nothing. It did tell us that Grave was founded in the 11th century and constantly invaded – by the French, by neighboring city-states, even by Spain. A ruling duke's son kidnapped and put his own father in a dungeon. The last human invaders were the Nazi's in World War II. The Maas River occasionally invaded the town too, flooding the town and cutting if off from the rest of the country until the large bridge, the Maasbrug, was built in 1929.

But what did the horse have to do with anything?

Later we walked into our favorite café for lunch, waving at the owner we'd nicknamed Toasti, a young woman with short burgundy colored hair. "Natural hair coloring" was apparently an oxymoron to European women. If one colors one's hair, why pretend otherwise?

"No *broodjes?*" we'd ask every time. Our guidebook told us these were great Dutch sandwiches. We'd look at each other, ready to play out our parts in an old Saturday Night Live skit about the Greek diner where only cheeseburgers and Pepsi were served.

"Only *Toastis.*"

"*Soupen?*"

"No, *toastis*," she'd say.

"Two *toastis*, please."

Tucking into our grilled ham and cheese sandwiches, we looked at each other and agreed that variety be damned, these *toastis* were tasty.

Friday was market day in Grave. Traveling vendors arrived early in the morning in compact white trucks, set up their stalls in the same spot every week and offered their specialties to the town. There were four flower stalls alone, along with an assortment of tents offering clothes, fresh fish, cheeses, vacuum cleaner bags, shoes, meats, music cassettes, produce, bedding and fresh roasted nuts. We never missed it. Each Friday I picked out a bouquet of peppery-scented apricot-colored roses for the equivalent of three U.S. dollars – a fraction of what they would cost in the States. I bought herb plants – basil, parsley and thyme. And while it was getting late to plant annuals, I located some red geraniums and deep purple lobelia in wicker baskets and fragrant petunias in shades of velvet purple, wine red, cobalt blue, and creamy white for planters on our boat's aircraft-carrier-sized deck. After all, we were in Holland. How could we not have flowers?

With the pilothouse rewired and the switches fixed, our electrician proudly showed us the labels he'd made for us in English: DASHLIGT (dash light) FLOADLIGHT (floodlight) ANKERLIGHT (anchor light) lIGHTSTEERINGHOUSE (lights for the steering house – pilot house). These were great, but my favorites were WHIPER (windshield wiper) and finally, the HOORN. I wouldn't let Paul remove the labels to correct them.

Progress continued. Tiny moments of triumph occurred more frequently with a series of firsts– a working faucet, a load of laundry done on board, and a bathroom wall erected. Plywood bed frames appeared and a new cook top installed.

But one eyesore remained. The ugly blue plywood box containing the old generator stayed on deck. When I'd ask Ben to remove it, he'd just shrugged.

"I have nowhere to put it," he'd said with a smirk.

I had an idea, but kept it to myself. "Can't you sell it?"

He'd snort. "Maybe you can take it home with you on the plane."

One day Paul came running for me. "Grab your camera. You're about to get your wish."

The big crane rolled down the tracks, beeped its inane safety beeps, and finally stopped by our barge. I let out whoops, snapped a bunch of pictures and in the middle of the shipyard did a Generator Removal Dance, a cross between a war dance and Riverdance. Only a few men in blue jumpsuits cast me a quizzical look. They seemed inured to me by then. The straps appeared secure...but as the box swung precariously 50 feet above our boat I began to do the Generator Don't Fall Dance, a combination swaying waltz and moon walk glide. The generator reminded me of the airlifted cow in "Apocalypse Now" before it plunked safely ashore.

On board our boat, I studied the tidy aft bathroom, which I'd just painted periwinkle and remembered the dirty, dark storage area it had been only a few weeks before. Harry, our carpenter, fabricated a shower for us, and at a turn of the handle, water flowed into the tiny sink. I smiled as I remembered a last-minute conversation with Paul about a way to economize.

"We can save three thousand dollars if we get manual toilets," he'd said.

"But can you put toilet paper down them?" I remembered all too well what had happened on our training barge.

"Ah....no."

It hadn't been much of a decision for me.

I put my foot on the pedal, my cats perched next to me, as we watched the paper swirl around and around and then disappear to the satisfying whir of the electric toilet.

We had one more job to do. Paul scraped off the decals that spelled *Pelletier.* I produced the stick-on white letters in Times New Roman font.

Together, we adjusted and measured, bent over the stern and the bow and pressed. Paul carefully pulled the cork from a bottle of Domein Van Stockoom and took out the two wine glasses we'd brought.

It had been my job to name our barge. We loved Monet's series of paintings and I'd mulled over calling her *Water Lily*. But lilies don't move and our barge definitely would. I'd liked *Escargot*, but a well-known hotel barge already had the name. Then it had come to me. We both loved the John Lennon song and its sentiment of peace and world unity. Webster defines the verb as "to form a mental image of, to picture in one's mind."

"To us," Paul said and we clinked our glasses. My eyes filled with tears, as they had many times in the last few weeks.

But this time was different.

These were tears of joy.

I caressed the smooth sun-warmed steel bow, poured a little wine over it and said, "I hereby christen you *Imagine.*"

We said goodbye to Toasti and Pet Shop Lady and had one more dinner at our former hotel. Our young waitress, her blonde hair in a chignon, wore a starched black uniform. All she needed were a pair of wooden shoes to become the quintessential Dutch Maiden. She remembered us and asked us if we'd enjoyed our visit.

"Oh yes, very much," Paul said. "Grave is wonderful but our boat is now ready."

"Where will you go?"

"We will cruise down the rivers and canals of Holland to France."

She bit her lip, as if trying to think of something positive to say. After a few seconds she said, "You will see many cows."

4 - *Bon Voyage*

July 2000

> *A ship in port is safe, but that's not what ships are built for.*
> *-Grace Hopper*

The Sunday morning of our shakedown cruise, St. Elizabeth's bells chimed nine times. I threw my empty coffee cup in the sink, grabbed my bright pink windbreaker, and bounded up the stairs of the apartment as I followed Paul to *Imagine*.

I glanced around at the empty yard. Any workday, I could envision fifty welders and electricians in their bright blue overhauls staring at us if we did something dumb like hit a dock. Or worse yet, another boat. And the odds were good we would do something wrong on our first trip aboard *Imagine*. We were headed to Cuijk, a town 10 minutes away by car where we often shopped for Edam cheeses and *kip schnitzels*. It would take us two hours by boat, Paul estimated. Barge travel is not for those in a hurry. It is a phrase I would often find myself chanting over the years. Patience is not one of my strong points.

Paul turned the key in the ignition. I held my breath for the few seconds before the engine caught and rumbled to life. A puff of gray-blue diesel smoke blew into the wheelhouse. We grinned and gave each other high fives.

"Cast off," Paul said. I untied the lines in the front, he undid the stern and *Imagine* glided smoothly off the pier. The azure sky was clean and crisp. A stiff breeze sent vanilla-tinted cumulous clouds scuttling over the Maas River. I inhaled the fishy river scent, accented with a hint of saltiness from the North Sea. First the shipyard receded from view. Then the tiny center of Grave slipped by on shore, the church cast its shadow over herringbone brick streets.

Behind granite 12th century shops, tawny houses with white windowpanes lined the linden-shaded lanes. As our boat glided along close to shore, carefully tended hydrangeas gave way to flat verdant fields of hay.

My heart pounded. A year ago, this scene had been a dream. Only a few weeks ago, we thought we might not cruise at all this season.

"Pinch me, I can't believe this is happening," I said to Paul.

He smiled as he spun the oak steering wheel hand over hand. His sneaker-clad feet were planted firmly apart. I stood behind him and peered over his shoulder.

But just watching wasn't enough. I couldn't wait any longer. "Please, please, let me steer." I tugged on his sleeve.

He stepped aside and I grabbed the wheel. Strong currents tugged randomly at the rudder. I stood tiptoe in my sneakers to peer toward the bow and steered to and fro, weaving the barge in a serpentine course across the wide gentle river, just to get the feel of how she handled.

I felt a huge grin spread across my face. "This is fantastic. I can't believe how easy she is to steer." I bounced up and down on my toes, spun the wheel and hooted with joy. *Imagine* felt like a car with power steering. She went where I aimed her bow, responding exactly where I asked her to go, albeit slowly. Not like a sailboat heeling over, not like a powerboat bouncing through the waves. She glided across the water with a gait smooth as a Tennessee Walker's.

Paul grinned back and gave me a hug.

" I'm not so sure about shifting gears, though." I eyed the 4-foot length of pipe that stuck out of the floor next to the wheel.

Using two hands, Paul shifted the boat into neutral.

"Put the boat in forward gear when I tell you, so I can see which way our propeller is turning." He climbed toward the back to study the prop.

Now, which way is forward? I thought. I could have asked Paul. But I didn't.

I just guessed…or assumed…or just thought I ought to know, from which it was a short step to assuming I DID know. Maybe it was my pride. Or my impatience. "Patience is a virtue, Michelle," my mother would singsong at me. I'd grumble something about my lack of many virtues. Pushing the gear forward should go forward, I reasoned. I let go of the wheel to use both hands, shoving the gear pipe forward with an unladylike grunt.

Paul called, "OK. Now back to neutral." He returned, shaking his head. "I'm surprised, I thought we had a left turning propeller. That's going to affect how I steer this thing. Hmmmm…"

Knowing I hadn't a hope of understanding physics, I never took the class in high school. Whenever people (usually men) get into discussions about inertia, momentum, mass and volume, well, I just zone out. I get the general idea of a few of the basics, like momentum, for instance. When things move, they're tougher to stop. But during our barge training, our teacher, Roger, kept talking about propellers and their effect on something called "torque" when the boat was put in reverse. He even used a demonstration model of his boat to explain it. I just mused at how cute the boat model was and tuned out. I knew Paul would understand. I never bothered to comprehend how the direction a propeller turned affected torque.

And my laziness was about to come back and bite me.

For two hours we glided on the Maas, passing by flat fields punctuated with brick bell-shaped windmills spinning wooden lattice blades. Holsteins grazed on the riverbanks and raised up their thick heads. "Many cows," I said to Paul and we laughed.

Suntanned Dutch couples in skimpy bathing suits passed us in their cabin cruisers. They waved and we waved back. Boaters everywhere have terms for each other – powerboats are "stinkpots" to sailors, sailboats are "tubs" to powerboaters. Although often plastic fiberglass cruisers cost multiples of our old steel boat, we'd nicknamed all cruisers with a slightly derisive term – "Tupperware."

At Cuijk, Paul made a wide turn in the middle of the river and started chugging back. He timed our progress upstream and downstream. When we reached the boatyard, Paul made his first entry in the *Jachtjournal,* his ship's log: "Cruised up Maas to Cuijk – 14 Kilometers per hour. Top speed against current 12 KPH, 2 hours elapsed time." Although we hadn't attempted any locks, we felt we had given the engine a good workout. Our only remaining trial would be mooring at our shipyard.

Sporting my new suede work gloves, I stood on the foredeck ready to toss the lines. As we neared the pier, Paul reversed the engine to slow us, and *Imagine* angled toward the sharp corner of the floating dry dock. The midsection of our boat closed in to the corner, as if drawn by a magnet. I gulped. Would the edge puncture the hull?

Paul jammed the boat in neutral, catapulted from the pilothouse, and ran forward. He did what our barge teacher had told us never to do. Never, never, never. Paul grabbed the edge of the dock, and with a Herculean effort, shoved the barge out of the path of sure destruction. All 70 tons. Like driving a dump truck on ice, not bad when it's moving, but a bitch to stop. I shifted from worrying about the boat and started to fear for Paul.

I ran up to him, trying not to slip on the deck. "Can I help?"

He shook his head. "I'm going to make another try at it. The stern's coming in instead of the bow. Everything's going the wrong way, like left is right and right is left. I just don't understand…"

I moved back to the foredeck while Paul reversed, then inched forward…then ..again, the boat twisted, and narrowly missed the dock corner. Paul ran out and held on to the dock instead of shoving us away. "Get the line around a bollard. Hurry."

With shaking hands, I tossed the line toward the metal post on the dock…and missed. I did it again. And again. Finally, I lassoed the bollard, wrapped it around *Imagine*'s bollard and held on tight. From the corner of my eye, I saw Paul, hanging on to the dock as if he were Atlas holding up the world, a grim look of determination creasing his face.

What the hell was wrong? Feeling more than ever like total amateurs, we manhandled the boat into an awkward position and somehow managed to get her tied up. I glanced around. No one in sight, thank God, not even the commercial barge family who had been staying at the yard.

"What was the problem?" I resisted adding it seemed like he'd never moored at a dock before. He could easily counter that it looked like I'd never worked a line.

"When I put the boat in reverse to stop, I turned the wheel to balance the twisting effect of torque. But our stern kept pulling the opposite way than I expected. That's why we almost crashed into the corner of the dock." Frowning and shaking his head in confusion, he went below and dug out the photographs he'd taken when the boat was in dry dock.

"It sure looks like a left turning prop in these pictures," he said. I took his word for it. I couldn't tell. It just looked like a huge propeller to me.

He started up the engine again and he had me put the boat into forward gear.

This time I asked. "I push the gear lever forward, right?"

He looked at me for a few long seconds. A flush crept up my neck. I felt like a kid who'd been caught cheating on a test. He shook his head. I yanked the lever back and he decided we did indeed have left turning prop.

I lowered my head and looked up at him. "Oops."

"Not just 'oops.' I don't care about the boat being scraped as much as I care about us. We could get hurt – badly – if we don't communicate. Right?" He hugged me and I shook my head 'yes' into his shoulder, my face hot with embarrassment.

"Forgive me?"

We'd worked together long enough to know that yelling was bad form for us. I didn't need Paul to raise his voice. His disappointment with my judgment was palpable.

"Sure." It sounded half-hearted. I just wanted his approval and trust and now I'd have to work a long time to gain it back. I realized that being alone together and working together in stressful times would highlight any of our problems in our relationship. There was no place to hide.

I hoped this would be the last time the subject of our communication would come up. But then again, I've always been an optimist.

The day before we left Grave, the local furniture maker in town delivered our last purchase, a small pine bookcase. His business card had a drawing of the same crude wooden horse in front of the Grave church.

"What is this horse about?" I asked him.

"Ahh. You see how sharp its back is?" he asked. I nodded and recalled the life-sized plywood horse, its body a large triangle with the point along its back. "Well Grave, you see, is a very old town. My business and home is in a building from the 12th century. Anyway, in those old days, to punish soldiers who disobeyed, they would make them sit on the horse for hours at a time. He gave me a big grin. "And to make it hurt more, they would attach weights to their feet."

I tried to imagine this picturesque, quaint town ruled by degenerate sons of dukes who would throw their fathers in dungeons and cruelly torture their own soldiers, and I realized that these kind, friendly people were probably the descendents of both the dukes and the tortured military. The downside to living in the same timeless place would be your ancestors' histories would follow you. You might own a pet shop, but be descended from a man who sat in agony on a horse your next-door neighbor's ancestor designed. Did they carry long-held grudges? There was something refreshing about having a clean slate in a new town, with a new life. Something Grave's inhabitants might never have.

Our first night aboard Imagine, I slipped into the new nightshirt I'd bought in Grave, in remembrance of Desirée. Silk-screened across it were three fishes outlined in red and written below them, in English, *"There're more fish in the sea."*

"Is that a message for me?" Paul said as I climbed into the bed Harry made for us.

"Definitely not." I snuggled up against him beneath the soft cobalt blue duvet and then kissed him. "Definitely not."

Six weeks after we arrived, on the Monday morning following our test drive, we were ready to leave the Grave shipyard. Ben, our project leader was there, of course, back from vacation now that our work was done. He tried to talk us out of leaving the area. "It is hotter down to the south and it rains more. You should stay here."

"No, no, no." I shook my head. "We are in a hurry to get to France now where we are supposed to pick up our first guests." I resisted the urge to say it was the shipyard's fault we were six weeks behind our original schedule.

Ben shrugged his thin shoulders. "Your guests will enjoy Holland. We are a wonderful people." Who don't believe in project planning, I silently added.

"But these people are paying us to come along. They are expecting to be in France, not Holland."

"What do you care? You are rich." We'd had this conversation once before. I'd told him then we'd sold everything we owned to buy *Imagine* and to pay for the work his shipyard did. Additionally, we were going to run this as a charter boat.

I sighed and shook my head. "No, we are *not* rich."

At 10:22 a.m., I waved at the shipyard workers who'd come out to say goodbye. Ben and his secretary waved back. Our blue-coverall-clad electricians gave more manly nods and lifted their hands. Our carpenter Harry, already working on another boat, saw us and smiled.

Paul turned the key in the pilothouse, *Imagine* powered up, the engine rumbled comfortingly as we glided away in blue puff of diesel smoke.

"Good bye Grra-a-a-va." I tried to mimic the women in the shipyard's office who'd spent time teaching me how to say "Grave." Every time I struggled with the language, I thought of a joke. What's someone who speaks three languages called? Trilingual. Someone who speaks two languages? Bilingual. Someone who speaks one language? An American.

Imagine floated down the Maas toward the now familiar way to Cuijk. My navigation chart, the *"Limburgse Maas,"* detailed but exclusively in Dutch, had been translated for us by Ben. There was a *Motorkabelpont*, a ferry that operated on a cable just the other side of Cuijk and it had the right of way. We would go through one lock, 32 kilometers up river. And of course, we had to find a place to moor for the night, probably at a *Loswal,* a river wall with bollards for tying up barges.

I hung out the pilothouse door and took photographs of the windmills along the river. Other cabin cruisers passed by and we waved to each other. The Dutch registry flag ruffled on the aft deck. There wasn't much to do but watch the scenery and make sure we didn't turn off the river onto a side waterway.

We spotted the ferry up ahead. It inched its way across the river. Paul guided *Imagine* well off to one side of it. Both ships moved slowly like an encounter between a two lumbering elephants doing a mating dance.

"Plenty of time," Paul said with a grin. "Not even close."

Our first lock loomed ahead – much larger than the French Napoleonic ones in which we'd trained – 40 feet wide, 700 feet long. Instead of a lockkeeper standing at the lock gate, a concrete control tower loomed over us, with only the eerie silhouettes of men visible inside. It reminded me of a prison guard tower.

Paul threaded *Imagine* between seven other boats, including a small sailboat, cruisers and two commercial barges. I stood on the foredeck, took my boat hook, stretched and stretched…and caught a bollard atop the wall. We were going up about 10 feet. My job was to hold the bow in while Paul minded the stern. With all the boats around us, it was important to keep *Imagine* steady.

There was a familiar roar of water, a yank on my line as *Imagine* was first shoved back, then forward. I held on tight, heard the creak of tension on rope, and smelled the fishy, fecund decay of rushing river water. I looked around me at all those boats …and lost my concentration just enough to let my line slip off my bollard. I tried frantically to catch the line again, but the bow had swung out too far to reach it.

"Damn it, damn it." I ran over to see how close we were to the commercial barge next to us. Our wooden fenders bumped harmlessly against their boat, but the sturdy woman hanging her wash out on the back of the barge gave me a dirty look. I didn't blame her.

Mooring that evening was straightforward. We found a *Jachthaven,* a yacht haven, near the town of Wanssum. Set off the river, a small wall abutted a park filled with salmon-colored roses, orange marigolds and pale blue cosmos. Now that Paul understood *Imagine*'s torque, he put the boat smoothly against the wall. I tossed a line and caught a bollard on the first try. This is easy, I thought, a piece of *gateau.* We should be in France in no time.

We ran on our own electric power for the first time using the new batteries we'd had installed. If we were not connected to shore power, like tonight, we only needed to use our generator for appliances that drew a lot of electric current – our combination microwave and convection oven, the electric coffee pot, the washer and dryer and my blow dryer. Paul had topped off our fresh water tank and fuel tank back in Grave.

He lined up the satellite dish and we watched some television including British news and a travel channel. One Dutch station ran subtitled episodes of "South Park" nightly. Judging by the quantity of "Who killed Kenny?" merchandise carried by market vendors, the show was very popular in Holland. "The Simpsons" also appeared to be all the rage as many stores sold clocks with Bart Simpson wiping his bare behind with a towel. I prepared a dinner of *kip fillet,* a breaded chicken breast, accompanied by fries and a salad. Paul opened a bottle of wine.

"To our first day of cruising," we toasted and clinked our glasses together.

We took time the next morning to wander around Wanssum, the town with cobblestone streets and immaculate chocolate brick houses surrounded by pastel roses and phthalo blue hydrangeas. Casually, we got underway around 11:30, with the promise of an easy twenty kilometers up the river without a lock. The day passed smoothly as we viewed the bucolic landscape dotted with windmills, small towns like Grave and Wanssum and more herds of grazing cows.

As we approached the mooring at the *Industriehaven*, however, we realized this was a different situation from the previous night. The entire *haven* looked to be strictly for commercial barges. The bollards were difficult to reach and not spaced very well for a boat our size, so it took us a half hour to tie up. Certain we were secure, Paul climbed a long ladder up to the top of the wall. *Imagine* was dwarfed by the huge black hull of a commercial barge next to us being loaded with gravel by three men. Paul returned a half hour later, climbed down the ladder and said, "We can't stay here. The harbormaster won't let us. We'd be in the way of more commercial loading. But he told me where we can moor."

We undid the lines and pulled out again into the stream of constant commercial traffic on the Maas. The harbormaster directed us to go 3 kilometers down to the *Passantenhaven,* pleasure boat harbor, where he'd assured Paul we would fit. He'd said emphatically in English, "That is where you belong."

Paul studied the chart of the harbor. "It's eighty centimeters deep and we draw a hundred centimeters."

"It should be too shallow, but a harbormaster in the area should know what he's talking about, right?"

He shrugged. "We'll just take it slow. Go up front and let me know what you see."

At the narrow entrance to the harbor, three steel pilings about three feet in diameter stood near the bank. These gray dolphins were meant for holding but not permanent mooring.

I couldn't see anything around the sharp bend to the harbor entrance. I felt uneasy; this just didn't look right and I shouted into the speaker, "What do you think?" We moved forward. Cabin cruisers sped out of the harbor past us and I yelled out, "Can we stay here?" One elderly man in a Speedo shrugged and another called back, "No one is allowed overnight."

I peered in. The harbor was lined with tall walls on three sides, about as high as the commercial *Loswal* and the only way to shore was up ladders. I didn't see a spot big enough for us.

"This doesn't look good to me," I said into the intercom.

"OK. Let's look somewhere else. We'll turn around. Come back in."

We looked at the chart and calculated *Imagine* should be able to turn in the harbor entrance. Paul tried the turn then stopped and straightened out again.

"I need you up front with the big balloon bumper to help me," Paul said. "We'll try to pivot off the wall to make the turn."

In position, I held the bumper and the bow flattened the soft balloon as Paul again tried the turn. The engine burped a blue cloud of diesel smoke. My hands shook. I looked up and spotted people peering down from atop the wall.

We stopped turning. *Imagine* blocked the entire harbor entrance. I still held the bumper, now pinned between the bow and wall. Paul came out of the pilothouse, walked up to me and said, "We're stuck. I think the rudder is in the muck at the bottom."

"What'll we do?" He shrugged and went back in. He revved the engine and spun the wheel hard. More diesel smoke poured out the back. I started to wonder if we would need a tugboat to get us. And if so, how would we find one? We had no cell phone, no dinghy and therefore no way to get to shore. More people appeared above. Mud roiled up from the bottom. We must be putting on quite a show, I thought. The harbormaster was lucky he was several kilometers away from me. No matter how proficient his English, I think he would've understood what I had to say to him.

Then with a jolt we broke loose but were back in the original position. Paul backed the boat up. We tied up to the dolphins to give us some time to think. There was only one way out – steering in reverse for about three hundred feet. Navigating a barge backward was not like steering a car in reverse; it's much harder since propeller torque twisted the boat. To stop the twisting action, Paul would slow to a stop, wait for the boat to straighten out, and then start up again. Additionally, we would back into a busy river with rapidly moving commercial traffic, like backing onto an interstate highway.

Slowly Paul reversed out, inched *Imagine* along, starting and stopping. I stood aft with my field glasses and watched for traffic as we approached the river. I held up my hand for Paul to stop and we waited as a commercial barge steamed by. I gave the sign and we backed out into the current. Paul shifted into forward and made a large U turn. Exhausted but relieved, we still needed a place to moor for the night.

Our chart showed mooring bollards at the locks. There was one lock ahead, more work than we'd expected on this supposedly "light" day. We had no other choice– it was dangerous to tie up along a bank of river as busy as the Maas. I chanted a litany as I worked the lines in the lock: Concentrate. This is where people get hurt. Concentrate.

We made it through and tied the boat up for the third time in one day. Paul came back with permission from one of the lockkeepers to spend the night. It wasn't scenic and we felt the wakes of commercial barges all night but exhaustion insured our sleep. Over dinner, we evaluated the day and decided we learned a vital lesson. In the future, we would trust our charts and our first instincts as much as any "authority."

We fell into a pattern of traveling 30 to 40 kilometers a day and doing one or two locks. We took the straight canal *Juliana kanaal* through the more industrial section of the Netherlands. The Maas snaked beside the canal.

Belgium was just off to the west. Often we locked with the same pleasure boaters during the day and assumed the same positions at each lock. A small sailboat, single-handed by a young guy, hung back too far behind the boat in front of him and was scolded forward by two older Dutch couples. I imagined they called him a chicken – a *kip* – in Dutch. We even had some time to chat with the other boaters in the locks. They'd start out in Dutch, and we'd explain we were Americans, not Dutch as our flag indicated, and were new to cruising. They'd adroitly switch to English and explain they were retired and spending the summer on the water.

Once, an unusual barge with gleaming wood trim pulled up next to us in a lock. It was a *Tjalk* pronounced "chau-luk." Rigged for sailing, with its large mast down and polished leeboards on the side, it was tiller-steered by a blonde pony-tailed man outside on his aft deck. Decorative painted scrollwork embellished the sides of the boat; every lace-curtained window was framed with diamond-patterned shutters. I was so entranced I lost my concentration and my line slipped off the bollard in the lock. Damn it. It was a repeat of our first river lock. I couldn't catch the bollard as our bow swung over toward the immaculate boat.

Both men on the barge rushed with their rubber bumpers and fended us off to avoid scraping their impeccable finish and paint job.

"I'm really, really sorry," I said. "Your boat is gorgeous…I lost my line while admiring it. I'm really, really sorry."

Ponytail stared at me icily, but the man with the shorter hair said, "Thank you very much. We've owned this barge for over 30 years. Where are you from? England?"

"No, America."

"Ah. We have been there, with this boat. We were invited to bring this ship to your Bi-Centennial celebration in 1976 when the tall ships sailed in New York Harbor. It was a wonderful experience."

It was obviously not only a well-maintained barge, but also a rare, historic, valuable boat. And I'd almost crashed into it.

Despite this incident, I improved my line handling and Paul gained more competence piloting *Imagine*. I graded us on our lock performances and we went from a "D" at the first lock, to mostly "Cs" and "C pluses." In five days we handled seven locks very different from the ones we experienced in our training course. They were easier than the smaller French locks because their width gave Paul some margin for error on entry. But some were deep – between 20 and 30 feet. And we had to tie to bollards to keep from banging our boat around. The word "bollard" sounded like a manly word, probably dreamed up by an ill-tempered pirate with termites in his leg.

Since it wouldn't be possible to catch the elusive mushroom-shaped metal posts at the top of the wall, someone had designed a clever system. Bollards slid between channels in the walls, ingeniously perched on wood. As the water level rose, I could easily catch a nearby post that floated up the wall with me like an obedient puppy on a leash.

In some of the shallower locks, bollards were recessed in the wall so we used a hand-over- hand method. With this technique we worked two lines, caught a bollard, held on until we rose up to the next one, caught it and let the first one go. The trick was to not lose the bollard while we held on and yet drop it when it disappeared under water. And not tangle the two lines. We'd learned this method in our training; I didn't like to think how we would've handled this trip without Roger's instruction.

On our sixth day out, we were poised to leave the Netherlands and enter Belgium. The entrance from the *Lanaye* lock, just south of Maastricht, would raise us from flat Holland into the hills and cliffs of Belgium. Our chart said it was fourteen meters high, over forty-five feet, one of the deepest locks in Europe. It looked higher.

Paul moved *Imagine* forward at a crawl. It was a triple lock, with two large lock entrances to our port side. The cluster of waiting commercial barges and pleasure boats chugged into these two entrances. We held back, not sure which group we should join. The lights above both entrances turned red.

"Now what?" I asked.

Paul shook his head, squinted through the field glasses and studied the lock. "I'm not going in till I'm sure. I don't want to be wrong and have to back up."

A green light appeared above smaller entrance to the starboard. The invisible lockkeepers up in the control tower wanted us in the narrower lock to our right side. We waited a while. Waves slapped at the side of the barge. As no one else was around, we figured the green light must be for us.

As we drew near, the gloomy interior made it difficult to tell if the lock door was even open – it seemed like one big menacing black hole. Paul said, "There must be a top on this lock, it's so dark."

"It looks like the sign over the entrance should read 'Abandon all hope ye who enter here.'"

Paul nosed *Imagine* in while I stood on the deck and craned my neck. A tiny square of light appeared at the top. It seemed miles above me. I shouted into the intercom, "There's no top on this lock; it's murky because it's just so damn deep!"

I looked up at 50 feet of wet slimy concrete with…oh my God, bollards embedded in the wall, like mushrooms growing on a mossy, rotting log. I couldn't believe a lock this cavernous didn't have floating bollards. There was no time to dwell on the lack of accommodation. Enormous metal doors banged shut behind us. I thought of the gates of hell. As I caught the first bollard, water streamed and drowned out my chants with a deafening roar. "Oh my God." I snagged the next one and held on tight as *Imagine* yanked and pulled toward the lock doors like a wild bronco.

My heart pounded as I counted the bollards above me; I would have to repeat this maneuver successfully at least seven more times. If I missed, or dropped a line, our boat could smash into a lock wall or damage a lock gate. I snuck a look at Paul, doing the identical maneuver in the rear of the boat.

The only positive thing I could say about this lock – it was quick. It felt as though we'd ridden the express elevator to the top of the Sears Tower. My hands shook with adrenaline as I set my lines down, took a deep breath and waited for the doors to open so we could get out of there.

Nothing happened. The exit light didn't turn green. We stared at each other and wondered why we were being held in a concrete cage. "Oh, I know what's happening," Paul said running into the pilothouse for paperwork. Oh, yeah, I knew now what was going on.

We were in Belgium.

5 - *Les Dames de Meuse*

Every man has two countries and one of them is France.
- Ben Franklin

One lock and everything changed – the language switched from Dutch to French, the flat landscape gave way to high chalk cliffs along steep pine-covered hills, and the Maas became the Meuse River. Paul exchanged our Dutch chart to a Belgium guide with its descriptions of points of interest in French, German and English. The weather also altered.

As Ben had predicted, it started to rain and didn't stop.

It wasn't bad inside the pilothouse as we steamed along, the small windshield wiper (labeled "whiper") sloshing back and forth. Heat poured from a radiator to help ward off the damp chill.

Outside, however, it was miserable. My rain-soaked gloves made it difficult to handle the thick slimy ropes as we prepared to cast off. My sneakers were waterlogged after a few minutes on deck and my pink nylon jacket and baseball cap were as effective as wearing a t-shirt and sun visor. We'd seen foul weather gear for sale in Holland, but had optimistically decided to postpone the purchase. I switched from the pink jacket to my full-length raincoat and a rain hat of Paul's, my feet and hands still saturated.

The chart and guidebooks raved about the scenery, how beautiful this stretch of the Meuse was, and it probably was, if only we could've seen it through the pouring rain. For amusement, I devised descriptions for the nuances of rain – at worst, a driving rain made it impossible to see the shore, diminishing to a downpour, then a steady rain, but it never stopped. Perversely, the rain seemed to intensify whenever I needed to do a lock or moor.

The locks also changed and were smaller. After the monster lock at Maastricht, we were relieved to have the locks mostly to ourselves. As we pulled into a lock near Huy, I caught my bollard ready to rise in the lock. It was, of course, raining. I would describe it as somewhere between steady and pouring. A lockkeeper sauntered from a small building next to the lock and asked us how many meters long we were. Paul raised two fingers on one hand and five on the other – twenty-five meters. The lockkeeper motioned us forward and pointed at a boat behind us. We'd noticed *Sea Lion* before, a pretty loden green converted barge with a lush garden of red geraniums. I caught the next bollard forward and watched *Sea Lion* come closer.

The lockkeeper shouted something to the woman on the deck and she put up two fingers twice – twenty-two. *Sea Lion* was twenty-two meters long and we were twenty-five meters. I shouted to Paul, asked him how long this lock was supposed to be. "Forty-seven and a half meters," he yelled back. Eighteen inches of leeway for two barges. Paul shrugged. I held my breath and hoped the lockkeeper knew what he was doing as *Sea Lion* nosed her way into the lock behind us.

The lockkeeper yelled something to *Sea Lion*, then gave the large lever a push, and the back door started to close. He stopped. He couldn't close the back door without hitting *Sea Lion*.

Sea Lion's pilot stepped from his pilothouse, crawled to the aft deck and grabbed the foot-long flagpole on the stern. Paul turned our rudder full to the side. The two boats snuggled next to each other and almost touched the gates in front and behind. But we fit. The ride was an example of how gentle the rise in a lock can be when a lockkeeper takes pity on you. He controlled the water flow as if he were filling a bathtub, with a minimum of sloshing back and forth. I carefully watched slack in the line, grunted as I pulled it tight. I kept peering over the bow, praying we wouldn't damage it or the lock door. Paul worked the lines in the back and kept an eye on the boat behind us. The back gates were *Sea Lion's* problem.

At the top, while still in the lock, the trim brunette from *Sea Lion* came to the front walkway over the gate with her camera and took a picture of our boats crammed in the lock. She smiled and greeted me with a distinctive

Australian accent. I looked at her, wiped the rain dripping in rivulets from my face with one hand while holding on tight to the line with the other and asked, "Are we having fun yet?"

We did more locks together and then both moored north of Namur near *Sea Lion.* When Fran, her husband Steven and her twelve-year-old daughter, Patti invited us on board for a beer or a glass of wine, we readily agreed. After those tight locks we could use a drink.

They'd lived on *Sea Lion* since the previous December, when they'd first purchased the boat. Unaware that not much canal cruising takes place anywhere but the Mediterranean in the winter, they sat in harbor until April when they could begin cruising.

Fran said, "You two were great to lock with in such tight conditions. You're both so calm and your attitude was downright relaxed."

Numb with cold was more like it, I thought.

"You've been obviously cruising for a while," Stewart said.

"We've been on the water a week," Paul said. They looked at each other and raised their eyebrows, probably thinking they might have not locked with us had they known. Then they smiled.

"How in the world did you two ever get up to speed so fast?" Fran asked.

"Barge training," Paul said. "Without it, I don't know what we'd have done."

And even with it, we'd had some harrowing times, I thought.

While Stewart and Paul explored the engine room, we chatted girl talk for a while and I realized how much I'd missed my woman friends. But something was on her mind. She leaned forward, put her hand on my arm and asked, "Have you heard any of the stories of the women who've been hurt working the lines?"

I nodded. Some of our barge training put the fear of God in me. Entering a lock, the pilots were safe inside the pilothouse – usually the male in a couple. And the women were up front working the bowlines. Not that a man couldn't get hurt, but all of the stories so far had been about wounded women. "You can easily lose a part of a finger if it gets caught in a line between the bollard," I said.

"Fingers, whole hands, women fall off the bow in locks and break bones, get crippled for life, even..." She stopped and shuddered.

Now I couldn't help myself, like sitting at a campfire listening to ghost stories. Scare me more, I thought. "Even what?"

"There was one woman who, when a steel cable snapped, well...it cut her in two, right up the middle."

Stewart and Paul returned. They had an animated discussion of the electrical equipment we had on *Imagine*. "Why do you need all of it?" Stewart asked Paul. We had an electric coffeepot, Stewart said he boiled water and made drip coffee. And we had the combination microwave convection oven, the television, and the satellite system. Stewart used a propane oven and rarely bothered with a radio, much less TV.

Finally, Paul said, "We need all of this because we are Americans."

Stewart laughed and said, "Well, at least you know it."

We began a ritual that would be played whenever we met fellow boaters – we needed to tell our horror stories. We started with our tale of being caught sideways in the harbor our second night. Our audience liked that one; they nodded approvingly. Then it was their turn.

"Stewart ran aground in the river," Fran said. "He got too close to shore when another boat passed. We sat there a while but he couldn't figure out how to get loose." Stewart glared at Fran, clearly wishing her to remain silent.

"So his solution," said Fran, "was to have Patti swim across the river with a line and tie it to a tree on the other side so he could work the bow loose." I imagined this petite girl swimming across the strong current with a line in her teeth despite the river traffic. The diminutive Patti grinned proudly, but I looked at Fran in amazement.

"He felt this was the most low-key way to handle the problem, rather than ask anyone for help. He was too embarrassed to let the other boaters around us know what he'd done." But not too embarrassed to put your daughter in danger, I thought.

Paul and I decided to spend some time in Namur and catch up on our shopping. We moored along the wall in town past a lock ominously named *"écluse des grands maladies,"* the lock of the large sicknesses. Perched atop the highest hill, an enormous 17th century citadel dominated the town.

We went for lunch at a small café along the river. Eager to try Belgium's specialty *moules et frites*, mussels and fries, we were one week too soon and they would not serve the shellfish out of season. Instead, we ordered a carafe of house white wine and the *plat du jour*, *Blanquette du Veau*, veal in a white cream sauce over rice. The steam rose from the hot food, the fragrance of meat and cream surrounded me. I felt the warmth of the wine all the way to my toes. The Belgians have a saying that they eat as much as the Germans and as well as the French. This meal convinced me.

"Oh my God, oh my God," I said as the warm comfort food hit bottom. "This is so good, oh God."

"Careful," Paul said. "You're starting to sound like Meg Ryan in the deli scene of *When Harry Met Sally*."

The café's small Formica tables were mostly unoccupied. A young woman ate the *plat du jour* in a corner. A balding man sat kitty-corner across from us. He sipped his Belgian Leffe beer while eying his girly magazine. Occasionally, he sat back in the orange banquette with his eyes closed, his face reddened, he breathed deeply for a while and then he sat up to study another nude photograph. He apparently enjoyed his magazine as much as I enjoyed my meal.

Back on the river it continued to rain. We cruised by the Marche-les-Dames, where our guidebooks told us King Albert of Belgium died while climbing the high cliffs in 1934. I used our field glasses to spot the cross that marked where the accident occurred, stared at the sheer face of rock and wondered what would make a popular king do this for fun.

We headed south toward Dinant, and at each lock, Paul dutifully brought our tax receipt into the office. Each official looked us up in his computer, entered our information in a handwritten log and stamped our tax receipt. We'd paid a fee to use the eleven Belgium locks on our way to France – the equivalent of less than one dollar U.S.

Paul spotted the church spire ahead. "Look at the chart." I studied the map and realized we were a few kilometers away from France. It'd only been eight days since we'd left Grave but it'd been a long, soggy eight days. I studied the landscape and looked for a crucial difference between the countries. Another citadel rose above us, reminding me the lovely river was not only a source of trade and transport but also a route for invasion. I remembered when we'd driven here barge shopping. The borders were ruins of concrete buildings to be circumvented, shadowy remnants of pre-European Union customs and immigration.

"Yes, yes, yes, we did it," I said as we entered the town of Givet. With soggy work gloves, we gave each other high-fives. We hugged and the water dripped off my jacket onto Paul. On the foredeck while the rain pelted me, I got down to the business of mooring. It was almost an enjoyable task as the water trickled down my neck.

We'd made it to France.

The next morning, using French francs for the first time, we purchased our *Péage Plaisance,* an annual permit to use the French waterways, for the equivalent of four hundred dollars. I stuck the small sign in the pilothouse window, making us official for French cruising. The locks were automatic. Radar detectors resembling E. T. space aliens recorded approaching boats. Boaters followed red and green lights. The locks filled or emptied by yanking on a blue rod on the side of the lock wall. An emergency red rod next to the blue one should be pulled, as our chart in translated English explained, "in case of false maneuver or accident. The sluices will close, the cycle will be interrupted and cannot continue until the intervention of the waterways officer."

When we arrived at a lock near Montigny-sur-Meuse, the signal lights were double red, something we'd never seen before.

"What's wrong with this picture?" Paul squinted behind the field glasses.

"Let's see..hmmm.. Doesn't double red mean 'broken lock'?"

He nodded. "Or some dummy pulled the emergency red lever by mistake." On the river several boats circled like frantic ducks holding their positions against the current. We waited for an hour and a half, wondering what was going on. Although we had VHF radios on board, no one spoke anything but rapid-fire French and we couldn't make out what was being said. Finally, the lights turned green and boats entered the lock.

"Whoa," Paul said as he jammed the gearshift into reverse. A huge black hull of a commercial barge loomed on our tail with a matching one chugging behind it.

"Don't feel like playing chicken with 400 tons of boat, huh?" I grinned at him. Commercials had priority and knew it. We groaned as we sat for another half an hour while the *péniches* lumbered through the slow lock. In six hours, we'd traveled only seventeen kilometers, a third of our average daily distance. I multiplied kilometers by point six to get a rough number of miles….that's about ten miles today, I thought. Would we ever get to Paris to pick up guests, let alone homeport, hundreds of miles south of here in Burgundy?

Patience is a virtue, Michelle, I told myself. At this pace, I was certain to be canonized.

We expected Fumay to be a popular mooring as it was the largest town of any size for several kilometers in either direction. The locks would be closed for Bastille Day on July 14, the French equivalent of our Fourth of July. And as we approached the quay, the wall along the river was already full of boats. We cruised by, made a sweeping turn and came back.

"What should we do? Go on or try to moor next to someone?" Paul asked.

"You expect me to know? You're the captain." I stared through field glasses. Tying next to miniscule Tupperwares lining the wall would be bad form. "There's one barge, but it's smaller than us."

Paul grabbed the binoculars. "They're flying a Dutch flag and someone's in the pilothouse." Two good things – they probably spoke English and we wanted to ask the owner for permission to raft. Parallel parking against someone's boat would be a first for us, and a maneuver I dreaded. It was one thing to scrape your own boat, another to potentially mar a stranger's.

On the foredeck I tried to get the man's attention by yelling, "OK? OK?" and pointing at the bollards on his deck. He turned away. Since it wasn't a "No," I yelled back to Paul, "I guess so." Most boaters let other boats tie alongside when there's absolutely no other choice. I hoped this *bargée* agreed with the custom.

We backed off to prepare and discuss our plan. We put all the fenders and bumpers on the side we'd tie up to. I held my two rubber bumpers – a balloon and a smaller deflated one. I had to throw a line over the front bollard of the other barge, put the balloon between us as a cushion, and hold tight while Paul pivoted the stern in. I also had to watch the Tupperware in front of us so we didn't crush it like a plastic Evian bottle.

As we approached, the man in the pilothouse glanced at us, then down to his newspaper. Odd. Usually people helped, especially when their boat's paint job was at stake. But fortunately, another man from a cruiser appeared on the barge's deck to grab a line or put down a fender. As if following a perfectly choreographed dance, we did exactly as we'd planned. *Imagine* sidled next to the smaller barge as if they were old friends. Maybe they'd moored together somewhere, long ago, on the Zuider Zee, each of them laden with a load of potatoes or grain or coal, their sails flapping in the breeze, Dutch captains and their families exchanging tales of life on the water.

I ran down, grabbed a couple of bottles of Côtes du Rhône, and then climbed back up on deck where the sturdy young man helped Paul with lines. "Here," I said thrusting the two bottles at him. "This is for you, and one for the man in the pilot house. Thank you for your help." I shakily handed the bottles over.

We crawled over the other barge to shore and joined a group of Dutch boaters who asked, "Did you have any trouble in Givet?"

No, we had no problem at all, what kind of trouble? Some type of labor unrest and rocks thrown at boaters in the Givet lock. Also, just two nights before we arrived, a commercial barge sunk in the river near here. To help the distressed boat, the French waterways officials lowered the water level three feet, enough to cause all the moored and rafted boats here to lean crazily to one side until the lines could be loosened. What a mess. And did we know this was the rainiest summer in over forty years?

I could believe it.

We told them our story of the hour and a half wait for the disabled lock. They knew what happened there too. They told us someone had pulled the emergency lever by mistake. They were sure it had been a German.

On Bastille Day, I studied the Dutch couple next door and guessed them to be in their seventies or eighties. How did they ever manage this journey down from Holland? We, who were decades younger, found it physically demanding. The locks alone must be a real stretch for two older people. He sat in the pilothouse in front of the TV smoking hand-rolled cigarette after cigarette while she worked acrostic puzzles.

I went down to our cabin and took a long hot shower and then rubbed Arnica gel over the storm-colored bruises on my body. I'd thought to bring this herbal remedy from the States after my training experiences with some sharp corners of *Vertrouwen.* I'd always bruised easily. Once a Chinese-American friend told me the Chinese thought each bruise took some time off your life. I told him I should be dead already. A steel boat has sharp corners everywhere and I'd managed to bump into most of them as I walked up and down the decks, bent over the lines, and knelt on the steel to tie off or grab a line.

I dressed and threw on my new hooded yellow slicker. At least I'd found part of my foul weather gear yesterday here in Fumay. But it was too late; I'd already caught a cold and Paul had one too. I knew colds came from viruses not cold and damp but sometimes, in my heart, I knew my mother might have been right about keeping feet dry to keep up resistance to disease.

On a mission for breakfast pastries and fresh bread, I left the pilothouse, crawled over the boat next to us (neither of our neighbors looked at me) and headed to the *boulangerie*. Ahead on the river, the cliffs of *Les Dames de Meuse*, women of the river, were supposedly the most beautiful part of this river according to three different guidebooks. Hodieme, Berthe, and Iges inspired the legend of unfaithful soldiers' wives who were turned into rocks by divine wrath. Who ever thought up this morality story? Who would look at rocks and see infidelity? Did three women run away with their lovers and then someone decided they'd turned to stone?

I pondered this while I walked through Fumay. Everything was in shades of gray. The hills were covered in gray- green conifers. The houses' slate roofs glowed luminously in the rainy half-light, the sun peeked out and pieces of low clouds hung over the hillsides like feather boas. I grabbed a red climbing rose drooped over a mossy river stone wall and inhaled the musky scent. The roses looked drowned, fallen petals covered carpets of grass as smooth as putting greens. But hydrangeas thrived, bloomed in blue and pink profusion, masses of color against soft-looking stone houses as if they were offerings to the *Dames de Meuse* for their terrible end.

I climbed the steep cobblestone streets, smelled the aroma of baked chicken wafting from the shuttered windows. The geraniums in window boxes were spindly from lack of sunshine. Inside, families were gathering for the holiday, and I realized the Fourth of July had come and gone. I was used to spending the day with friends and family, watching parade of kids on bikes decorated with red white and blue crepe paper, barbequing burgers and hot dogs, and oohing and ahing at the firework displays painting the night sky.

Instead, the Fourth here had been another day of grueling drudgery through the rain. My eyes stung as a wave of homesickness gripped me. I missed my house in Boulder, my routines, but most of all, I missed my friends and family.

I took my place in line inside the tiny *boulangerie*'s warm, yeasty interior. I nodded as six sets of curious eyes studied me. I glanced at my reflection in the immaculate plate glass window, and thought that dressed in my yellow pointy-hooded jacket, I resembled the garden gnomes scattered in all of the local front yards. *Etranger*, I thought. Foreigner. Stranger. I'd been through worse, I reminded myself. Like once in Penang at Lei Lei, the department store. It'd been Chinese New Year and the disk jockey had greeted us, trying to be friendly by shouting over the PA system, "Hello Foreigners!" We'd cringed as we stood out literally above the rest of the crowd while everyone turned and stared.

Carrying my bread and *pain au chocolat*, I crawled across the deck, through the pilothouse and down *Imagine's* steep stairs. The salon's antique pine flooring had withstood the onslaught of sometimes-careless workmen (I once found cigarette butts ground into it, and had lividly complained to Ben) and I'd managed to vacuum most of the sawdust and screws from the construction embedded between the planks. On my hands and knees, I'd washed it with the remains of a floor care product Desirée left for me so it gleamed and smelled of wax.

Royal blue velvet curtains framed the windows. Closed, they shut out the rest of the world and made *Imagine* cocoon-cozy. In the dining area, six rattan chairs surrounded a reproduction of an antique Dutch table with a dark wooden top and wrought iron legs, all purchased at our favorite immigrant's store, Quantum. Like all things Dutch – even an imitation – the table was built to last. It weighed so much that two grunting workmen had to help us load it down the hatch. The wrought iron chandelier over the table with six votive candles promised romantic meals. I'd had to beg Desirée to leave it. "It wasn't expensive," she'd said.

"But I love it. I'll never find one exactly like it. Please, please Desirée." I'd given her my best pleading look. I didn't know how to tell her it'd been the center of my dreams after we'd first seen her boat. "You can take anything else, anything…just please leave it." I think I'd worn her out and reluctantly, she'd let go of it.

My refrigerator was the size of an office model, with the freezer capacity of a loaf of bread. I set my pastry and bread on top of the cabinets painted in the original Desirée sap green and Prussian blue. I wasn't sure I would keep the color scheme but we'd run out of time for niceties.

I shook my head as I look at the velvet couch and two side chairs we'd purchased from Desirée and Teuce. The furniture on our first – and only – visit had been covered in simple throws. When Paul went back for the survey, Teuce and Desirée offered it as part of a separate package deal along with the washing machine. On one of our long-distance phone calls, Paul had suggested we buy them

"At least we'll have something to sit on for now," he'd said.

"What color are they?" I'd asked.

"Green," he'd said. "A very vivid green."

When I'd first seen them, I'd gasped. Not only were they an intense lime, but also, in an effort to incorporate them into her color scheme, Desirée had tried to use blue wall paint on one of the chairs, creating a strange hard surface. We'd covered that one with a throw but tried to live with the other pieces. They looked like what they were – old Dutch people's parlor furniture, with curves and fringes and a scrollwork design of deeper green. I thought I might enter the couch into a contest I'd found on the Internet for the ugliest sofa in the world. I think it would have won.

Sundae slept contentedly curled on a chair, her red-gold fur clashing with the lime green. Bear greeted me as his tail wrapped around my leg. The odor of fresh coffee filled the galley and I gave Paul a hug. George Carlin once said, "Home is where the stuff is." And, to some extent he was right. But for me, right then, home was where my cats and Paul were.

Later that night, in bed, we heard a loud boom and peered from the cabin window. Almost directly above us despite the weather, Bastille Day fireworks rained down over the river like streams of quartz, diamonds, rubies and sapphires. It wasn't the Fourth of July celebrations we'd missed but it helped soften the longing.

6 - Breakdown

The only aspect of our travels that is interesting to others is disaster.
-   Martha Gellman

The deep-forested hills of the French Ardennes were shrouded in mist. Rain poured down and I squinted to see the bank of the River Meuse only ten yards away. The atmosphere lent itself to the legends that permeated the region. I could imagine Ardueanna, the Gaelic goddess of hunting and the forest, astride a wild boar tearing through the primeval woods.

"Do you smell something?" Paul asked wrinkling his nose.

I sniffed the air and inhaled an acrid metallic odor. "Yeah…yeah I do." Looking around, the windows seemed more fogged than usual. I glanced down outside the side of the pilothouse. Steam – or was it smoke? – poured from an engine room vent. "Oh my God, something's burning."

"Take the helm." Paul scrambled down to the engine room.

I clutched the oak wheel.

"It isn't a fire," he shouted. I let out the breath I'd been holding. Thank God, not our worst fear realized. He stuck his head out of the engine room door. "The boat's overheating. We have to stop – now!"

Paul ran up the stairs and took the helm. "You catch a tree along side the bank as soon as we get close enough." He inched the boat next to shore. I winced at the loud scrape as *Imagine* nosed into the rocky bottom. The bow smashed into the overhanging branches of a maple. Like a cowgirl, I lassoed the nearest good-sized limb and managed to tie us off. I ducked the broken branches threatening to spear me and brushed off a pile of broken twigs. Paul killed the engine.

I sat in the pilothouse while Paul tinkered below. I shook my head. Not only were we six weeks late getting on to the water, we planned to pick up our first guests in a few days in Reims, miles away.

He came up the stairs, a smear of grease on his left cheek. "What's wrong?" I asked. He shrugged. "What are we going to do?" I had visions of sitting in the river, surrounded by primordial forest, waiting for help. No one would stop. First we would run out of food. Then water. Then...

Paul studied the chart. "There're towns ahead. We'll try to get to them after the engine cools down."

For an hour we sat in silence. I knew from past experience Paul needed time to think. He also didn't want me chattering or peppering him with questions he couldn't answer. "Let's try again." Paul said. I untied the bowline, the engine rumbled to life and I came back to the dry pilothouse, shaking the rain from my bright yellow foul weather jacket.

He stared down at the instrument panel and tapped it with his fingers. "Damn. The temperature gauge is broken. Probably burned out."

We didn't need the gauge to tell us we were in trouble. Within fifteen minutes, the harsh odor returned, along with the telltale steam from the vent. We took turns running to the engine room to look at the haze. It seemed about the same, but who could tell?

We pulled over, tied to a tree, and sat for another hour. Once again, we went underway and limped the boat into the small town of Monthermé with a public *quai*, a wall with bollards. After an hour of fussing with our mooring lines, Paul shook his head and frowned. "I don't like the rocky bottom here. When there's more traffic tomorrow, the boat wakes may bang us around too much. We'd better find another mooring."

Our boat was overheating and he wanted to move again. Bone-tired and chilled through, I wanted to let the bottom take the scraping. So what if we sank? Mutiny was more likely than sinking. Hot anger flooded me. I wanted to scream this adventure had been interesting, but I was through as of that moment, he could find a new crew, I would leave as soon as I figured out where we were and how I would get home.

Except, I didn't know where "home" was anymore.

I gritted my teeth and shook my head. "You can't be serious." Damn it, he was. I bit my bottom lip until it almost bled as I untied all of our hard-won mooring. I thought about our friends and family. They were divided almost evenly into two camps – those who thought we were doing something admirable and those who thought we were crazy. Right then, I agreed with the latter group.

Imagine inched along as her engine temperature built. In spurts, we came into the small town of Château Regnault. Its empty floating metal pontoon dock, designed for the smaller Tupperware cruisers, looked fragile. *Imagine* came to an abrupt halt as Paul pulled her in against the pontoon.

"Did you feel like we'd hit something when we stopped?" Paul asked. I nodded. We went over to the edge of the dock and peered down. One of our 6" X 6" X 36" wooden fenders we used to absorb bumps in the locks was wedged firmly under the edge of the dock. Paul gave it a few tugs. It wouldn't budge. A fitting end to the day.

Our fender was stuck and so were we.

Paul disappeared in the engine room. After an hour banging and clanging on pipes, he held the trophy in his grimy hands, a mangled piece of black rubber. "This is supposed to have fins around it." I studied it and saw a few tiny points left, but mostly the edge was smooth. "It's the water cooling impeller. The rest of it's in shreds."

"Do you have a spare?" I felt a faint glimmer of hope.

He shook his head. "Uh….no. Spare hoses, belts and hardware, but not an impeller." My face fell. "But don't worry, Honey. Our chart shows a boat repair garage in Charleville-Mezieres only about twenty kilometers south on the river."

Awed by Paul's ingenuity and mechanical ability, my hope returned. Maybe we could fix the boat after all, maybe the weather would get better and I wouldn't leave and go back to the States. I gave him a huge hug and ignored his greasy hands on my back. "How in the world did you ever figure this out? I am so impressed." You big, strong, handsome and oh so smart man. My man.

With a wink he said, "This boat is one big Lotus Super Seven." I knew what he meant. English sports cars equated with constant repairs.

Whatever the analogy, he'd done it.

We took a reconnaissance mission through town. A water spigot and a power outlet were located on shore, with no sign of a charge for mooring. Sweet. Up a set of stairs, a city park overlooked the water. One block contained the extent of commerce in Château Regnault: a small grocery store, a post office, a phone booth, a restaurant, Café Bayard, and a pharmacy. Across the bridge was a *Tabac*, a tobacco store, with a bar. I had the eerie feeling that we'd entered an adventure game, like the ones Paul and I played on our computer. Years before, they were text only with lines like, "You're standing in front of a house. There's a mailbox outside." The newer games had graphics, showing small towns with puzzles to solve. We'd played them in unison, not competitively, which kept our marriage intact.

"Just like an adventure game," Paul said.

"I was just thinking the same thing. But these puzzles might take days to solve."

He nodded.

I did notice, however, one thing – the rain had stopped.

The next morning was Monday, and refreshed by a good night's sleep, we were ready to take on the challenge of getting the impeller replaced. A pleasure boat flying the Belgium flag moored in front of us. Two brothers aboard helped Paul call the garage listed in our chart.

"What's the scoop?" I asked when they returned from the payphone across the street. I already knew the news wasn't good by the look Paul's face.

"Well, we asked if a mechanic come and fix *Imagine*. They said we have to bring the boat to the garage. We couldn't get it across to them that the boat was unmovable – or they didn't care." He rubbed his hand across his forehead.

"It's time for Plan B. We'll go to the garage, order the part and I'll install it myself."

Our Belgian friends had moved on. Our French was good enough when we stood in front of someone – after all, more than half of communication is through body language. But when the phone cut out the extra channel and we needed technical terms we never learned in school – impeller is "*turbine*" – the challenge overwhelmed us.

We conveyed to the postmistress that our *bateau* was broken and asked if she could order a taxi to go to Château Regnault. She made the call for us.

Within ten minutes a taxi squealed to a stop in front of the post office. Paul pointed to the chart with the map and the address of the garage. *Oui, oui,* the driver nodded. We hopped in the cab and introduced ourselves – one of the few actually useful phrases I'd committed to memory back in the East Leyden High language lab. "*Je m'appelle Michelle, il s'appelle Paul.*" He called himself Joel, pronounced it like it rhymed with "Noël." A pine atomizer hung from the rear view mirror and perfumed his immaculate cab with a redundant fragrance, as pine trees surrounded us on all sides.

We took off over the hills, through deep forests on wet two-lane twisty roads. Joel drove as though he was in a competitive road rally. He shook his head at slower drivers as he slammed on his brakes and then narrowly passed the little Peugeots and Fiats while he muttered French phrases I never learned in language lab. And I wouldn't want them translated.

We were belted into our corners of the back seat. I reached across, grabbed Paul's hand and said, "We're going to die."

He grinned. "Yep, we're all going to die."

"No, I mean now – right now." I felt the blood leave my face.

He shook his head. "Nah. Only the good die young. Besides, he's driving the line pretty well." In an effort to increase his speed, Joel drove in the middle of the road. Good for speed, bad if another car came in the opposite direction.

"Easy for you to say, Mr. Race Car Driver."

I moaned. A wave of carsickness passed over me as the taxi careened around tight S-curves. I thought of how Paul and I had recently updated our wills and at least wouldn't leave a paperwork mess for our heirs when we were killed on the slick roadway, our taxi found wrapped around one of the tall oak trees, our still-steaming bodies sniffed at by a wild boar or two. "How ironic and how tragic," our friends and family would say between heaving sobs. "They only had two days in France and the weather wasn't even good."

Miraculously, we arrived in Charleville-Mezieres intact and Joel slowed enough so only three pedestrians had to jump out of our way. One elderly man with a cane refused to budge from a crosswalk. He avoided eye contact with Joel and played a dangerous game of chicken. Fortunately, Joel relented and let the man cross.

Our cab screeched to a halt at the garage's address on the chart. No marine repair shop. Not even close. Joel jumped out and spoke to workers repairing the street, returned and pointed to a new area on the map. The garage had moved since the chart was printed. This wasn't the first time the chart had let us down. It wouldn't be the last. We circled the town, headed back toward the *port de plaisance*, where the workers said it would be. It wasn't. Undeterred, Joel found a pay phone and called the number on the chart for the garage. On the other side of town, we found Garage Ponsot.

Joel came in with us and stood in the background like a bodyguard, arms crossed. A mechanic in royal blue coveralls walked over, looked at the shredded impeller Paul produced and shook his head. We thought this meant he had none in stock. He grabbed a parts book the size of the Chicago Yellow Pages, looked up our part number and made a few phone calls.

"*Téléphone demain,*" he said to us, simplifying his French to match our command of the language. Call him on the phone tomorrow. Our part should be here. That wouldn't be too bad. Two unplanned days of no progress, but still plenty of time to make it to Reims if we moved along at a good pace.

Joel drove at the same hair-raising speed and pulled in front of *Imagine* an hour later. We asked for his card and told him we would like him to drive us back when the part came in. We paid him and tipped him generously for the extra effort he put into helping us find the garage. He shook Paul's hand, then mine and told us he will be back to check with us tomorrow. *"Au revoir, mon ami,"* Paul called out as he drove off. Joel waved and smiled broadly at us for the first time. He would be back.

Without email, we were out of touch, cut off from our family, friends and customers. The best solution Paul had found for communications was a combination of "Pocket-mail," a Palm PDA and a public phone. Public pay phones didn't take coins or US credit cards. Instead, we'd bought prepaid phone cards, available at *Tabacs* or local *Postes*. We did our first e-mail download since we'd left Holland. Our first guests had gone from "guests" to "guest" – the couple had broken up in the last few days and our friend, Suzanne, was coming alone. We wrote her back and told her to meet us in Reims.

With nothing to do but wait, we merged with the ebb and flow of the small town. A short, thin, somber young man owned Café Bayard. He curtly nodded at us as we entered for lunch. His young daughter with disheveled chestnut hair ran through the restaurant, playing with a wooly apricot-colored poodle. Three men in Prussian blue serge coveralls walked by, nodded to us and said, *"Bon appétit Madame et Monsieur."* We were used to the pleasantries of greeting everyone in this small town, but didn't know the custom of wishing someone a good meal. *"Merci."* Our meal stretched an hour and a half, but with nowhere to go, we relaxed, ate and sipped some wine.

Across the street in the park, under pruned sycamores, wizened men in dark suits, white shirts, ties and berets sat on the benches. They watched us go by in silence and then resumed their conversation. The small grocery store had everything we needed to provision – fresh bread, produce, cat food, canned goods and a butcher willing to cut meat to order. The checkout woman greeted me with *"Bonjour Madame"* every time I entered the shop, as did the butcher.

They'd looked at me knowingly the first time I responded, *"Bonjour."* My accent was a dead giveaway in only two words. *"Je suis américaine,"* I explained as I pointed across the street. *"Avec le bateau, Imagine."* Ah, they nodded, and raised their eyebrows as if they were impressed with our big boat. The butcher did his best to get me the cuts of meat I needed and when he was done, *"Voilà."* French numbers baffled me, so when the cashier finished ringing up and rattled off the total, I glanced at the cash register display to see what I owed her. She wished me, *"Bonne journée, Madame."* I thought she was wishing me a good journey. No, that's *bon voyage.* Hmmmm. I had to look the phrase up in our dictionary. It meant have a good day. Just like the States.

Other boaters stopped for the night on the pontoon. Since we took half the dock space, some also rafted next to us, including the cruiser *Déesse,* flying the New Zealand flag. The couple aboard introduced themselves as Val and Roland, recent retirees who'd come to travel the waterways of Europe. We joined them for cheese and wine and met their two women guests. One of the women hobbled around with her bare foot wrapped in a towel.

"What happened to her?" I asked Val after the limping woman went top.

She ran a hand through her short silvery hair. "Stepped on a coiled line to stop it from running out, silly goose. Should've known better being a sailor and all. The rope wrapped around her foot, pulled taught, and almost dragged her off the boat."

I winced. "How bad is it?"

"Could be broken – it hurts enough. She won't see a doctor until she goes home in a couple of days."

I shook my head and made sympathetic noises.

"You know, we women need to be careful. There're plenty of us who've been hurt by the lines – lots of lost fingers," Val said.

"Oh, I know, I know. I even heard a grisly story last week about a steel line that cut one woman in two."

Val was silent for a few seconds, and then asked, "Do you know if she was sliced from the top down or the bottom up?"

Paul and Rolly came back, and I had an inspiration. "Say, do either of you speak French?"

"Well, yes," Rolly said. "I worked as a construction manager in France for several years, along with a stint in Algeria." He had the erect carriage of a leader.

I knew Paul would hesitate to ask. "Would you mind helping Paul on the phone with our garage?"

"Not at all."

I smiled at Paul. Maybe we would solve the impeller problem after all.

We went to lunch at Café Bayard. The same three men were eating lunch here again and two others joined us. The weather was good enough to sit outside at one of the tables. The owner's unkempt poodle unabashedly begged us for food. The small chalkboard outside read: *plat du jour – langue.*

"What's that?" Paul asked. "I don't remember the word 'langue.'"

"Oh…I do. It's ah…tongue."

He wrinkled his nose. "Oh boy."

Tongue. I had nothing on board for lunch and the grocery store was closed, as it always was for two hours at midday. I gave myself the same speech I always did when eating something unfamiliar. What's in hot dogs and sausages? You probably don't want to know. I remembered my mom made calf's tongue when I was young. I'd studied the taste buds like a science project, running my fingers over them until my mom shooed me away. In Beijing, we had Peking duck, and were served everything in eight courses: the feet, the beak, the wings, the breast, the thighs, the drumsticks, the tongue, and the brain. We stopped at the brain. When we returned from Asia, one of our friends asked us if we ever had monkey brains there. Paul replied, "I don't know. But whatever we ate was delicious if we did."

At any rate, the tongue at Café Bayard was meaty, much of its flavor camouflaged by a spicy red tomato sauce, all served over rotini pasta. Red Côtes du Rhône wine rinsed it down. It was a good lunch.

That afternoon, while we sat on deck, Joel's cab screeched to a stop, a fare sitting in the back seat. He jumped from the taxi, waving us over. *"Mon ami,"* he said as shook Paul's hand. We told him the part wasn't in yet – could he call the garage and ask them to call him when the part arrived?

Bien sur, mon ami. Of course.

The next morning, Thursday, Paul called the garage again. Another torrent of French by the obviously distraught office woman filled his ear. He walked back to the boat to discuss a strategy with me. We decided the best approach was to ask her questions requiring either a "yes" or "no" response.

La turbine arrive, Madame? Oui ou non, s'il vous plaît.

It didn't work. At first she said, *"Oui"* but then began to rant. She was in a frenzy at this point, French pouring from her like water rushing over a lock gate.

We waited for Rolly and Val to return from their daylong hike. Would he mind talking to the garage? The woman in the garage's office was relieved to have someone who understood. A part did arrive via the overnight service; unfortunately, the one we ordered was two inches in diameter and the one that arrived was two feet in diameter, big enough for an ocean liner. The impeller had been reordered and it should arrive tomorrow or perhaps Saturday when they would be open until noon. She'd talked to Joel and knew to call him when it the part showed up.

At this point, we gave up hope of getting *Imagine* to Reims to pick up Suzanne on Monday. In fact, we might be docked in Château Regnault for the next week. Paul wasn't sure the impeller would fix the problem and wouldn't know until he installed it and tested the engine. Fortunately, there was a train station within walking distance and after decoding the schedule, we emailed Suzanne to tell her we would come by train to meet her in Reims and bring her back to the boat.

After our frustration came relaxation. My bruises faded to yellow-green and my sore muscles started to uncoil. In Château Regnault, time wasn't spent and lost like currency; it only passed. The town's pace was slow and steady.

At seven o'clock in the morning the foundry across the river produced rhythmic percussive deep booms. People walked from the market carrying their fresh *baguettes*. Around ten, the old timers gathered at the park benches and remained until lunch, which lasted for two hours. All shops were closed for two-and-a half hours at midday and on Sunday and most Mondays as well. Children played on the grass in the park; mothers walked their smaller children out on the dock to look at our boat. The foundry booming stopped at four, then traffic on the road signaled the end of the workday. People gathered at the park, fed the ducks and fished. Some stood on the bank and looked at the river. Occasionally, a teenager brought a boom box to the nearby parking lot and the sound of French rap music invaded the quiet for an hour or so until the party moved on.

We hung around our boat on Friday waiting for Joel. No sign of him. The other boaters took off, including Val and Roland. A small sailboat docked in front of us and a calico cat jumped off the boat followed by a wizened older man, who chased the feline along the shore. Paul ran out to see if he could help, and the sailor spoke to him first in Dutch, and then switched easily to English. He was from Madeira on his way to the Mediterranean and said, "Don't worry about the cat, it's a little game we play for exercise. She's twenty years old and won't get very far." Later we spotted him sitting on the park bench conversing easily in French with the local men. Still no Joel.

By eleven o'clock Saturday morning we'd given up hope of getting to the garage that day. Maybe on Monday we'd be able to pick up our part. Then Paul spotted Joel's cab. "*La turbine! Elle est arrive!*" Joel yelled at us, pointed at his watch, yes we understood, the impeller had arrived and the garage would close in less than an hour. In the cab, I realized Joel was trying to make even better time than he did on our first trip to Charleville-Mezieres. People leapt out of our path as we sped through Château Regnault. At least he had an admirable sense of urgency.

We did arrive on time, they had the right part and yes, we'd ordered two impellers so we had a spare. On the way back, to celebrate, Joel gave us an impromptu tour of Charleville-Mezieres, pointing out the surreal-looking building that housed the international society of puppeteers. The edifice was meant to resemble a big puppet and the whole structure sat on a set of bright red legs. But as Joel attempted to act as a tour guide, we noticed he had the same tendency as many Americans; when he couldn't make himself understood, he increased the volume until he was shouting.

In only a few minutes, Paul put in the new impeller, ran the engine, and gunned it. No signs of overheating. He pronounced *Imagine* cured and said, "Well, we can go now. We could easily make Charleville-Mezieres' *Port de Plaisance* this afternoon."

"What do we gain? A shorter train ride on Monday to pick up Suzanne, maybe saving ten minutes each way." I liked it here. "After all, what's the hurry?"

Paul raised his eyebrows. "You know, you're right. I could use an afternoon off."

And for the first time since we arrived in Europe, we ignored a deadline, and relaxed.

We were curious about the legends of the Ardennes *Quatre Fils*, the four brothers who were sons of the Duke Eymonn: Reynard, Roland, Ogier and Namon. Reynard wanted to fight Charlemagne, but the king wouldn't do it. So Reynard made another plan. He played chess with the favorite nephew of Charlemagne, Berthelot, and after six games, took the heavy gold chessboard, smashed the nephew over the head and then "used his sword to clave Berthelot's skull to the brain and left him dead at his feet." This image uncomfortably reminded me of the woman *bargée* sliced down the middle by the steel cable.

The brothers and their men fought off over a thousand of Charlemagne's knights, but eventually the brother's forces were either killed or taken prisoner. All of the brother's steeds were slain in the battle, except Reynard's horse, Bayard, whose back stretched magically to hold all four brothers. They then fled Charlemagne's men riding on Bayard's strong back, his hoofs splitting huge boulders along the way, to the forest of the Ardennes where they built the Castle of Mountayneford, safely out of the reach of Charlemagne.

We climbed to the top of a hill to see the local marble statue of the *Quatre Fils*. Three brothers sat on Bayard's sturdy back, one held the reins. I'm sure the artist had rejected the idea of sculpting the horse so unnaturally out of proportion had he tried to fit all four of them on its back.

From the high hill, we gazed at the serpentine Meuse as it wound through the deeply forested valley. We could see the town, the dock and *Imagine.*

I sighed. "It looks like a fairy tale village from here, doesn't it?"

Paul smiled at me. "I wonder if you'd feel that way if the boat was still broken."

"Probably not." I kissed him. "But it's fixed now."

We walked down the steep gravel path, arm in arm, giggling over our own name for the statue – "Four Brothers and the Horse They Rode In On".

7 - Champagne at a Snail's Pace

Come quickly, I am tasting the stars!

- Dom Perignon, at the moment he discovered champagne

Boy am I ever glad to see you two," Suzanne said as she hugged me then Paul in the Reims Ibis Hotel lobby.

I stood back, and took in her lopsided grin, chestnut eyes and long straight mane. "Oh, you don't know how glad I am to see you too." Tears filled my eyes. "Let's go get some coffee. What do you think? A latté?" We'd often stopped for a designer coffee when we worked together.

She snorted. "I tried that already. Instead of coffee I ended up with a cup of warm milk. I didn't realize how different Spanish is from French. If it hadn't been for some guy who spoke some English, I'm not sure I'd have made it out of that train station in Paris, the Gare de whatever."

We knew the feeling.

After an espresso, we walked to the center of Reims. We fortified ourselves at a café with a lunch of *moules et frites*, tender juicy mussels and fries, accompanied by a bottle of white wine.

"Better?" I asked her.

"Mucho, mucho better," she grinned.

"We thought we'd tour the cathedral here. Okay?" Paul asked.

She shrugged. "You guys are the tour guides. My friends warned me not to come back with too many photos of churches. After a while, you can't tell them apart. AFC – Another French Church. And that's the clean version." She grinned her wicked grin.

The Cathedral of Notre Dame was decorated with gargoyles, fantastic figures and drain spouts disguised as statues, protectors from evil spirits and educational tools for the illiterate medieval peasants. Inside was a living church with people praying in alcoves. I inhaled the sweet scent of incense and fresh flowers in front of the Blessed Virgin Mary's statue, where I made a donation and lit a candle for my mother.

The coronations of the French monarchy were held here for hundreds of years and I could imagine the processions under the vaulted ceilings over one hundred and twenty feet above, royalty marching up the aisle to the altar where the symbols of temporal and spiritual power met. The original church on this site was built around 700 AD and it continued to change and evolve. The current cathedral was started in 1211 and took eighty years and five different architects to complete it. Dramatic changes like expansions and more decorative work continued for centuries.

Shelling during World War I seriously damaged all this grandeur, but some replacements were better than the originals. A rainbow of light streamed through Marc Chagall windows of vibrant ultramarine overlaid with images of the Old Testament. While the subject matter was common ground for both Judaism and Catholicism, I pondered why a Jewish artist made such a spectacular contribution to this monument of Christianity.

Other changes to the cathedral were more subtle: the stone steps and floor worn and grooved by the millions of footsteps trod over the centuries, the patina of wear on the pews and the exterior limestone blackened from the acid rain of modern pollution. We were relieved this structure withstood the Allied bombing during World War II, but later someone told us the reason our forces left French cathedrals unscathed for the most part was not an effort to save national treasures but for a more practical motive: pilots could visually navigate across France using the large cathedrals as points of reference for their bombing runs.

Next we took a guided tour of a champagne house. The cool, crypt-like cellars were filled with magnums of champagne stored on their sides. It smelled musty as an old basement. Our tour guide was a petite French young woman, her warm brown hair pulled back into a stylish chignon. Adroitly she switched back and forth from French to English while she told her spiel.

Most of the actual production took place closer to the vineyards but millions of bottles were stored here. We learned the appellation "Champagne" could only be used in this region and it was illegal for any other bubbly wine, or even Yves Saint Laurent's perfume, to use the name. In the late 17th century, the *Champenois*, Champagne producers, experimented with blends of grapes from different villages or *crus*. They noticed certain *crus* were more effervescent, while others produced stronger, fruitier grapes.

Like all wine producing areas, Champagne had annual variations in the acidity and sugar content of grapes due to the weather. These characteristics varied from vintage to vintage and from *cru* to *cru*. By blending base wines made from Pinot Noir, Pinot Meunier and Chardonnay grapes from several villages and vintages, the *Champenois* discovered that they could create a more balanced consistent wine. Blending allowed producers to develop their own unique style – some known for their lightness and elegance, others for medium-body wines or for rich, mature wines with great depth.

The wine first fermented in stainless steel vats and then was transferred to pressurized vats or dark bottles. Other wines from previous vintages were blended in. On rare occasions, grapes were judged to be of such quality that no blending was needed – and voilà "vintage" champagne. Next, sugar and yeast were added. This second fermentation created the characteristic bubbles and took anywhere from a few weeks to a few months.

The wine was bottled and stored while it matured. The bottles were shaken daily and turned exactly the right amount until dark sediment forms at the bottom of the cork. In the past, only skilled laborers performed this operation, called "riddling." Like much of manufacturing, the process had been mechanized for the most part except for the most expensive makes of the bubbly. Finally, in a procedure called *dégorgement,* the sediment was removed by carefully taking the cork out of the bottles. The pressure of the champagne shot the sediment into the air. The champagne was sweetened, corked and then aged for up to seven years before it was considered drinkable.

"And now," our tour guide said, "we arrive at the tasting."

"Finally," I muttered.

We sipped the champagne, felt the bubbles explode in our mouths. I thought of old monks stumbling on the discovery and wondered at all of the culinary inventions of the world. Who figured out how to eat the first snail, artichoke, or even the first egg? I raised my glass in silent salute to the brave pioneers of the past. A sign hung on the wall, a quote from Madame Bollinger, one of the *grandes dames* of Champagne: "I drink Champagne when I'm happy and when I'm sad. Sometimes I drink it when I'm alone. When I have company, I consider it obligatory. I trifle with it if I'm not hungry and drink it when I am. Otherwise I never touch it – unless I'm thirsty."

After a thirty-minute train ride back to Château Regnault, we walked to the dock from the station.

"Wow this boat is huge! The pictures don't do it justice." Suzanne stared at *Imagine* while we beamed like proud parents. We climbed into the pilothouse. "I remember this guy. You bought him at coffee shop in Golden just before you left, didn't you?" she said pointing at the little rubber Buddha sitting on the dash. In one hand he held a latté and a cell phone in the other. This sign in the shop had read, "Squeeze me and I will chant for you."

"Yep. He's our good luck charm." I squeezed him and he emitted a high-pitched squeak. "Unfortunately, his chanting doesn't always work." I thought of our latest engine trouble.

Suzanne unpacked then promptly fell asleep, jetlagged and emotionally drained by her recent breakup with her boyfriend. Combined with Desirée's sad tale, I considered changing the barge's name to *Heartbreak Hotel.*

On Monday, July 25th, while the engine warmed, a man in a suit approached Paul who nodded emphatically. Later I asked him what the official-looking man had wanted. The town spokesperson had hoped we were leaving soon as they needed the dock space for a festival later in the week. They'd been reluctant to ask us to go because they knew we had trouble with the *bateau*. So they must have been relieved to see the engine running but no more than we were.

"How 'bout dat engine?" I asked Paul as we sniffed for signs of overheating. He grinned at the punch line from a story when we'd been barge shopping. We'd just seen the barge with no shower and the barge broker Mr. Doeve had taken a drag on his hand rolled cigarette. Through a haze of smoke he'd said, "How 'bout dat engine?"

It'd been the only positive thing we could've agreed with.

We'd casually warned Suzanne we'd hit "a bit of trouble," but it appeared we'd fixed the problem. She shrugged. "I'm in France and on a beautiful boat with friends. I don't care where we start, where we go, or how far we get." Good attitude for barging with us on our maiden voyage.

Our wooden fender remained wedged under the dock. The past week we'd tried everything from a hammer and chisel to one dramatic move when Paul put the boat in reverse to yank the fender out. I'd stood on the metal dock and felt the surface lift. Oh my God, we're going to pull the dock from the bank, I thought. I'd frantically waved at Paul while I tried to maintain my footing. He'd stopped in time. We remedied the situation the only way we could without destroying the dock – we cut the lines to the fender leaving the piece of wood behind as a souvenir for Château Regnault from *Imagine.*

Suzanne was a willing student on the lines. I gave her a speech about safety and included the stories of missing digits trying to scare her a bit so she didn't do anything foolhardy. The same age as Desirée, she was athletic and fit with a strong enough sense of adventure to have moved to Costa Rica for two years without knowing much about it beforehand. The cliché "falling on deaf ears" occurred to me as she stared at me unimpressed with my horror story. "Is that so?" she asked.

Our first destination was a port at Pont-a-Bar, the entrance to the Canal des Ardennes, eight locks and thirty kilometers away. It felt good to be cruising and although chilly at least it wasn't raining. The wooded hills occasionally gave way to pastures and fields. We chugged through Charleville-Mezieres and spotted the places near the *port de plaisance* where we searched for the garage in vain. The perspective from the canal was vastly different than charging through the streets with Joel. Although the view was limited we could see more details moving at only about four miles an hour.

When we went through locks in towns we noticed we were providing the local entertainment. Entire families lined up along the edge of the locks and watched as we caught – and missed – bollards and then rose up to their level. All of the locks were automatic so I showed Suzanne how to twist the pole hanging from the wire in the middle of the canal to start the locking sequence. We started singing "Twist and Shout" and twisting away on the front deck.

We laughed and danced through town.

"You know," Suzanne said. "Paul sure is serious when he's driving this boat."

I thought about it a bit. Paul was an Eagle Scout and a trained lifeguard. He and I have a history of rescuing people on the water. Once we helped a group of young people fend their twenty-eight foot sailboat off the rocks in Lake Geneva. One night, we'd followed a boat without running lights in order to save it from potential collision.

"Hmmm. Most of our savings is floating down the canal in the form of this barge, so I guess he's serious." I hadn't noticed because most of the time I made myself serious too. Even though I'd kidded about it, I didn't want to hurt myself or see anyone else injured either. Almost as if to prove the point as we descended a lock the bowline caught in a crack in the lock wall. Try as I might it wouldn't pull loose. It was wedged in tight.

The boat continued dropping. The strong line began to creak.

"Oh God, oh God," I chanted as I yanked on the line. I knew what could happen. Roger, our instructor, had told us the story of a pleasure boat tied up in a lock, something you never should do. As the water dropped the boat hung on its side suspended from above. Astonished, he'd watched a woman climb the ropes out of the lock. That had been a Tupperware, not a barge.

The creak grew louder and the line sung. It couldn't possibly hold all 70 tons of *Imagine.* At some point it would snap and I didn't want to be anywhere near it if it did.

I yelled out for Paul. Thank God he heard me. He came at a slow run carrying a hatchet in his left hand.

Suzanne stepped away, her mouth agape.

"Stand back." He swung and cut the line in two.

He may be serious but I like that in a person when there's a problem.

The Canals des Ardennes narrowed to a width of about twenty meters, or sixty-five feet, much like the canals where we'd trained. A blue heron stood on stilt legs along the bank waiting for us. As we neared, the bird flew up and then swooped down and dove in front of the bow. Then it flew up ahead, landed on the opposite bank, and repeated the process. It came up fishless every time.

Now that we were on the narrower canals, I studied the banks and noticed the erosion. I knew the culprits – wakes from boats going too fast. There was supposed to be a speed limit on the canals; unfortunately no one enforced the law. We'd seen a variety of bank-liners designed to stop erosion: wooden posts driven into the bottom with perpendicular corrugated metal strips attached, piles of rock, broken concrete, poured concrete, chicken wire holding piles of rock and concrete, even old tires staked into the banks. Where there were natural banks, I'd occasionally see a passing boat's wake tear at the earth and fill the canal with more silt.

On these narrow waterways Paul observed the speed limit, particularly when the canal was narrow as it was near Le Chesne where we planned our next stop. As we approached port a large Tupperware cabin cruiser flying a Belgium flag sped up behind us honking its horn. This boat aptly named for a bird of prey was determined to fly by us in order to find a spot in the port and get there before we did. I winced as it passed us and its wake carved away at the shore. On board, three suntanned couples in brief bathing suits and loads of gold jewelry lounged. The women had the audacity to wave at us as they passed us and tossed our boat about in their wake.

When we arrived at the quay it was almost full. The Belgian Tupperware sat in the largest spot while its passengers sipped cocktails. Two people on a familiar looking boat waved to us. I recognized them and grinned.

"Roland and Val! Hello," I shouted.

"Hey, you got your boat fixed. Good for you."

They joined us at an outdoor café where over a dinner of duck, veal, and salmon, we entertained Suzanne with our stories of survival. I told Val I'd passed on the gory lore of the locks to my trainee and I'd decided we should have a club for the women who work the lines. Our name will be "*Les Dames des l'écluses,*" the women of the locks and we will have a secret hand signal to each other. I folded down a couple of my fingers and turned my hand so it looked like I'd lost a few digits. She saluted me back the same way.

Since the best spots on the quay had been taken we'd turned around in a wide spot in the canal and gone back about a kilometer facing the direction from which we'd arrived. The next morning we needed to turn back around. The spot where we turned yesterday was out of the question. "No way could I back this thing up a kilometer through heavy Monday morning traffic," Paul said. "Besides, turning should be no problem." He pointed at his chart showing the "turning basin" or widened spot on the canal created for that purpose.

We started our turn and then stopped. The engine revved, mud bubbled up from the bottom. I walked back to the pilothouse. "Too shallow?"

Paul nodded, his brow furrowed with concentration. "They probably haven't dredged this turnaround since Napoleon's time."

There was a convenient bollard on shore. I threw a line around it and Paul tried to pivot to swing the stern around. A family living nearby in a small beat-up caravan stared at us. The woman hung laundry on a makeshift clothesline with a dirty toddler wrapped around her feet. She looked at us vacantly. Two boys around six and twelve years of age tried to grab the lines. "*Non, non,*" I shouted. One finger between the line and a bollard and... They had a guttural sound to their speech and kept shouting at us. I didn't understand what they were saying. So they got louder. In the meantime we were dodging pleasure boat and commercial traffic. We blocked the canal every time we attempted a turn. No matter what we tried, one end of the boat or the other ended up stuck in the muck.

We gave up. I wrestled the lines away from the boys. We'd noticed another spot several kilometers back up the canal. Again it was neither wide enough nor deep enough as we discovered after we spent another hour trying. We hated to backtrack, but we had no choice. We retraced yesterday's route, trying spots that looked large enough for us to turn around. Finally, fifteen kilometers back in the direction we'd come from the day before, we found a wide spot and made our turn. As the bow moved across the shallow area, hundreds of silver fish leapt a foot into the air as we passed. Suzanne and I whooped and cheered.

"Let's do the Turn Around Dance," Suzanne said and we made up a kind of Motown dance where we spun around waving our hands in the air singing..... then we noticed a boatload of fishermen staring at us. At least we flew the Dutch flag and they wouldn't know we were crazy Americans.

Once we turned around and retraced our route it was too late in the day to get to another port before dark. We moored in the exact same spot as the night before, with an important difference – we faced the right way this time.

Suzanne came here to heal her broken heart. "You know," she said. "I'm having a great time with you two. But I sure would like to go out with a guy on a date." She munched on her croissant sandwich stuffed with scrambled eggs and sausage.

"Suzanne, it's not going to happen. We are out in the middle of Nowhere France where you don't even speak the language." I chewed for a while. The sandwich was great. I've never been a sweet tooth – give me fats and spice. "Besides, you should save your energy for the twenty-eight locks we have to go through tomorrow."

She raised her eyebrows and kept chomping.

All along this trip we'd been ascending. Finally we were at the summit of the area. At the top near Le Chesne was Lac de Bairon, the lake that fed this canal and kept the water level stable. Before this system was developed a long drought could close the canals. The lake not only provided water for the canal but also was a leisure center with a swimming beach and kayak rental. On our chart Paul showed us the series of locks we were going to do.

"Twenty-six locks in the flight series," he said. "Plus two additional ones. All in one day. Once we start, we can't stop. The chart says to allow seven hours to descend. So, let's get an early start tomorrow."

At the first lock in the chain, I felt as if I was at the top of a steep set of stairs. Each lock was three meters deep, about nine or ten feet. It looked like as we exited one chamber we'd start entering the next. The first lock had a lockkeeper who handed us a sheet explaining how the automatic locks would work.

We were told to obey the lights and pull the blue lever (*not* the red emergency one) to activate the process of letting the water out. We had to push a bar just above the water near the exit lock door to start the next lock in the series. We knew smaller boats often had a crewmember (the wife) use a boat hook to manually push the bar. But for once our larger size could work to our advantage and *Imagine*'s hull should shove the bar as we exited each lock.

We made it through the first two locks with no problem. I timed us and found we could go through a lock in about ten minutes. At that rate, we should be through the series in less than half the time the chart told us it would take. I was optimistic as usual. The lock door for the lock number three opened and a full-sized *péniche* lumbered out of the door directly at us.

This is where a commercial barge might run us aground, I thought.

Paul steered *Imagine* as close to the bank as he could. The *péniche* practically filled the canal. It would first push us up against the bank with the water it displaced. Then, as it passed, its propeller would pull our stern towards it. How violently all this happened depended on how kind the commercial pilot was. If he was careful and slow I could use rubber bumpers to fend us off the other boat. If the *péniche* pilot gunned his engine as he passed us we would run aground.

I remembered the commercial captain who pulled us out of the banks on our training voyage. I gulped as the black hulk neared.

But this pilot took pity on us and eased past us with his engine just above an idle.

We got back in the rhythm of going through a few more locks until we exited one where the right-hand lock door didn't retract fully into the wall when opened. Paul maneuvered to the left and narrowly avoided scraping the door against the side of *Imagine*. As we approached the next lock, the signal light was red, not the combination of red and green that showed the lock was filling for us. Usually this meant there was either a boat already in the lock, or another craft had signaled first from the oncoming direction.

But it was clearly empty and there wasn't another boat in sight. We waited and speculated as to what the problem might be. If in that last maneuver to avoid the door we failed to catch the bar, this lock wouldn't activate. There was a small building next to the lock with a phone in it to call the French Waterway Authority, the VNF. There was no easy way to get off the boat but Suzanne was willing to jump to shore and make the call. We coached her so she could tell them in French the number of the lock and convey it wouldn't open.

She made the emergency call. "Hey," she yelled from shore. "He's coming. Some guy spoke enough English to tell me he'll be here in a few minutes."

A white moped zoomed up the towpath and a dark haired man dismounted, went into the control room and started the sequence. He and Suzanne talked animatedly, grinning all the while. She hopped back on board and said, "His name's Christian and he speaks good English. He told me to tell you he likes your boat." We waved at him and shouted, "*Merci*."

Four locks down there wasn't a red light, or a double red light, there were no signal lights at all. Paul and I were stumped. What could be wrong now?

I was beginning to understand the seven-hour estimate to pass through this stretch.

In an effort to save money, the VNF hired part-time workers with a goal of automatic locks everywhere. When the locks worked it was the most efficient and cost effective way to operate. Still I preferred someone to talk to when things invariably went wrong.

Suzanne jumped to shore, made the call, and we waited. Two men on VNF mopeds zoomed up, including Christian. He told us there'd been a power outage and several locks weren't working. It should be fixed shortly. In the meantime he and Suzanne chatted on shore. The power came back on.

"I'm going to walk the towpath for a while," Suzanne shouted. She and Christian meandered off. I began to get the idea.

Suzanne rejoined us but by the end of the series Christian hung with us "just to see how we are doing." In a final conversation they agreed to go out to dinner together. I'm not sure who asked whom out but I was happy for Suzanne. After we moored Christian arrived in a Mercedes sedan (his father's we found out later) to take her to a restaurant in his village. I took the car as a good sign and realized I felt responsible for my friend. At least I knew where he worked and even where he lived

I heard her close the pilothouse door late in the night. The next morning I shook my head in disbelief. "Only you," I said, "could find someone out here in the middle of the country."

She shrugged and smiled. "He spoke enough English."

On Friday we arrived in Rethel where Suzanne and I took a train to Paris for the last two days of her visit. I felt a little guilty leaving Paul to spend the weekend doing maintenance on the boat but not guilty enough to not go. We had dinner in a simple sidewalk café, ordered the *plat du jour* and sipped on Côtes du Rhône. Back at the hotel we changed for a night out on the town – Suzanne looked like Sarah Jessica Parker in her clinging sheath and three-inch high-heeled strappy sandals. In contrast, I wore a skirt down to my ankles and a pair of flats. *Vive la différence.* I used to wear high heels, I thought, let me see, how many years ago was that? I probably couldn't even stand up in them now. I didn't wear underwear that pinched, shoes that hurt or even panty hose if I could avoid it. I didn't know if it was the wisdom of age, the casual life style I led or being happily married for almost fifteen years. Whatever.

Suzanne picked out a jazz club in the Latin Quarter within walking distance. Downstairs in the smoke-filled cave a quartet played something resembling jazz. I grabbed a glass of red wine, found a bench along the wall and sat there thinking about how much I hated bars. Suzanne danced with a variety of guys and at least she seemed to be having fun. An older, paunchy man next to me leaned over and said in a British accent, "Unsavory looking chap your friend is dancing with – I'd watch out for him." He continued to critique of all the characters and soon I was giggling.

When I told him I spent the summer on our barge, he told me he also owned one in Dover.

"Our barge is steel," I said.

"Mine is iron." This was the height of the ultimate in barges; rare, very old and considered by many to be the strongest hull to have. I was impressed.

"Ours is twenty-five meters long."

"Mine is twenty–two," he said.

"Ah," I said, "yours is harder but ours is longer."

Touché.

It was fun talking to him but I noticed Suzanne had disappeared. In the other bar upstairs, I found her engrossed in a conversation with several people. They looked at me with expressions of awe as Suzanne introduced me. What *had* she been telling them? They were fast track Silicon Valley software people. I recounted my work history and what we were doing now. One particularly burnt-out looking young guy said, "You mean after working sixty hour weeks for years at least there's hope and a light at the end of the tunnel?"

Most people postpone what they really want to do for a variety of reasons. Sometimes they live in a place they dislike because they feel tied to it because of work or family or both. Or they hate their job but feel it's the only thing that will provide them with the income they need to survive. I can relate to all of the reasons because they have been mine too, sometimes for good reasons, sometimes for self-created ones.

I nodded yes, there was light at the end of the tunnel and the light could be nearer than you thought if you really wanted something.

"What's the name of the barge?" they asked.

"*Imagine.*"

"For the song?"

I nodded. For the song and for imagining the possibilities in life that could be yours if you're willing to take a risk.

Suzanne's feet were blistered from her high heels so she took her shoes off and walked the seven blocks back to the hotel barefoot. I resisted the impulse to gloat (aloud anyway) as I clumped along on my sensible flats. Instead, I focused on praying she didn't cut her foot on a piece of glass or step on a fresh dog turd along the way. France is a beautiful country with little litter in the street. The people are refined, polite and they are justifiably proud of their rich cultural heritage. There is, however, one aspect of their culture the French could stand to change – the custom of letting their dogs poop anywhere on the sidewalk or street and not picking it up. Instead street and sidewalk cleaners come by periodically, cleaning up the poodle poop along the way. In the meantime walking anywhere can sometimes be like picking your way through minefields of *merde.*

The next day was Sunday. My plans included the Musée d'Orsay, the Eiffel Tower, and dinner in the Latin Quarter. There was much to see and do in this city but instead of trying to see too much I wanted my friend to see something in depth and the Musée d'Orsay was it. We waited in line for about a half an hour to enter the elegant 1900 Beaux Arts interior with its immense glass-vaulted ceiling.

Originally a train station, it was closed during the 1970's because of diminishing train travel and was almost demolished. The French government wisely decided to save and renovate the beautiful structure that opened as a museum in 1986. It contained mid-nineteenth century through early twentieth century paintings and sculptures. The Impressionist paintings from the Jeu de Paume Museum were transferred here, along with some works from the Louvre and the National d'Art Moderne that fit into the time period from 1848 to 1914.

But before we began our tour we had to eat. And there was nowhere better than the Restaurant d'Orsay, a grand room with lofty figure-painted ceiling outlined in gilded gold from which hung enormous crystal chandeliers. The food was grand too – rare tuna steaks in cream sauce with braised endive and pureed fennel accompanied by a bottle of chilled white wine.

"Now we're ready to see the art," I said.

We wandered the lower floors viewing the Romantic and heroic paintings, masterpieces by Ingres, Delacroix and Millet, all setting the stage for the art revolution to come. There were interesting models of the Paris Opera and of Paris as seen by a hot air balloon in 1848. At last, we trekked upstairs to the Impressionists: Manet, Monet, Degas, Renoir, Van Gogh, and a new favorite, Albert Sisley, an English painter who'd lived in France and used the canals and barges of Moret-sur-Loing as subject matter. The barges, canals and locks hadn't changed appreciably and some of the paintings might be of *Imagine* today.

It was hard to believe these artists were once reviled and banned by the establishment; their work was so popular we had to thread our way through crowded rooms, walking from one dazzling painting to another. I felt dizzy as if I were overdosing on the beauty. I enjoyed Suzanne's stunned reaction to the paintings as we walked slowly and spoke softly, almost reverently. We stood for a long time in front of Van Gogh's oil of his small bedroom in Arles, which vibrated with color and brushwork. Suzanne returned to Van Gogh again and again.

"What do you like about him?" I asked, expecting answers an art student might give –his use of color, form, texture, composition, or brush strokes.

She studied the painting, so near she might touch it.

"His godliness," she said.

We took the metro to the Eiffel Tower and craned our necks to gape at the massive structure. Aggressive vendors at the base sold all kinds of cheap souvenirs: mechanical birds that careened wildly, designer knock-off watches, plastic miniatures of the tower. What is it about traveling outside hometown city limits that causes all good taste to go by the wayside? Tourist junk is everywhere tourists are, so people must buy it. In Colorado and the West it's cheap "Indian" artifacts: beads, pottery, moccasins, shot glasses, coffee mugs, wind chimes, drums and cowboy statues. Come to think of it, Lake Geneva, Wisconsin had pretty much the same stuff. Maybe there's a huge factory manufacturing universal tourist trinkets for the world in Malaysia or Thailand.

Over a glass of wine in a café, Suzanne told me she had decided not to revitalize her relationship with her boyfriend and to go her own way. I thought this was a good idea from some of the stories she'd confided in me over the week but I've learned over the years not to be too harsh on anyone's ex or soon-to-be-ex. The couple may get back together and your friend will usually forgive her boyfriend or husband his past transgressions, but she will unerringly remember all the negative things you said about him while they were broken up. I cautiously said I thought this a good decision. The biggest problem with their relationship seemed to be a common one – perversely, the qualities that attracted him to Suzanne in the first place were those he'd rigorously been trying to change.

Then she gave me her own advice when I mentioned we had to get going down the canal soon to pick up the next guests.

"Slow down and take the false pressure off yourselves. Look at Val and Rolland," she said. "They're never in a hurry. They stop for days at a time when they feel like it, to go for a hike or explore a local church. What's the rush? Isn't that why you're here?"

She was right, of course. After thirty years of business deadlines and quotas, hurrying had become a habit and it was second nature for us to set a measurable objective and meet it even if the real goal was something else.

On the train station platform, we hugged goodbye. She stood back and looked me deep in the eyes. "I don't know how people stay married."

"What?" A chill ran down my spine. Suzanne was second only to my mom in near-clairvoyant empathy. "Where did that come from?"

"Oh, I didn't mean you, just people in general." She shrugged.

I rushed to my train. Most of the French people around me read. Teenagers sat with closed eyes, headphones plugged into their ears. As the quiet train raced through the countryside, I sat with my eyes wide open.

Had Suzanne seen something I refused to admit even to myself?

8 - The Lesson of Château Regnault

For my part, I travel not to go anywhere, but to go. I travel for travel's sake. The great affair is to move; to feel the needs and hitches of our life more nearly; to come down off this feather-bed of civilization, and find the globe granite underfoot and strewn with cutting flints.
                                                    -Robert Louis Stevenson

urprise!" Paul said as he removed his hands from my eyes.

"Wow, how did you ever do all this in two days?" I shook my head. He'd painted the entire topside of our eighty-foot barge while I'd been in Paris. *Imagine*'s superstructure was now a pristine white. The rusty stains from the Grave shipyard welding by-product were gone. Mismatched window trim was now an identical royal blue on both sides of the barge. Large black gaps where Desirée had stopped painting were replaced with solid deep reddish orange side decks.

Over a glass of Côtes du Rhône that night I said, "You know, Suzanne reminded me we're not on a software business schedule anymore."

"I do know," said Paul. "But it's tough not to be compulsive."

"Like painting the entire boat while I'm gone for two days? Like that?" I smiled and held his hand.

We'd known this intellectually but now we were ready to take Suzanne's advice and Roland and Val's example to heart.

"Yeah. And remember how we had fun in Château Regnault because we hung around the extra day?"

Paul nodded and talked about how we could change our approach to cruising. We decided on a strategy – we would go fewer kilometers and locks each day and would spend at least two days a week in port. We both agreed this would improve the quality of our time in France dramatically.

We raised our glasses and clinked them together.

"To 'The Lesson of Château Regnault'," I said. "May we never forget it."

Something else about us had changed. Slowly and gradually without either of us trying – we'd been losing weight. Paul had lost the most and was down to the last hole on his belt and he needed a size smaller pair of jeans. A pair of shorts I bought in Grave hung loosely on me especially in the waist. We didn't have a scale on board but Paul had weighed himself at a hardware store on a commercial scale in Holland and had lost about twenty-five pounds then. Now he looked appreciably slimmer.

In a way we weren't surprised, as Roger Van Dyken had told us he'd lost about thirty-five pounds when he was barging in Europe for seventeen months with his family. But, it was ironic after years of trying to be "good" eating low-fat or no-fat food, the most dramatic weight loss occurred while we happily feasted daily on chocolate butter-laden pastries, Brie and Gruyere cheese, liver pâté, all washed down with Côtes du Rhône.

The Barge Diet – An effective weight loss program.

1. Buy a barge built in 1906.
2. Thoroughly clean the barge yourself preferably spending a great deal of time on your hands and knees, swearing some dirt dates back to 1906.
3. Paint every square inch of its eighty-foot length by fifteen-foot width inside.
4. Repeat the above process outside.
5. Go up the stairs from the aft cabin to the pilothouse and then down the steep stairs to the salon area. Repeat many times a day.
6. Haul lines for locks and mooring. Sometimes repeat mooring steps several times in one day if moorings are found to be unacceptable after tying up. Bonus for using heavy water-soaked ropes.
7. Don't own a car – walk or bike ride everywhere.
8. Go to the local villages on foot.
9. Get lost in local villages and walk even more.
10. Eat as much French food as you like and nothing labeled "Low-fat", even if you can find it.
11. Consume plenty of good French wine.
12. Relax and watch the world go by.

We stood on the train platform in Rethel as the local train screeched to a halt. "I see Paul," I said, spotting him above the crowd. "And there's Margaret." We ran over to them and I hugged Paul's son. Margaret and I exchanged triple kisses on our cheeks. She looked more French than a Frenchwoman with her dark hair and ivory skin. She enhanced her European look by wearing black except for a burgundy scarf knotted at her throat. "*Bonjour, mes amis*," she said. She not only looked French, she spoke it well enough to teach it at a college level and was pursuing her PHD in the language.

We had a bunch of tasks for her where her language expertise would come in handy. After they settled on board, we went about the daunting job of finding out how to get a cell phone and how to communicate wirelessly on the Internet. First we planned to try in Rethel, a fairly good-sized town. Then, if we couldn't find what we needed, we'd give it a go in Reims.

Paul and Margaret set out several times to visit French Telecom to get a cell phone and an Internet connection. On the first visit, the phone store was closed for an exceptional reason – "*fermé exceptional*" read the sign, with no further explanation. The next attempt was thwarted when a long line wound out the door because the store had been closed the day before.

"It usually takes three tries to be successful in France," Margaret told us.

The third try worked and we became the proud owners of a cell phone, with a "pay as you go" plan. But we still couldn't figure out how to connect to the Internet with it, nor could people at phone stores or computer stores. After a few more attempts along the way, trying different stores and different approaches, we were defeated in going wireless. It seemed we were on the "bleeding edge of technology," not for the first time in our lives.

Margaret and I completed a second quest more successfully – we both got haircuts and I had mine highlighted. It was easy enough to say "blonde" and point, but I never could've answered the more subtle questions about shades like, "More honey or more ash? More around the face than the back?" No one in the shop spoke English. The hairstylists did a careful job and we both walked out of the shop satisfied and feeling very chic.

At night, after dinner on board, we sat around the table under our candle lit chandelier.

"I'm worried about the language, there're too many English words creeping in," Margaret said as she ran her fingers through her chic new haircut.

"So? What's the big deal?" Paul III asked.

She banged her hand on the table and we all jumped. "Because it's more than just words, it's a symptom. First it's the cute American phrase like 'Bon Weekend.' Then another McDonald's opens up down the street." She shuddered. "Then before you know it, they'll want to turn your restaurant table instead of letting you have it all night."

"Language always evolves and changes. Look at what we speak. 'American' isn't 'English.' Language constantly takes on new slang, like it or not," I said.

She shook her head then sighed. "Let's have this discussion again, after you've lived here longer. I have a feeling you'll change your mind."

I thought about the supermarkets and discount stores we'd seen here and knew cultures were being homogenized. I didn't know how to solve the problem. How do you insulate any country, especially one in Western Europe, from the onslaught of modern communications?

"And the metric system. Why didn't America adapt it, huh? No, we always have to be different," she said. She poured herself another glass of Côtes du Rhône.

Paul nodded. "Yeah, it's great."

"You know, it's important to get used to things being done differently in another country," she said.

"Right," Paul says. "It's a great system. Makes a lot more sense than ours."

"It's wrong to expect everything to be done like it is in America. Ridiculous," she said. "Get used to it...."

Paul III and I looked at each other trying to figure out how to straighten out this conversation.

Finally Paul said, "I'm *not* complaining. As an engineer, I *like* the metric system, Margaret, better than our measurement at home. In fact the metric system makes perfect sense to me."

"Oh," is all Margaret could say when she realized she'd been arguing about nothing, and we all breathed a sigh of relief the non-argument was over.

I sniffed at the sweet smell in the air when we stopped to moor in Blanzy-la-Salonnaise. I spotted the source – a nearby sugar processing plant surrounded by sugar beet fields. The four of us set out to find stores in the small town of Asfeld and wandered until we were lost. For over an hour in the fading evening light we walked through beet fields studded with fireflies.

"You know what this looks like around here?" Paul III asked.

I studied the pastoral landscape. "Yeah, farmland."

He nodded. "Like the farmland around Madison, Wisconsin – with older buildings."

Finally we spotted the sugar factory and using it as our marker found *Imagine* moored along the bank. I sighed with relief and climbed on board.

Then it struck me. I hadn't been afraid of being lost. I knew better. Paul had a great sense of direction, unlike me. For the first time, I realized how much this barge had become home to me.

Home, I thought. We weren't homeless as we often joked. I had a new home that never left me.

Our chart showed a ship's chandlery in the town of Barry-au-Bac where we could buy some much needed supplies, like lines, boat paint, and more foul weather gear.

I squinted through the field glasses. "I see a store, all right, but I'm not sure if it's a boat store."

"I'll pull her over. Think you can jump to shore?"

Paul nosed *Imagine* as close to the bank as he could. I stared down at the ground a good six feet below me. Suzanne had jumped off the bow several times. Why couldn't I? I took a leap, hung in the air for a moment, landed on the weedy bank… and my knee collapsed. Nettles stung at my bare legs and I looked up to see three people staring at me with concern.

"You OK?" Margaret shouted.

"Fine, fine." I turned away before the tears sprang from my eyes. I wasn't hurt as much as embarrassed. Much as I'd always prided myself on a youthful attitude, the fifteen years between Suzanne and me made a difference. I had to admit daring feats of physical prowess were out of the question at my age.

Even if the "daring feat" was only a leap from the bow of my boat.

I managed to catch a line and tied the boat to a tree. The four of us walked to the store I'd spotted. Its stucco walls were painted with faded signs advertising marine supplies but inside it was a small grocery store with no nautical items in sight.

Margaret asked the man behind the counter for marine supplies. He scowled and said they haven't had boat items for years. Paul and I began to recognize a pattern. This chandlery was a grocery store and had been for years, the marine garage in Charleville-Mezieres wasn't where it was supposed to be according to our chart.

Our guidebooks and charts were seriously out of date, despite the current year printed on the cover. They couldn't be trusted.

And I'd jumped to shore for nothing.

In our aft cabin that night, I confessed to Paul. "I was afraid to jump ashore in the first place."

"Why didn't you tell me?"

"I don't know. I feel as if I'm letting you down."

"You only let me down if we can't talk. I can't do this without you." He kissed me. "So no more jumping off the boat, OK?"

"Never, ever."

Along this stretch of the canal Paul had trouble entering the locks. Every time he lined up *Imagine* as straight as possible, an invisible force shoved the boat from one side to the other. We'd bang a wooden fender on port against the granite wall, and then ricochet off the starboard. Or vice versa.

I thought Paul had lost his knack for piloting. "Want me to take over?"

"Thanks for your vote of confidence, but I don't think you'd do any better." He explained the problem. Spillways for the water above each lock in the canal were close to each lock entrance. "Look," he said as he pointed to the water gushing in by the side of the lock entrance. Sure enough, as Paul slowed down for entry the turbulence grabbed our barge and shoved her hard to the right. I held on as the boat banged against the lock.

"The engineer who designed these locks never drove a boat our size," Paul said through gritted teeth. "If he ever piloted a boat at all."

And the engineer certainly had been a student of the Marquis de Sade.

Paul decided to use more power to counter the effect of the spillways. I held my breath at each entry. Instead of slowing *Imagine*, Paul gunned the engine. The granite lock corners seemed to rush at me. As the bow would come in, I jumped up and fended off the largest smacks with our rubber bumpers, trying to keep the sides of the boat from scraping the sides of the lock and ruining our paint job, or worse yet, denting our steel hull. We weren't alone – the entrances were smudged with bright red and blue paint scraped from other boats that had trouble as well. We discussed various approaches. I was pro going slowly, but Paul insisted the speed was necessary for control. No matter what he tried, we bumped gracelessly as we entered every single lock.

After several of these locks I was on my usual station, up on the bow. My stomach clenched and I had to remember to breathe. As we approached the lock, it seemed to me we were heading directly into the stone corner of the entrance. And it felt like we were going fast, way too fast. I looked back at the pilothouse seventy feet away, but I couldn't see Paul clearly. What was going on?

Seventy tons of boat was about to hit an inflexible stone wall. I sat in horror wondering what I could possibly do. I clenched my large rubber bumper in my hand. I could put it between the boat and the wall. This might save the boat from damage. It might.

It looked like we were going to hit on the starboard, right near me. But what if I lost my footing in the crash? Within a second, I made the decision of a lifetime.

I would let the boat take the blow. I grabbed a sturdy pipe and braced myself.

Bang! *Imagine* shuddered, granite chips flew into the air, I held up my arm to shield my face. With a shiver, the realization came to me. Had I stood near the impact, I would've likely been thrown overboard and crushed in the lock between my boat and the lock wall.

Were we taking on water? I hung over the edge of the boat. I couldn't see anything other than a new six-inch long, several-inch-deep dent in the chin of our bow. Pieces of granite lock wall lay scattered on the deck.

I tied up the bow with adrenaline-shaking hands then rushed downstairs to see what'd happened inside. We weren't sinking, but the impact had been so strong it'd knocked Margaret over while she washed the morning's dishes.

"I'm OK, fine." She stood up, brushing off her derriere. "Just startled, that's all. What happened?"

I found a light fixture lying on the salon floor, popped out of the ceiling from the force of the impact. Not too much damage…except the dent of course.

But better a dent in my beloved *Imagine* than in me.

Paul III was a natural working the lines. I could sit on the deck or visit with "my Paul" in the pilothouse instead of running out to work the lines every few minutes. Margaret avoided the lines as if they were snakes, but helped in her area of expertise. We always had problems asking lockkeepers about mooring – was it deep enough for our draft, did the marina accept a boat of our size, what was the charge for mooring? Even the word "mooring" wasn't something we'd learned in school. Our chart translated some words, but we could tell by the puzzled expressions of those we've attempted to ask, that we weren't using *quai*, quay, the correct way.

In Reims there was a *Halte Nautique*, a boat harbor, with full services. We were worried we wouldn't fit. Instead, we found a spot along the wall and tried mooring. *Imagine* stopped about six feet away from the wall. I walked back and saw mud churning up behind us. I knew the signs by then – too shallow. No markers, nothing on the charts.

"I'll check it out for you," Margaret said. I winced as she leapt ashore but she landed as gracefully as a gazelle.

She returned in a few minutes. "We're in luck. There's a space our size with electric, right over there." She pointed next to a boating school.

The harbormaster hurried out of his office, the *capitainerie*, to warn us in a mixture of English and French to steer clear of the fence and the school boats.

Paul squeezed *Imagine* into his parallel parking spot and I lassoed the bollards like a cowgirl. I felt a rush of pride and a new feeling about us. Something like confidence combined with competence.

There was no sign of activity next door at the school. I read the sign. It was closed for the month of August, prime time on the water. Paul and I shook our heads and wondered at the difference between the States and France. So what if was the middle of summer? There was a vacation to consider first and foremost. We'd learned that lesson in Grave.

And yet, even with this non-profit attitude, commerce seemed to survive. Paul and I couldn't turn off our business minds. How did the smaller places stay open? The tiny Bayard Café, with only five customers for lunch, seemed to provide a living for the owner and his family. In America, we often got a check before a meal was finished. Filling the restaurant and turning a table over were critical in order to make the overhead and profit margins. In most of the rest of the world, it was unthinkably rude to deliver the bill until it was requested and most tables are occupied only for a single seating.

Perhaps the proprietors owned their buildings for generations, eliminating the overhead of steep mortgage payments or rent. They often worked the businesses themselves, rather than hire people. The Bayard Café offered only a single meal. The smaller stores keep limited inventory. If we bought a toaster, the dusty floor model might be the only one in stock. They would reorder a replacement the next day. In the unlikely event another customer comes in to purchase a toaster today, they would have to wait until the replacement arrived or go elsewhere. It was a simple version of "Just in time" inventory every manufacturer strives to achieve.

Do we need so many choices? I remember coming back from Asia, feeling like an alien from another planet when I was overwhelmed by all of the rows and rows of stuff on the shelves at the local discount store. And wandering through a supermarket where I counted seventeen kinds of canned kidney beans –aren't one or two brands enough? Or when I opened a menu the size of a small book, I had to wonder at the freshness of the ingredients or the preparation that involves a bank of microwave ovens, thawing out dishes in perfect portion-controlled sizes. It was efficient, based on carefully studied volumes, but it was an emptier way to live. We were hurried into finishing our nuked food, frustrated in long lines at our supermarket or discount check-out lines, cajoled into working more and more hours so we can attain enough wealth to "live the good life." The question was – when were we supposed to start living?

In Reims, we shopped for good French/English dictionaries and settled on *Le Robert and Collins Dictionnaire* recommended by Margaret. The large hardcover edition came with a small pocket sized one - they would help, as did our electronic language translator and our CD Rom interactive training tool "Learn to Speak French." I practiced using the dictionary to translate the cookbook that came with my combination microwave/convection oven.

Margaret taught us how to use more colloquial French than we'd learned in High School. It was more common to use "*Merci bien*" to thank someone very much, instead of what we learned in school, "*Merci beaucoup.*"

There were even more ways to say the word "yes" than I'd ever imagined.

"Parisian ladies," Margaret said, "say 'yes' this way." She inhaled quickly, like a gasp. "Now you try it."

I inhaled. She shook her head. I tried again, this time like I'd spotted a mouse on my foot.

"You've got it," she said as she nodded.

The word for "yeah" in French sounded like "way." Just as in the States, "yeah" was as popular or more so than the formal "yes" or "*oui.*" I would have thought the lockkeepers were trying to sound like California Valley Girls if I hadn't known.

Of course, sometimes it might be a detriment to really understand the language. One evening Margaret crawled down to the salon, fuming.

"What's wrong?" I asked.

"There's a bunch of teenaged boys and girls out by the dock, smoking cigarettes and swearing. I came in when they started talking about me. I wanted to tell them off, but they might come back later tonight and graffiti your boat."

I appreciated the thought and so did Paul after all the painting he'd done.

We had a view of the Reims Cathedral from our port. But the park next to the *Haulte Nautique* was home to a few men who drank their wine out of paper bags and staggered around the streets late at night into the early morning hours. When Margaret and I went for *baguettes* in the morning, we spotted one of them lying on his side in the park relieving himself on the grass. We gave them all wide berth, and especially him.

We left port and headed south down the Canal de l'Aisne a la Marne toward Chalons-en-Champagne, first through the industrial part of Reims where commercial barges picked up their loads of grain or coal. Eventually, the canal wound again through quiet countryside.

Ahead was a 2,302-meter long tunnel at the *Souterrain de Mont-de-Billy*, near the town of Billy-le-Grand. The tunnel was only wide enough for one boat at a time, so it was a one-way trip through a mountaintop. As we approached, we saw a green light and Paul switched on our searchlight. Paul

III and Margaret sat on the deck as we entered the dark, dripping, tunnel only inches wider than our boat.

Paul and I had been through another tunnel on the way here and it had been a challenge. If either of us had been claustrophobic I don't know how we'd have fared. Since the way was so narrow, the torque effect was dramatically increased; if we went too fast, the boat pulled to the right and we'd hit the wooden rub strip installed along the wall of the tunnel. We'd ricocheted to the other side, hit the rub strip and bumped until Paul put the boat in neutral and stopped. We'd had to do this several times whenever we got off kilter.

Our wooden fenders designed to protect the boat worked well until one of them caught on a rough part of the wall. The breakaway lines did what they were supposed to do with a loud snap. We'd stopped the boat and spotted our fender floating about twenty-five feet behind us. Paul had jumped on to the muddy emergency walkway along the right hand side of the tunnel. I'd held the flashlight for him as he'd fished out the fender with a boat hook.

This tunnel wasn't too bad. *Imagine* crawled thorough with only a few bumps and came out to daylight on the other side, forty minutes later.

Near Conde-sur-Marne, we dropped Margaret off at a lock and sent her ahead to scout out the port. When we arrived, she was chatting and laughing with a couple of fishermen.

"They want a beer," she said.

"But can we moor here?" Paul asked as our barge hovered in neutral.

"Ah, I haven't found out yet. They don't know." She scouted around and returned with the *captainaire.* He nodded, caught the lines for us and we neatly tied up.

We offered the fishermen a couple of cold 1664 beers as a good-will gesture. Fishermen were often the bane of our cruising. If they fished with poles long enough to reach the middle of the canals, we unavoidably disturbed them just by passing through. And perversely, they often placed multiple poles at the only wall with mooring bollards, in which case, Paul would send me to ask them to move.

As nicely as I could, in my best French, I'd shrug and apologize by saying "Désolée." I liked that phrase, it always sounded like "desolate." Most of the time, they'd move but reacted anywhere from gracious to grudging. And most of the time, they'd accept my offer of a cold beer as a peace offering.

We planned to stop in Chalons-en-Champagne for two days. Paul III wanted to push on to Vitry Le-Francois, the next large town.

"Why leave?" Paul said.

"I want to keep boating and see more villages," Paul III said.

Sticking with our new approach Paul said, "This is much more relaxing. Staying here, soaking up the sights of this town."

Paul III looked skeptical. It would be more relaxing – at least for Paul and me. We moored next to a park, the town center within easy walking distance. Our guidebooks were at least accurate about this city – it was charming. The St. Etienne Cathedral, built in the 13th century, had a collection of antiquities, including Roman stained glass and 12th century baptismal fonts and some odder relics– the slipper of the Irish apostle St Malachi and the reed mat of St. Bernard.

The smaller church, the Notre Dame en Vaux, was more elegant than the cathedral. Next door to it, a museum showcased a collection of recently excavated medieval art from a cloister built on the site in 1170 A.D.

The center of town was outlined in half-timbered buildings, exposed wooden beams surrounded by stucco and stone. At the Tourist Information Office, we discovered the town had a project to renovate these 15th century buildings. At one point, the half-timber facades went out of fashion and had been covered over. Now they were removing the stucco building-by-building, exposing the skeletal structure of the hand-hewn wood.

Huge baskets of hot-pink and purple petunias hung on every lamppost. In marked contrast to the dark wood and white stucco of the half-timbered facades, red geraniums with trailing vinca vines filled the window boxes. I half-expected to see Heidi or Hansel and Gretel traipsing down the cobblestones.

The Hotel de Ville, the 18th century city hall, was as ornate as a wedding cake. Tri-color flags fluttered above the Tomb of the Unknown Soldier in the middle of the square. Every French city and small village we'd visited had a war memorial, usually in a park with carefully tended flowers adorning the monument. It was often a small bronze statue of a soldier with the engraving "*Les Enfants de France.*" Plaques below were engraved with the individual names of those who died in each war. The list for World War I here was, as usual, five times as long as the total number of names listed for all of the other wars combined.

At the train station, we hugged and kissed Paul III and Margaret goodbye. They climbed on board the TGV headed to Paris. For the end of their holiday, Margaret intended to give Paul III a guided tour of the city she considered her second home.

"*Au revoir,*" we called out and waved at them until the train disappeared.

"That was a great visit," I said to Paul, wiping tears from my eyes.

"Then why are you crying? Sad at the thought of being alone with me again?" He smiled.

I grabbed his hand and said, "Not one bit, *mon chérie. Je t'aime.*"

And we strolled back to our barge hand-in-hand through petunia-scented boulevards.

Photos

Imagine in a lock.

Helping the lockkeeper open a lock, (picture taken from the bow.)

A classic lockkeeper's tiny cottage.

Our lockkeeper and friend M. Alain DeNuit in his lock house museum.

Imagine cruising under the plane trees.

St. Jean de Losne, near homeport.

Walking the towpath beside *Imagine*

Our main Salon.

9 - The Ditch

*Through travel I first became aware of the outside world; it was
through travel that I found my own introspective way into becoming a
part of it.*
--Eudora Welty

Whomp, whomp, whomp.

What the heck is that? I thought as I woke from a deep sleep. As I listened to the percussive beats, light reflected off the canal and created a wave-pattern on the aft cabin ceiling. Rubbing the sleep from my eyes, I crawled up the stairs to the pilothouse of *Imagine* and peered out the window. A mute swan thumped his wings on the water, then circled closer in an ice sculpture position with cocked neck, wings up and off his back. Like spoiled supermodels, swans seemed to expect to be handed the necessities of life on the sole basis of their beauty. I threw him some leftover *baguette* and his slightly smaller mate swam up to share in the bounty.

Only six months ago, I would have been sitting at my desk by this time of the morning while I gulped down my coffee. Or worse yet, driving off to an airport to catch a flight to visit another manufacturing company. I'd have spent hours replying to emails and voice mails, returning calls on my cell phone, updating my daily planner with everything to be accomplished. All the time, I would have stared out the sealed office window thinking of all of the places I would rather be.

On the canal it was an Impressionist morning; the warm sun lifted the fog off the water, plane trees lined the banks, the scent of wood smoke hung in the air. Stone houses were surrounded by lush gardens that would make Monet proud: soft color swirls of climbing roses, delphiniums, and larkspur. Only the small fish feeding just below the surface disturbed the water. The smell of Paul's freshly brewed coffee enticed me down to the galley where croissants and *pain au chocolat* awaited me. Over breakfast, he and I would discuss where we would go, study the charts and plan our day.

No phones, no emails, just our whims.

We'd stayed at Chalons-en-Champagne an extra day. Our earlier plans to go west toward Epernay and Paris had been scrapped. We traded long days of cruising for touring by heading down the Canal Latéral a la Marne instead toward our final destination, St. Symphorien sur Saône – homeport. The Canal's no-nonsense approach made it straight as a rail and earned its nickname – The Ditch. Its design seemed to shout utilitarian, built to move cargo from one place to another

We cruised past Vitry-le-Francois. Although the city dated from the 16th century, most of it had been destroyed during World War II. Ugly concrete block post-war buildings dominated the skyline. Nearby, the small village of Vitry-en-Perthois had been razed to the ground three times since it was fortified in the 10th century. We decided the area must have been strategic since it was near the junction of three canals and where main North-South and East-West waterways met.

"Good thing we didn't rush to get here," I said, nodding at the post-war buildings.

Paul smiled. "I'll have to tell Paul III he didn't miss anything."

Coming out of Vitry we needed to make tight turns where the Canal de la Marne a la Saône split off the Canal de la Marne au Rhin. The chart showed two bridges before the lock. As we approached, we cruised beneath an Autoroute highway bridge. The cars rumbled above us. Then we glided under the train bridge. It was dark; water dripped down from last night's rain. We both jumped as a TGV train thundered over us.

"Spooky," I said.

He nodded as he squinted through the binoculars. "I can't see the lock, can't see a signal light. There's nothing." The canal was so narrow, two boats couldn't pass.

"What if there's a boat coming out of the lock?"

"We're hosed." I knew Paul hated to back this boat up, especially around tight turns.

There wasn't another boat, the gates opened and we entered. I stood on the bow with the bollards at least ten feet above me. I waited for the lockkeeper to come and catch the lines. He walked by me. Odd, I thought. Oh well, I guessed I had to do it myself. I balanced on my tiptoes, used my boat hook, and looped the line over the top. I managed to wrap the line around *Imagine*'s bollard, just as the water poured in from the open gates.

My line ripped from my grip as he cranked the water gates to full open.

What the hell?

I spotted Paul yanking the back lines as *Imagine* was shoved toward the back wall. The rope burn on my hands stung as I tried to keep the boat under control. I shortened and rewrapped the lines as best I could as the boat kept surging back and forth.

I caught the lockkeeper's glance and pointed at my lines. "*Doucement, doucement*" I shouted. Gently, gently.

He squinted at me behind the Gauloise cigarette hanging from his mouth and shrugged. Then, I knew what was going on. He could control the flow but he was lazy and wanted us to get out of there as soon as possible. My hands throbbed and I shook from adrenaline and anger. We usually tipped the lockkeepers with a can of cold pop, but this time I wanted to throw the can at him and smack him in the head with it. I didn't say "*Merci. Au revoir*," as I always did when we left the lock we'd christened "The Lock from Hell."

In Orconte, we decided to stay for two days and enjoy the hot weather. The port bordered a large field of corn, the cicadas chattered and it felt like summer in the Midwest to me. I liked the cultivated gardens we'd seen, but I equally enjoyed the volunteer wild flowers at the edge of the fields – daylilies, Queen Anne's lace, chicory, milkweed.

Two people in port waved at us as we finished mooring and the man came over and introduced himself as Barry. While he sanded his cruiser the *Lady Jane*, he and Paul chatted. His wife Jane sat in the shade of a birch sewing a piece of complex-looking needlework, a tiny petit point. She reminded me of a titled English lady, her white hair piled high on her head.

"That looks tough. I'm not sure I'd have the patience." I said. Actually, I knew I didn't have the patience. Whenever I've crocheted or done needlework, simple and quick were my bywords.

"It is slow. But it lasts much longer this way." She threaded the tiny needle. "Just like it's good to have a book in English with lots of pages."

She had a point. Since everything took longer than we expected our entertainment had to last as well. My addiction to reading had been assuaged when Suzanne had brought paperbacks stashed in her suitcase. Paul III had delivered all of my back issues of "The New Yorker," including the summer fiction edition. I'd been in Reader's Heaven for a while until these too ran out. Now in Reading Limbo I waited for a future delivery from the next guests in a couple of weeks.

Barry and Jane invited us for a cold beer on a hot Saturday night. We set up chairs by a picnic table along the bank. Barry, a burly man with cobalt blue eyes, sucked down the brew with relish.

"What's your line of work, Paul?" he said.

Paul hadn't thought about "work" in a while, nor had I.

"We're retired from computer software. But we plan on chartering our boat."

Barry raised his eyebrows and glanced at our barge. "It's big enough all right. I've just retired from the shipping industry." He sighed and took another swig. "Don't you miss the excitement of it all?"

Paul shook his head. "This is exciting enough for me."

We all griped about our inaccurate charts.

"Have you noticed," Jane said, "the planned improvements along the way scheduled for completion in 1986?"

"Yeah," I nodded. "And the cover's printed with the current year. That must be all they update. I can't tell you how many stores are long gone." I thought about the hypothetical ship's chandlery in Berry-au-Bac where I'd jumped to shore for nothing.

It seemed inevitable that the conversation turned to other tales of woe. We admitted stupid things we'd done (getting stuck in the harbor in Holland) and they countered with managing to get turned around 180 degrees inside a lock (no small feat). We all complained about The Lock from Hell.

Barry warmed up. "We sailed the *Lady Jane* across the English Channel."

Paul raised his eyebrows. A trip across The Channel was a quest we wouldn't dare to take in our flat-bottomed boat. Combined with rough seas and loads of commercial traffic, it was a challenging voyage for the best of boaters. And like us, this was Barry's first year full-time in his boat.

"It went fine until a German sailboat decided to overtake me in a tight channel in France. Then the idiot ran aground right in front of me." He shook his head. "What else could I do? I hit him right in the middle of his hull." I imagined the cruiser's steel bow hitting fiberglass with a crunch. It wouldn't have been much of a contest.

"We had a few words. But of course, the German eventually admitted everything was his fault."

Paul and I exchanged glances. How close had Barry followed the German? How fast had Barry been going that he couldn't avoid hitting another boat?

"Then in Belgium, we were moored when a commercial pulled up. The barge captain kept yelling the mooring was 'Commercial only! Commercial only!'" Barry snorted. "I didn't know what he was talking about. The barge kept coming as he tried to moor at the quay. I'd yelled back, 'If you hit my bow...! Don't you hit my boat,'" Barry's face reddened as he retold the tale. "Eventually, of course, the barge captain apologized."

"Tell them the rest of the story," Jane said.

"Well, I guess the apology was undeserved. I found the sign later that reserved the quay exclusively for commercial barges. I just hadn't noticed it."

Paul and I stole another glance at each other as we sipped our beers.

"I'm anxious to get going, but the damn canal's closed tomorrow," Barry said. "You know the French and their days off. Just because it's Sunday, they can't work. Christ, I could've never run my shipping business this way." He shook his head and swigged on another beer. "I can't just sit here. You want to bike over with us to a lake tomorrow?"

We shook our heads. We planned on doing nothing much the next day, maybe wandering into town. After all, it was Sunday in France.

Sunday in Orconte was like Sunday used to be when I was growing up in the 50's before the advent of shopping malls open seven days a week for our shopping convenience. Tantalized by the aroma of fresh baked goodies, we meandered into the local *boulangerie* to buy some croissants, *pain au chocolate* and a fresh *baguette*. The bread was still warm. Grinning at each other, we each took a big bite out of the crispy loaf.

On sun-baked sidewalks, kids rode bikes to each other's homes, the sound of people singing at mass poured out of the church in the middle of town, the scent of family chicken dinners wafted from open windows framed by white lace curtains.

It reminded me of hot summer Sunday afternoons; our family dinners of ribs or fried chicken, televised baseball games provided background noise, the hypnotic quality of the announcer, "One strike, two balls, here comes the pitch." After dinner, the mid-afternoons games dragged on, I felt drugged by the heat and the hum of a fan. My father snored in his gold velour recliner; my eyes grew heavy as I listened to TV commercials for beer from the land of sky blue waters. The bedroom floor was cooler, I would lie down on it, windows wide open, cool wood on my arm, my leg, and I'd pray for a heat-braking rain while my mom in her sleeveless housedress would declare, "We're sweating bullets."

Jane and Barry returned exhausted that evening with their fair skin sunburned.

"The lake was further away than the damn signs showed," Barry said. "We rode a lot further than a couple of kilometers. We must've ridden over twenty kilometers each way."

Paul and I studied the map that night. It looked like they'd missed the closer lake and had found one further away.

"Barry would never admit it," I said, smiling. Paul grinned back.

We were certain he'd blame the map instead.

We continued down The Ditch, with traveling lockkeepers who were students working summer jobs. They scooted along on their VNF motorbikes on the towpaths after we left each lock and waited patiently for us at the next.

We'd occasionally see the portent of things to come – abandoned lock houses stripped of everything valuable, their doors cemented shut, windows boarded up and gardens in ruin, overrun with weeds.

Interspersed were full-time lockkeepers, mostly *Mesdames*, who lived in the quaint stone houses next to the locks as part of their compensation. Usually a lockkeeper held his or her job until retirement. Their well-tended gardens overflowed with roses, red climbers festooned most doorways. Coleus and masses of impatiens filled in the shadier sections. Baskets of petunias and geraniums hung on the lock doors.

None of the gardens was complete without an assortment of lawn ornamentation: plaster dogs, cats and ducks, small wishing wells, handmade flower containers made from tree stumps, and all sorts of fairy-tale characters and gnomes. The view was often comical; as we rose up in a lock more of the yard became visible until I stared eye-to-eye with Snow White and her entourage of seven dwarfs. Once, after seeing thousands of these little figures, a lock garden featured a foot-tall plaster gnome who held his robe open to "flash" me.

And he was anatomically correct.

Lockkeepers were notified of our arrival by the previous lockkeeper either by cell phone or by radio. The call-ahead system was handy as usually the next lockkeeper in the chain was waiting for us and had already filled or emptied the lock when we arrived. But there was a hitch – we had to let the lockkeepers know when we planned to stop for the night and start up again the next morning. So whenever Paul made an estimated time of departure in the morning, he tried to stick to it.

"I have a date with a lockkeeper," he'd say.

And then there was lunch to consider. The locks closed from noon until one every day. Sometimes, we arrived at a lock just before noon. The lockkeeper might pass us through. Otherwise, we would tie up in the lock and have our lunch while they had theirs. One man was willing to work through lunch and offered to let us through, but I could smell the delicious aroma of cooking chicken through the open door of his cottage where his wife stood at the stove. I knew the next lock ahead was probably closed anyway.

I shook my head, "*Non. Bon appétit, monsieur.*"

He grinned, wished us the same. He returned early to help us through.

We tried to help as much as we could with the heavy old locks dating from the mid-1800s. Once we rose up, one of us would hop off the boat and grab a huge paddle. Paul did more of the locks, but I'd tried too. I'd lean against the bar as soon as the lock filled and push hard while I walked in a big circle. Usually gravel gave my feet traction. I'd lean in harder and huge doors would open to let *Imagine* out. I'd hop aboard, untie the bowline and we'd glide out.

I was impressed that the lockkeepers were up to the physical challenge to do this for a living, especially older skinny men with cigarettes dangling from their mouths, heavy-set middle-aged women clad in dresses, sweaters and waterproof boots, and young college girls dressed in tight blue jeans and t-shirts who didn't weigh more than a hundred pounds.

If they could do it, so could we. Besides, it was one more step in the barge diet.

We watched television for our news and entertainment in the evenings. Our satellite, once it was lined up, had hundreds of available channels, but mostly Dutch. Our news and weather forecasts came from the BBC stations and CNN International. There was a presidential campaign going on in the States, mercifully, we'd had five minutes a night devoted to it on the news.

Instead, we heard more about what was going on in the rest of the world. Weather maps and satellite pictures were worldviews of every continent, the swirling motions of storms and high and low pressure areas flowed uninterrupted across the planet's surface instead of chopped off at country's borders.

Our favorite entertainment was watching British shows about food and travel. It was interesting to see how English people viewed French food, more open to the authentic dishes with all sorts of organ meats and tripe and sweetbreads, loads of lard and butter and real cream. But we couldn't bear to watch the English pub-cooking series with its greasy-looking food. It reminded me of the joke I'd heard while in Asia: The best things a man can have are an English house, a Chinese cook, a Japanese wife and an American paycheck. The worst? A Japanese house, an English cook, a Chinese paycheck and an American wife. I'd given the jokester a dirty look, as had his wife

We'd heard of a new series in America called "Survivor." It wasn't on our satellite. The most current shows featured were "Oprah" from two years before. "We may be the only Americans who haven't seen the show," I said to Paul.

"This won't be the first time we've been out of it."

Returning from Asia, during a layover in San Francisco, we'd sat in a jet-lagged stupor staring at children on TV performing a local ethnic dance. Later, we found out it was the Macarena.

We loved to view the programs where British people traveled to Las Vegas, New York and Chicago. They offered advice where to stay, ways to save money, and how to stay safe in the States. Barry had told us he'd had a hard time convincing Jane to go to America, she'd been afraid of being shot. They had visited South Carolina for business and had been pleasantly surprised by the graciousness and kindness they'd encountered.

When we told another British couple we owned an RV, similar to what they call a caravan, they wistfully said, "We'd love to travel in America by camper, but we don't own a gun."

"A *gun*?" I'd asked. We were astounded. We've traveled all around the country in our motor home and never had a problem. RV campgrounds were generally safe and friendly places. "Where did you get *that* idea?"

"A friend from Texas told us not to travel anywhere in the United States without a firearm," they told us. "And he warned us to be prepared to use it."

We continued down The Ditch toward the port at Saint-Dizier. Assumption Feast Day, a national holiday, meant staying put for a few days. Saint-Dizier was built on the site of an ancient stronghold famous for the siege of 1544 when 2,000 "brave lads" defended the town against 100,000 soldiers of Charles V. The expression "brave gars" in French has become the name the townspeople are known by today – the Bragards. Now, a huge Case International plant and a Miko ice cream factory along the banks of the canal dominated the large city.

As we cruised past the *port de plaisance*, I heard a yell.

"It's Barry and Jane," I said to Paul. "They're waving us to moor by them."

Paul shook his head. "Look," he said and pointed at the chart. "We're definitely not going to fit. And I'm not going through another episode trying to shoehorn in where we don't belong."

I agreed and stood on the deck pointing further down to a public quay where we knew we could moor. Barry kept waving.

After we'd tied off Paul said, "I'm going over to see if our British friends need anything." He grabbed a bike off the deck. "Barry looked a little frantic. Maybe something's wrong."

"He *always* looks a little frantic," I said as Paul pedaled off.

He found Barry pacing inside a chain link fence.

"I can't get out of here. We're locked in, dammit," Barry said.

"Let's see. There has to be a way out." Paul worked hard not to laugh.

"Can you believe we're penned in here for the entire holiday? They've gone home and left us." Barry's face reddened with outrage as he yanked on the padlocked gate.

Paul scouted out a hole in the fence.

"Thanks. You're a lifesaver." Barry breathed a sigh of relief as he crawled through. "Now I can get some beer before all the stores close."

And with that, he strode off.

On Assumption Feast Day, August 15th, Saint-Dizier shut down except for flower stores doing a booming business, some *patisseries, boulangeries* and *charcuteries*. Cafés and restaurants were also open and filled with families.

Because it was a holiday, we assumed The Ditch was closed. We glanced up when we heard the purr of a boat engine.

It was the *Lady Jane*.

"Do you want to cruise today?" Paul asked.

I thought for a nanosecond and shook my head. "Let's take the day off anyway; it's a holiday after all."

We waved at them and Barry called out, "We're moving on."

We knew they planned to end their season about the same time we did and wanted to go to Holland for some work on their boat. We'd quickly calculated they'd better start north *today* with as few stops as possible instead of going any further south this summer if they planned to meet this deadline.

"I can't stand the stress!" Barry shouted at us as he waved goodbye.

Laughter bubbled up in me and I shook my head. I'd found gliding down the waterways to be long stretches of relaxation occasionally punctuated by moments of terror. But stressful hanging around port for a holiday? Hardly.

He was a human mirror of us only a few weeks before. It was probably inevitable: we nicknamed him Bustling Barry.

10 - Convoy

The man who goes alone can start today, but he who travels with
another must wait till that other is ready.
--Henry David Thoreau

L et's tie up here and go out for lunch," Paul said, pointing at the bank
in Joinville.

"Twist my arm." But I didn't jump to shore to catch a tree. I let
Paul do that while I took the helm.

"Look at that cute boat." I said, pointing at an English "narrow boat," a 7-
foot wide, 30-foot long vessel parked nearby. Brightly decorated with hand-
painted flowers, lace curtains at the window and pots of red geraniums lining
the aft deck it looked like a toy boat, a craft for a tea party for dolls and teddy
bears.

A large man with a shock of ginger hair emerged. He jumped to shore
without bothering with a gangplank. A diminutive woman appeared and he
easily picked her up and set her down on shore like a cherished doll.

"I'm Eammon and this is Pat," he said. "I bet you're sick of hearing that
name with all of the legends around here. Eammon this and Eammon that,
especially if you've been through the Ardennes."

Ah, yes, we knew about the *Quatre Fils*, the four sons of Eammon. And
the horse they rode in on. I nodded. "We've been there. And stayed longer
than we expected."

They fell in step with us on our way to town.

"How did you get your narrow boat over here?" Paul asked. "You didn't
sail it across the English Channel did you?"

"No, no," Eammon said. "We had it shipped over here by freighter."

"How are the locks in your boat?" Paul asked.

"Most are pretty easy," Eammon said. "The lockkeepers love us. If we're
the only ones in a lock, they only have to open a single lock door for us. I bet

you have to squeeze in even with both doors open." He had a point. *Imagine* was almost twice as wide.

"But aren't you intimidated at least a little when you're in with a big commercial barge?" I said.

"Sure. But in fact even your boat looks like *The QE II* to us," he said.

"Would you like to join us for lunch?" Paul asked.

"We'd love to but we're on our way to market. We're out of wine and that won't do will it?" Eammon said with a smile. "Then we must be on our way."

We waved goodbye with regret. I'd taken an instant liking to them and hoped we could find them again along the way.

Joinville sat along the Marne River that meandered next to the canal. It was difficult to choose a restaurant since all of them took advantage of picturesque views of the river. We decided on a small outdoor café and ordered salads and grilled cheese sandwiches, *croque monsieur.*

"Maybe I'm missing my *toasti,*" I said between bites. "But the wine is better here than Holland." I poured from the carafe of house Chardonnay.

It was quiet along the cobblestone streets, people wandered into the small restaurant wishing everyone *Bon appetite Madame et Monsieur.* I felt drowsy in the sunshine while I gazed at the river.

This is the life, I thought. The one I'd dreamed of.

Our young lockkeeper, who'd traveled several locks with us, helped us moor near Froncles. "You must try to visit my town, if not today, perhaps over the weekend." He beamed. "It is a beautiful town. Promise me you will go."

I nodded. Why not?

Stone houses lined the canal in the peaceful village. All kinds of lace curtains decorated the windows: abstract medallions, designs of ducks, geese, cats, windmills, and flowers. So when we noted the lace curtains on the home across from our mooring it wasn't unusual. But the curtains were – the lace was woven into a picture of a barge on a canal.

In the small village of Froncles only one Tabac/bar/restaurant was open. Reggae music poured out. At the bar two women and two men smoked, and turned the bar into a smoky den.

I asked the bartender, "*Dejeuner possible?*"

"*Oui Madame,*" he said and rattled off the *plat de jour.* I heard "*frites*" – fries – and Paul heard tomato salad, but other than that, we weren't exactly sure what we were getting for lunch.

"I can't stay in here with the smoke. And you know how I feel about the smell of stale beer."

"I know," Paul said. He followed me outside to a lone cement table, its top decorated by a flower-shaped mosaic. The bartender came out and wiped down the table scattering flies, then dried off the white plastic chairs. The sun wasn't out after the earlier rain, but it'd brightened enough to make me wish I'd brought my sunglasses along.

A small wiry man with a beard emerged from the bar. He looked like he'd long ago decided most of his calories would come in liquid form. Doing a belly dance toward us, he twisted his hips back and forth while he sucked his bottle of 1664 beer. When he tried speaking to us in French, we conveyed we were American and spoke only a little French, "*un petite peu.*"

"Ah," he said, "*Americans.*"

"*Oui.*"

He danced around some more and said, "Election?"

We looked at each, trying to figure out how to say "primary elections." We couldn't come up with the right words.

"Ah, George Bush president!" he said.

"*Non.*" We struggled how to say George W. just won the Republican primary and wasn't president – yet.

We said, "Clinton. Bill Clinton is still president"

"Clinton?"

"*Oui.* Our president."

He digested that for a second or two and then, with a knowing grin on his face shook his head and wagged his finger. "Monica Lewinsky!"

"*Oui.*" We shrugged and shook our heads in dismay. Was there no place remote enough on earth, no human being anywhere, who doesn't associate those two?

He pointed at himself. "Drink *beaucoup.*" We, with our uncanny powers of observation, had already figured that out. He introduced himself as Jean-Marie.

The bartender acted as cook and waiter. He carried out the salad – sliced tomatoes and canned tuna in vinaigrette. He frowned at Jean-Marie and herded him back inside so as not to bother us. The salad along with our carafe of house red wine and the omnipresent great bread would've be enough for lunch. But he asked us how we would like our meat prepared. What meat? we silently asked each other.

"*Medium,*" I said. I don't know what I'm getting, so medium seemed a safe enough choice.

"As long as it's not chicken we're in great shape." Paul grinned.

In a while, the bartender arrived with a tray carrying two steaks with fries. Jean- Marie followed the bartender out, and gestured to ask if he could sit with us. It was just too early in the day to communicate with a stranger who didn't speak much of my language and who was slurring his. He smiled to show no hard feelings and shrugged and returned to his friends at the bar. A *fromage* plate of Brie, Gruyere, and Camembert cheese was delivered. For desert there was a plastic container of crème caramel each. *Tres bien.* We went in to pay our bill. The total came to about $15 US.

Jean-Marie sat alone at the bar, sipped his beer, and hollered to the bartender when he moved to the kitchen.

"You'd think he'd be sleepy by now and pass out," I whispered to Paul. We'd been there for the usual two-hour lunch.

"He hasn't lost a bit of steam," Paul said as Jean-Marie waved at us again, stood up and started belly dancing.

I thought about traveling through small towns with our limited language ability and was reminded of one exchange Paul and I had witnessed a few years ago. We'd been driving through Iowa on one of our countless trips between Chicago and Boulder. We'd stopped for the night in a small town off Interstate 80 with its water tower embellished with a huge smiley face. For supper we'd gone to the only diner in town and overheard a couple with strong French accents attempting to order their steaks rare. After their dinner had been delivered, we'd watched the look of frustration cross their faces when they tasted the wine and then as they sawed at their well-done steaks. They'd grimly finished their meal, puzzled no doubt, as to how America's breadbasket can disappoint a serious diner.

We were the only people to lunch at the Bar/Restaurant. We poked our heads in and bid "*Au revoir*," to the bartender and to Jean-Marie, who'd waved spiritedly to us from behind his beer.

"*Au revoir, mes amis*," he said.

In the port at Bologne, there weren't many facilities, just a small building with toilets, showers and spigots of potable water. We pulled in behind a smaller barge with something unusual on its aft deck; in addition to the pots of flowers and herbs, a flourishing garden of tomatoes was ingeniously planted directly in the plastic bag of garden soil. I hadn't grown my own tomatoes in a long time. I had to console myself with the fact that tomatoes in the markets here – even the supermarkets – were as good as homegrown ones in the States.

We introduced ourselves. Jim and Ellen in the smaller barge flew the new Euro flag but had American accents.

"Where are you from?" Paul asked.

Jim said, "From Europe." Although it didn't answer the question directly we approved of the "World Citizen" view. "We live aboard full-time on our barge and have been for the past several years."

A smaller cruiser pulled in behind us. Aboard were Graham and Nancy, an English couple, who like us were new to cruising. Recently retired, Graham was a thin, nervous looking man with gray hair and matching gray beard.

"Oh no," said Nancy said as she came out of the shower room. "It's broken. No shower for me and I was so looking forward to it."

It was hot and sunny. "Would you like to use one of ours? We have three." Too late, I remembered Eammon's comment about *The QE II*.

"Thanks, but that won't be necessary," she said. Later, I spotted her in her black one-piece bathing suit dousing herself with her portable shower, which consisted of a plastic bag hanging from a tree limb. She looked considerably cooler but I couldn't see showering in tepid water wearing a bathing suit as a replacement for a good hot shower. I thought about my Grohe faucets, our great water pressure and all of our electricity including the electric toilets.

No public restrooms for me, I thought, let alone portable showers in my bathing suit.

We sat in folding chairs that evening as we visited our neighbors. I felt like kids around the campfire telling ghost stories or RV campgrounds where the transient lifestyle made for convivial introductions and shared interests inspired easy conversations.

"How about that lock up near Orconte? Couldn't see a thing until we were right in front of the lock," Paul said.

"And the lockkeeper is a sadist. He cranked open the gates so fast, my line ripped from my fingers." I showed them my rope burns, just now healing.

Graham and Nancy exchanged glances.

"It was," Graham said, "the worst lock we've ever been through. What could go wrong did go wrong."

As they'd approached the narrow channel under the bridges, Graham had let his wife off on shore to see if the lock was open and available. As Graham approached the lock, he'd heard his wife's urgent voice on his walkie-talkie.

"Back up, back up! There's a full-sized *péniche* leaving the lock, heading right for you."

He'd jammed his boat in reverse. "I heard an awful screech. I climbed out to find my antennas wedged on the train bridge. I grabbed some tools, and took the whole arch apart, while I kept one eye on the *péniche* as it approached."

"Did you make it in time?" I asked.

"I managed it, only just." He shook his head. "But then the barge's wake shoved me so hard I thought our cruiser was a goner. After I made it into the lock, well, you know. Somebody ought to report that lockkeeper."

"The Lockkeeper from Hell," I said nodding.

"Hey look at this," I said the next morning. The smaller barge seemed to be floating away from the dock, heading out toward the middle of the Ditch. I grabbed the field glasses. I couldn't see anyone at the controls in the pilothouse. "Maybe they've broken loose." I frowned. It didn't make sense. The weather was calm and no commercial barges had been by.

Paul ran out to see if they needed help. A few minutes later, through my field glasses, I saw Jim appear from below and take over the wheel.

Paul returned, shaking his head. "As near as I can figure out, this how they leave a mooring." Not our style, but then, they'd been barging longer. Maybe someday we'd be relaxed about maneuvers. Maybe.

If Jim and Ellen were casual boaters, Graham was the opposite.

While *Imagine*'s engine warmed up, Graham popped out of his cruiser.

"You need any help?" He eyed the distance between his boat and ours. "Do I need to move my boat?"

I shook my head as I untied the bowline and smiled. "Nope, we're fine."

"Exactly how long did you say you've been cruising?"

"Long enough," I said. "We haven't damaged another boat…yet."

Nancy stood on their deck with her buoy in hand ready to fend us off while Graham pranced on shore.

We felt smug. After so many screw-ups it was nice to have mastered some moves. And leaving a mooring was one we'd practiced a lot. I unwound the rear mooring lines, moved forward and put my big inflatable bumper against the pivot point on the wall to keep from scraping the paint. Paul revved up the engine, and the rear of *Imagine* moved out into the channel.

Once the aft was out far enough, Paul put the engine in reverse and eased our barge out into the middle of the canal. I cast off the front line. The bow swung out, and *voilà.* Paul shoved the gearshift into forward and we were on our way. I smiled to myself, knowing we'd done a good job of pulling out from our parallel parking space.

I snuck a look back at Graham, expecting to see admiration on his face, maybe even awe at how well we'd handled our large boat.

Instead, I spotted him coughing from our diesel fumes with a distinct look of disgust on his face. So much for impressing him.

On the way to Langres, we stopped at the port of Chaumont. The town perched high on a hilltop surrounding the ruins of a castle from 940 A.D. Away from the center of town, the city became increasingly modern until it ended in a sprawl of an immense shopping center of discount stores.

The port was neatly manicured with petunias planted in rows around a flagpole. In the office, the Madame behind the counter politely asked us to sign her guest book I tried to think of something interesting to inscribe but writing our United States address was probably enough, there were so few Americans here.

We went out to check out the port. Jim and Ellen were moored and Graham had bravely pulled in behind us again. Maybe he trusted us enough now not to hit him.

A café within walking distance provided another fine meal of *coq au vin*, chicken in wine sauce, a salad and a potato gratin. The weather was nice enough to sit under the flower-covered patio arbor. It was a busy Saturday. We greeted everyone who walked by, "*Bon appetite Mesdames et Monsieur.*" We received some quizzical looks, but they responded accordingly, thanking us and wishing us a good meal. We knew we couldn't pass for French once we opened our mouths, but we've been stopped several times and asked for directions in French. At least we didn't look too foreign. Sometimes we'd say we were American to explain we're only visitors like them. Other times, we'd surprise them with a short explanation of where to find the train station.

Whether or not they trusted us enough to follow our directions once they left was another matter.

Just before a short tunnel near Condes, we tried to get through one more lock before the lockkeeper's lunch break. As we waited, a *péniche* steamed out of the lock. As he passed us, the barge pilot gunned the engine and shoved us hard to starboard.

I coughed from the diesel fumes left in the barge's wake. Paul revved the engine, but *Imagine* didn't budge. Mud riled up off the bottom of the canal.

We'd run aground.

Paul left the pilothouse, grabbed a boathook, and tried to shove our 70 tons off the bank. Nothing. He went back in and revved the engine hard. Blue smoke poured out of the exhaust. Would we overheat again?

The lockkeeper watched us from the open, waiting lock. Finally, she walked over to us on the towpath and pointed to her watch. Maybe she thought we'd stopped for lunch.

I knew it was lunchtime. I tried to think of the words for, "Didn't you see it? The big boat ran us aground, the son-of-a-bitch gunned his engine right when he passed us."

Unfortunately – or fortunately – the words didn't come. I pointed in the direction of the large barge and said, "*Péniche.*" I shook my fist in his direction.

She nodded and pointed to her watch again.

I shrugged. "*Bon appetite, Mademoiselle.*" There was no telling how long we'd be hung up on the bank.

I put a bumper down to fend us off of the rough rocks along the edge of the canal. The rock had been put there to prevent erosion, but it made for a nasty shoreline. I tried to think of ideas to help Paul. It was too steep a jump for me to hop off the boat and tie around a tree on the opposite bank to pull us off the bank. I remembered Fran's daughter swimming across the river to free *Sea Lion* when it'd run aground. The canal was only about six feet deep, but the bottom was mud and muck. *Imagine* proved that – the water was murky with weeds and mud as Paul kept the engine revved. No way was I going to swim to the other side.

No, I would have to wait for Paul to figure it out. It was only a matter of time and patience I told myself. And then, inching forward and backward, bit-by-bit, Paul eventually worked us loose of the bank.

But something was wrong. *Imagine* floated in the middle of the canal but wasn't moving. I walked back to the pilothouse. "Now what?"

"Take the wheel while I check out some things." I waited, something I'd done a lot of lately.

He came back frowning. "I'm afraid we've damaged our propeller on the rocky bank."

"Do we have a spare?"

"Nope."

Not again. This is good, perfect, I thought. Here we were, away from a large city again, this time unable to move forward or backward at any speed. I looked around at the farms; the huge white Charolais cattle stared stupidly back at me. I had seen enough cows to last a lifetime. What I wanted was a big city, the bigger the better with a huge garage filled with spare parts.

I kept these thoughts to myself as Paul concentrated on the problem. He gunned the engine, shoved it in forward and reverse. Then he climbed out on the aft deck, trying to see through the murky water whether or not the prop turned. This went on for at least 20 minutes.

Finally, *Imagine* shuddered and moved forward. Paul and I gave each other high-fives. I stepped out and saw a cloud of sap green in the water.

"Weeds?"

Paul nodded. "Probably bamboo, like that stuff over there." He pointed to a particularly bushy patch of green along the shore. Bamboo had wrapped around our prop in a stranglehold when we'd been run aground.

"It might be a good idea to invest in a spare prop. What do you think?" I said as I hugged him.

He nodded. "But we can't do it right now. It has to be custom-made to exactly the right size and the pitch has to be perfect."

"And how do you find that out?"

"When the boat gets hauled out of the water. Or the current prop gets damaged. Whichever comes first."

"Then you better drive like a pro."

Except it had been a pro who got us into this mess.

11 - In the Rhythm

"I am going away with him to an unknown country where I shall have no past and no name, and where I shall be born again with a new face and an untried heart."

—Colette

The live-in lockkeepers, amid the gardens and lawn ornamentation, usually kept a menagerie of geese, chickens, dogs and cats. In an effort to be friendly, I'd once bought a box of dog biscuits at a grocery store. *"Pour le chien,"* I smiled and gave the first lockkeeper a biscuit for his poodle. The dog took it, held it briefly in its mouth, spit it out and walked away. A second elderly lab with a white muzzle wouldn't even pick up a biscuit. The owner had been so apologetic and obviously embarrassed I'd stopped trying to give out "treats." It was obvious French dogs didn't eat biscuits mass-produced for dogs. They were probably used to the delicious table scraps of their owners. I couldn't blame them.

Just before we reached Langres, in a lock near Humes, I spotted a kitten very much like a cat I'd once had, a pinto-like black and white. The kitten was no more than a few weeks old. Like many animals along the way, this kitten was curious. I wondered if it smelled my cats but before I could think much about it, the kitten jumped onto our deck as we lowered. I would've loved to keep it but I was sure the lockkeeper wouldn't appreciate losing her pet. Moreover, my two cats wouldn't take kindly to this young stranger. I kept our cats inside – I'd read enough horror stories about cats falling off the deck in a turbulent lock.

I gently lifted kitty up and set it back on the top of the lock. It mewed a while, then jumped down again, this time a further distance as we were lowering. Alarmed, I glanced at Paul. The last thing I wanted to see was a mashed kitty. I reached the cat up to shore. He headed back toward the stern – and made another jump aboard. Black-and-white was determined to stow away. Paul lifted him ashore. Madam, dressed in a pair of leggings with a long chenille sweater, noticed the problem, grabbed the kitten and brought him closer to where she worked the lock door. Not easily dissuaded from exploring, Black-and-white walked around the wheel his mistress turned and then climbed into the lock door mechanism, the hinge on which the huge door swung.

I gasped. I couldn't see the kitten anymore. He crawled about in a hole in a steel door with all kinds of hard, sharp turning action going on. I clutched my bowline. Madame stopped turning the wheel until a small black and white head emerged. She scooped him up and finished opening the door. As we drove away, I spotted Black-and-white looking at us, gauging whether or not to make one more try at boarding. I feared our stowaway-wannabe kitten was not long for this world.

When we arrived in the port of Langres, I was elated. Our convoy was here – Graham and Nancy, Jim and Ellen, Barry and Jane, and Eammon and Pat in the "narrow boat." We moored and I felt as if we'd arrived at a family reunion. We told our kitten story and found the little guy had jumped on every boat going through the locks. This confirmed my fear that was only a matter of time before Black-and-white got into serious trouble.

Lady Jane was here, but not Barry. When we asked around we were told, "Barry's taken up fishing. He's trying to settle down a bit."

Paul and I grinned at each other.

Eammon and Pat invited us on board their tiny boat. They had two dogs along – one smaller terrier and a large German Shepherd named "Kilo." I was cautious around dogs I didn't know. I've had my share of farmer's dogs coming after me on my bike, barking and nipping at my heels. Paul's response was always, "He's just a big puppy, and he wants to play." The dogs in question growled and snarled, hair standing up on their backs. This was not play behavior to me.

But Kilo was one of the sweetest dogs I'd ever met. As we chatted on the lawn by the port, Kilo brought her toy ball to me to throw it. I did, and she retrieved it, over and over. She never tired of playing and while she probably took up a quarter of the boat, I could see why her owners loved having her along.

Inside the narrow boat, a couple of steps down from the tiny aft deck, the salon was a miniaturized version of ours. Polished ash cabinets and shelves lined the walls. A built-in dining nook and a couch and chairs completed the salon. A narrow hallway led to a sleeping cabin with barely enough room for a double bed. Overflowing bookshelves lined the walls.

Over a cold beer, I commented on the lovely English boat, for a lovely English couple. Eammon said, "My dear, I'm not English, I'm Irish. And I can speak Gallic and Latin fluently, which helped me get my first job. In fact, I met Pat when I was a teacher at her girl's school."

Pat dimpled, and with her Pixie haircut and upturned nose, she looked like a mischievous elf. "That's right. The scoundrel seduced me, right in Sister Mary Theresa's office."

"Alas, some busybody noticed our reflection in the transom window in a rather compromising position." He sighed. "But do keep in mind I was fresh out of school, surrounded by a bevy of beautiful lasses. No one has that much willpower."

Nonetheless, he'd recently retired from a position of English school headmaster. They both loved to read and we spent a pleasant hour talking about all of the good books we'd read. Then, we moved on to the inevitable canal gossip.

"Do you know *Sea Lion*?" I asked.

"Oh, yes, I still speak to Stewart. He's selling the boat, you know."

No we didn't. Eammon kept in contact with Stewart, so I kept my opinions to myself.

"They're going to get a smaller cruiser for just the two of them next year and send Patti off to a boarding school." Different cultures, sending a teen off to boarding school. Everyone I know well in America loved to spend those years with their kids as much as they could. Knowing Stewart, I guessed he probably was glad to be rid of the intrusion of a teen-aged girl who wasn't his own daughter.

"He's quite a salesman," was the only positive thing I could think of to say about Stewart.

And yes, they knew Val and Rolly from the *Déesse*. We told them the story of how Roland had helped us out when our boat had broken down and how we had so much trouble communicating in French over the telephone.

"Ah, yes," Eammon says. "Roland has a great command of the language. Spent a great deal of time over in Algeria. He has quite the Algerian accent to his French, you know." We didn't know, but it makes sense since he has lived all over the world. "Yes, that Algerian accent gets the local's attention – they never know when he might send the men with the gel."

Short for gelatin, as in *plastique* explosives. No wonder the woman at the garage was so anxious to please us.

Langres perched on the northern edge of the limestone Langres Plateau, elevated 1500 feet above the river valley, a medieval walled fortress ready to defend itself against the invaders coming down the Marne River. It was a living antiquity; people did business, lived within the thick walls, went to school and attended mass at the Saint-Mammas Cathedral. The way up to the old city was steep, too steep to ride our bikes and too far to walk comfortably, but we were told there was a bus we could take to the old part of town to do some sightseeing.

First, Paul and I found the route to the local supermarket, as our provisions were low. To get there, we passed a junk store, then down a small street for several blocks to a path up a steep hill where the funicular railroad used to be. The railway would have been a much more convenient way to get to the top of this hill; instead, we clambered up the path through dense forest, the way littered with empty beer bottles, used condoms, signs of campfires.

Then the path widened between back yards adorned with flowers, dogs barked at us from behind iron fences, people sat on their patios drinking café, watching us trudge by. The way reminded me of another funicular railroad, the one in Penang, a remnant of the British rule. We'd ridden the train that crept up Penang hill, through ancient virgin rainforest, past waterfalls, into fog. Monkeys begged for food by the side of the track.

When this path ended, instead of Hindu temples and Muslim mosques at the top of Penang Hill, we found the *Intermarché*, the French supermarket. To get our shopping cart, we put a 10-franc coin into a lock on the chains holding the unused carts together. The lock released and we had our cart. When we were done shopping, we'd return the cart to the line, click the lock into place and *voilà;* we would have our 10 francs back.

We bought as much as we could carry and walked down the steep path back to port. We couldn't resist a visit to the junk shop and rummaged through three buildings of found objects. The rooms were filled with dusty treasures. A small cobalt blue coal-burning stove caught Paul's eye. *Imagine* used to have one in the salon as evidenced by a hole in the ceiling tile where the flue pipe had been. Even though we had central heating, it would be nice to have a fire on cold nights for the ambiance. If we were hoping for a deal in this junk store, we could go ahead and hope, but we were not going to get one. The owner spoke enough English and we spoke enough French to negotiate but we ended up at $200 US. A brand-new working stove was only a bit more. We could wait. Instead, for a few francs I bought some old tins, a small pitcher and a straw woven bag like the *Mesdames* used for shopping.

The next day, we decided to go into the downtown area and this involved figuring out the bus schedule. We walked over to the closest stop, the bus terminal itself. Like bus terminals everywhere, it had graffiti-covered walls and bathrooms used at night for activities I didn't like to think about. The bus pulled up on time and we hopped aboard.

As the vehicle climbed the steep incline, we looked back down the road and watched the river grow smaller. We chugged past the *Intermarché*, by the other modern stores and then into one of the gates to the walled city. We hopped off at the cathedral, located near the edge of the wall, not in the center of town as seemed usual to us. One of the church pamphlets described the patron saint of Langres, Saint Urban, as also the patron saint of vinedressers.

In art, he was shown as a bishop with a bunch of grapes or a vine at his side. "He is invoked against blight, frost, storm and faintness." I would remember to invoke him next time I was in the middle of a tornado watch, I thought.

Saturday shoppers and people enjoying the outdoor cafés filled the city. We walked atop the walls of the town, looked down on the vista below. The field-covered hills gently undulated down to the Marne. We traced the route we'd traveled by bus and located the port and spotted *Imagine* surrounded by smaller boats, like a swan encircled by her baby cygnets.

Back in the center of town, the famous Langres cheese was sold everywhere. I was anxious to try some of it – tall and round, reddish on the outside, concave in the middle. Two shopkeepers told us two different stories: one said the shape was meant to resemble the Langres Plateau, the other told us the indentation was for pouring champagne in the middle before eating it.

Whatever the reason for the shape, it was soft and creamy on the inside, with a pungent aroma similar to French Munster, which is much stronger in flavor than in the States. A prior in the local Dominican Abbey developed Langres cheese back in the 18th century from whole cow's milk that must have at least a 50% fat content. I tried not to think about sat fat and calories and bit in. Yummy. It was delicious, and got creamier closer to the center of the cheese.

Recommended accompanying wines were robust reds able to stand up to the cheese, such as Médoc or Nuits Saint Georges or Marc brandy from Bourgogne or Champagne. The French were so serious about this cheese that it was governed by a decree of appellation and the production limited to only three areas: Côte d'Or, Vosges, and here in the Haute Marne.

In port the next morning we waited for the bread truck to arrive. With no close *boulangeries* the bread must come to us. The French couldn't imagine life without a fresh *baguette* every day. Wonderful when fresh, but without any preservatives, the bread was stale the next morning and fit only to feed the ducks and swans. I knew I'd started to take this for granted but I made a promise to myself – I'd remember eating this well when back in the States eating some "French bread."

The white van honked its horn and like Pavlov's dogs trained to eat at the ring of a bell, most of the male boaters hopped off their boats and stood in line. The bread truck carried more than bread: croissants, *pain au chocolat*, dessert tarts, and brioche. Paul returned with the morning's goodies and told me all of the men are now referring to our boat as *The QE II*. Thanks Eammon. Graham found this nickname particularly funny. The local canal gossip said although he trusted us not to hit his boat, he hated the smell of our diesel exhaust enough not moor by us nor go through a lock behind us.

Then we spotted Barry, fishing pole in hand, looking sheepish. When we inquired about his new hobby, he shrugged. "I'm not very successful at it yet," he said. "But I'm trying really hard."

We weren't sure if he meant successful at catching fish or learning to relax. He walked away, a bit unhappily, I thought, and we wondered if his new hobby would help him unwind or not.

When we left Langres, we continued traveling with some of our convoy – Graham gave us wide berth and refused to go through locks with us. Eammon moved ahead, assuring us we would see him again. Most of our group planned to moor for the winter in the same area, either in ports at St. Jean de Losne or St. Symphorien. Barry and Jane had finally decided it would be wise to turn north and start the trip back.

"*Bon voyage*, Barry and Jane," I called out. "Will they make it to Holland in time?" I asked Paul.

"Just – if they hurry as fast as they can." He grinned at me.

"Then they'll make it," I said, grinning back.

A tunnel over 4,800 meters long, the *Souterrain de Balesmes*, loomed ahead. It went directly under the town of Balesmes-sur-Marne. Our chart explained we had to trigger radar to set the directional lights in our favor. At the lock before the tunnel, our *éclusier* lockkeeper said, "There'll be a red light there. Just ignore it and enter the tunnel." We hoped she knew what she was doing. It would be bad to run into some oncoming traffic, since the tunnels are only a boat width wide, making the tunnel definitely one way only. One of us would have a very long, very difficult job of reversing.

We approached the radar, which looked like a desolate alien on the side of the canal. Was it working or not? We couldn't tell. As we approached the tunnel entrance no directional lights shone. Spooky. We turned on the searchlight, took a deep breath, and entered.

Bouncing from side to side, *Imagine* crept along in the dripping darkness. The outside world disappeared. Cool as a cave, the ceiling was low enough to touch. Our chugging engine noise echoed off the tunnel walls. The smell of diesel grew thick and when I looked back at the entrance behind us, the weak light was diffused with exhaust.

I thought about the time before barges had diesel engines. Barge pilots would have to "leg" their barges through – they lay on their backs and moved the boat along by pushing against the wall or ceiling of the tunnel with their feet – literally walking the boat through. In *Horatio Hornblower*, Captain Hornblower had to leg through a long English tunnel in 'the strangest sort of mesmeric nightmare'." I understood how he felt; I had a headache when we emerged into the bright afternoon light after an hour of darkness.

A cruiser waited by the entrance for us to exit. I looked behind us and saw a room set into the hill above the tunnel. It was a manned control room and explained the mystery of who knew what traffic was inside. We passed Graham and Nancy pulled over having a bite of lunch along the shore. We stopped a little way up, considerately keeping our diesel fumes downwind.

Later that evening, when reading one of our books about barging, the authors described the tunnel we'd just traversed, the *Balesmes*. They'd followed a large commercial barge through the tunnel. When they'd exited, the barge pilot had been relieved to make it through.

"Because it was so long?" the authors had asked.

"No," said the commercial *bargée*. "Because this tunnel is a popular place for robbing slow moving boats. Like us."

I was glad I hadn't known before we'd gone in the tunnel.

With our new slower pace, we glided through the back yards of France, voyeuristically examining vegetable gardens, swimming pools, and terraces. In the country, we saw more fields of ripening wheat and grain elevators along the canal with huge chutes for loading barges with cargo.

As I waited for locks I sat up front on a resin chair and sunned myself. When we arrived at a lock, I could manage a conversation of sorts with the lockkeepers. If the lock was deep and no one offered help, I used my boat hook like a crochet hook to wrap the line around the bollard. Paul used a lasso technique. When he made it, it was an impressive toss. For me, the boat hook method was more reliable but less showy. I'd stopped grading our lock performances – they were nearly all A's. Usually I could get the line off when we were ready to go with a flick of my wrist, sit back down in my easy chair and watch the scenery unfold while I sipped my coffee.

As we headed toward Beaumont, the first town in Burgundy, the name reminded me of a story Paul had told me when we first met. He kept referring to "The Beaumont Law of Compensation." The theory stated all things in the universe are destined to be equal and so if things were going well, watch out – compensating bad will happen. The converse was also true. When you didn't like the way things were going in your life, equivalent good would occur.

"Of course," Paul had said, "there's no way of predicting exactly when the offsetting events will happen."

"I've never heard of it. Which philosopher devised this theory?" I'd asked.

"Charles Beaumont."

"Hmm. Nope never heard of him."

"Oh, you wouldn't have. Charlie Beaumont was one of my roommates at Yale."

Ahh, a theory probably developed over many beers. Nonetheless, I couldn't help but believe Beaumont's theory was at work as I sat on deck basking in the sun. Warblers sang in the trees while *Imagine*'s engine hummed along. Somewhere a lawnmower droned and the scent of fresh-cut grass wafted through the air.

I lifted my coffee cup, looked at the panorama around me and made a toast.

"Here's to you Beaumont. And here's to the compensation of a lifetime."

12 - Burgundy at Last

It is good to have an end to journey towards, but it is the journey that matters in the end.
--Ursula K. LeGuin

We left The Ditch behind and moved on to the wide Saône River. The river wound sinuously through gentle hills and fields downstream to our homeport in St. Symphorien. I'd loved Burgundy the first time we'd traveled here five years ago, a lifetime ago. We'd rented a car and traversed the county in five days.

We would be in homeport on September 1, just under two months after leaving Grave on July 3rd. We'd cruised 919 kilometers and worked 238 locks. *Imagine* had used two tanks of diesel fuel and we'd put 198.5 hours on her engine.

"Whoo hoo, we're almost there," I said as I danced across the pilothouse. "I remember that place." I pointed to a big house by the side of the canal.

"Yep, it's even featured on our chart." I peered over Paul's shoulder and read "*le maison isolée a l'aval de l'écluse de Saint-Symphorien*" – the isolated house. Three stories tall with stone steps from the river, a former hotel and restaurant, it had been converted to apartments. Too bad, as this would have given us a place within walking distance to eat. As it was, the only public buildings in St. Symphorien were the church, a school and the Mairie.

Through my field glasses, I spotted the lock to the Canal au Rhône au Rhin, which connected the Rhône River via the Saône in France, to the Rhine River in Germany. Just past this lock was our homeport.

I punched the number on our new cell phone for Bourgogne Marine. A familiar voice with a Yorkshire accent answered.

"Hello Roger? It's Michelle and Paul Caffrey, with our barge *Imagine.* We're here, just outside the lock. Can we come in to port?"

"Sure you can. I've been expecting you. But remember, the lock's closed for lunch from 12:30 to 1:30."

"Yeah we remember. Shouldn't be a problem. There's plenty of time, it's not even noon yet," I said glancing at my watch.

Roger told us to moor alongside another barge, the third one from the end. His port wasn't full, but he estimated about twenty boats of our type were in port. I sighed. *Imagine* would be in her homeport at last, no longer dwarfed by commercial barges or shunned by diminutive cruisers. Nestled in homeport *Imagine* will moor with like barges, transformed from an ugly duckling to a graceful swan.

I remembered our first trip here when we'd barge shopped. In our rental Peugeot, we'd driven down a sycamore-lined road, past golden rapeseed fields, and circled a roundabout. Paul had exited the spoke toward the tiny village of Maison Dieu where small stone houses with painted shutters hugged the road.

"How poetic is that?" I'd pointed to the *Auberge de Paradis.* "The Inn of Paradise in the House of God." Then to the village of St. Symphorien, its largest building the church. Incandescent yellow jonquils and forsythia contrasted with smoke-colored walls that divided garden from farmland. Chimneys puffed wood smoke and the scent had hung in the air. Just past a sign with a red slash through the 'St. Symphorien,' I'd spied a small notice for Bourgogne Marine.

"Turn here," I'd said. Fields of chartreuse sprouting crops had surrounded us; enormous white cattle dotted the pasture. "The road will come to a 'T,' then go right."

Through the budding poplars, I'd spotted more barges than I'd ever seen in one place, lined up one after the other.

"We're in Barge Heaven," I'd sighed.

We'd seen at least 40 barges moored against the grassy banks and then to each other, sometimes four abreast. They were painted in somber Dutch colors like *Vertrouwen,* or nautical shades. Behind us, an ancient mill stood by a stream where the only sound was that of a waterfall's splash. We'd walked toward a lock – twenty feet below was the River Saône. A sign next to it read, "*Bienvenue* - Welcome to the Canal du Rhône au Rhin." The marina was at a wide spot on the waterway linking the Rhône River to the Rhine.

As we'd walked back to the office, a man welding had waved at us.

"Y'all lookin' for a boat?"

We'd told him we were barge shopping.

"Glad to meet you," he said extending his grubby hand. "I'm Bill. If you find a barge, he's as good as any to deal with." He nodded in the direction of the office. "Otherwise, you could keep your boat here – we all have a good time, get together a lot."

We'd knocked on the door of *Cassiopeia* and Roger Walster had answered "Hello" in a British accent. As we'd sat below with him, I'd studied the pine floor planks, big skylights, and the kitchen open to the salon. Now this was more like it, I thought. But this barge wasn't for sale.

He'd taken us to see a barge for sale. "This boat isn't for us," Paul had said. "We want to charter, so we need two cabins with their own baths up front, and our cabin in the rear. But we like this port. We noticed a few barges have people living on them. Do some winter-over here?"

"Yeah, they do. We always have a handful year-round. I keep an eye on the boats left here and work on them too if you need things done."

"Would you have room for another barge? If we find our boat in Holland, we'd like to have a place to keep our boat in France," I said.

"A homeport?"

I'd savored the term and nodded.

"Yes, a homeport."

But to get there, we had to make it through this lock. The current was strong on the river and the lock angled upstream about 30 degrees.

Paul stared through the field glasses. "The light's red, but I think I spot a lockkeeper who's not taken off for lunch. Yet."

"Great, we're going to make it." A small rental Tupperware cruiser joined us while we station-kept and waited, fighting the current. The couple on board waved at us but I had limited trust in rental boat drivers. They didn't need to pass a boating test in France so we assumed renters may or may not be familiar with the boating rules. I stood on deck wearing my work gloves with bumper in hand and watched the rental boat, trying to decide if I needed to call out to them. They should let us go first not only because we arrived first, but also because we were bigger. If they bumped our stern in a lock it would be much less of a disaster than the other way around.

"The light's green – we're goin' in," Paul said to me over the intercom. I stood at the bow ready to explain things to the renters, but they followed behind us. Paul and I had already talked about a method for this tricky lock. Because of the current, Paul warned me that he'd use more speed than usual. I would use my deflated bumper to cushion when we scraped the lock wall, which was almost inevitable with *Imagine*'s stern being dragged hard by the current.

We're doing fine, I thought, psyched at the perfect approach. Then within a hundred yards of entering, the light changed from green to red. A slim stylish woman ran to the side of the lock and waved us off. Paul veered off hard to port and the little rental boat did as well. The huge lock doors clanged shut in front of us.

The rental boat people look confused and we shrugged. None of us had an idea what was happening. Puzzled, we checked our watches; it wasn't lunchtime. We'd never been waved off when we were so close to entering a lock. It reminded me of aborted landings on airplanes, my seat in an upright position, tray stowed, my seatbelt fastened low and tight across the lap, descending and then the engines roaring at what felt like the last possible second. I'd left my stomach behind on several occasions due to storms and severe crosswinds and once when "an obstacle" (another plane) sat on the runway where we were to land.

We continued to station-keep and watched the lock through our field glasses. No other boat came out.

"What's this?" Paul said staring through the field glasses. I saw an enormous white hull coming upstream. A restaurant boat with the name *Beatrice* emblazoned on her hull steamed up, swung in front of us and stopped. The lock light turned green, the doors swung open as if someone had said, "Open sesame!" and the big boat headed in. It took skilled maneuvering as the strong current dragged *Beatrice*'s stern out. Two crewmembers on deck caught side bollards on an outside the wall to get the bow in.

Beatrice finally squeezed her way into the lock, like a Madame squeezing into too-small a girdle. The doors closed, the water filled the lock, but she didn't move out. Instead, she sat in the lock for about ten minutes. Some of the passengers walked around the top of the lock.

"They're probably looking at our homeport," I said to Paul. "At least they can see it." I shook my head, glanced at my watch.

"I just don't understand what the heck they're doing," Paul said with a furrowed brow.

Then water poured like a waterfall back into the Saône, *Beatrice* lowered, the doors opened, the restaurant boat backed out, and steamed upstream. *Beatrice* either had a specific time she did this trick or had radioed ahead to the lockkeeper. All so passengers could appreciate "the lock experience."

It was now lunchtime. My hard-won equanimity evaporated like mist on the canal. "I could bite through the steel hull," I muttered to Paul as I climbed to the galley to try to put together lunch from our scrawny provisions. I imagined the passengers on *Beatrice* eating a fine French *dejeuner* served with a good Côtes du Rhône, their appetites whetted by their lock experience. We tied to a bollard near the isolated house while we gnawed our lunch of leftover bits of Brie and day-old bread.

With strong feelings of déjà vu, at 1:30 we assumed the same position with the rental boat. Finally, *Imagine* slid into the cavernous lock with the Tupperware following behind.

I waited for help with the lines but the lockkeeper remained in her glass room. I tried to catch her eye. She turned her bleached blonde head away and stared out over the river. I reached the bollards with my hook by standing on my tiptoes. I didn't like to do this. It's one of the most popular ways for people to fall into locks.

As we rose up in the lock, I spotted her reading a paperback book with a cover straight from a Harlequin romance novel – a French bodice ripper. Maybe she was engrossed in her book since she didn't come out when our gates opened either, which was a good thing for her. I had no intention of tipping her. If I had a better command of the language, I might have asked her how long the pampered passengers of *Beatrice* would've had to wait if she had let us through before they arrived.

Paul was quick to remind me we would see this *éclusier* again, perhaps many times, and she could make our lives miserable if she wanted. I sullenly agreed with his logic, but he couldn't make me say, "*Merci Madame*" and wave when we left like I usually did.

I had to let my frustration go – our port was so close to the lock we had to get ready to moor. I counted the rows, spotted where we belonged, and prepared to raft to a nice-looking barge, without a dent on it, or a paint scratch. I made sure their paint job remained unscratched with my bumper, and Paul drove *Imagine* in like he was parking his car.

After we tied up, Paul asked, "Does this boat look familiar?" He nodded toward the barge next door.

"Yeah, kind of." But I never remembered boats like he did.

"Remember the boat we looked at outside our price range and already under contract? This is it." The name had been changed, but it did seem to be one of our former candidates.

"From the barge center with the snotty woman?" I asked.

Paul nodded. I remembered the day we'd gone barge shopping all too well.

Paul had made an appointment to look at boats from a boat broker in St. Jean de Losne. We'd followed a French platinum blonde's trail of Chanel Number 5 to view a barge called *Oceanide*, already under contract. The barge had been *Vertrouwen* on steroids, twenty feet longer, crisply painted in ultramarine and white, with a varnished teak wheelhouse – and at the absolute top of our price range.

"If we bought this boat," I'd whispered to Paul, "we'd have to name it *Our Entire Home Equity*."

She'd shown us the kitchen, a separate room. I didn't comment. It wasn't my kind of layout – I like an open floor plan with kitchen and living area combined.

"There was a trend for a while to have an open kitchen, *a la Américain*." She'd sniffed and winced, as if insulted by the very idea. "But many French prefer the separate room to keep unsightly mess and odors from the rest of the house." Obviously she considered Americans unsophisticated boors who didn't know an odor from an aroma.

I'm glad we hadn't bought a barge there and had to deal with them; I'd had my fill of snotty women for the day.

Jeff and Maureen, a young American couple from Vermont, had purchased *Oceanide.* They planned to spend at least a full year aboard with their three little girls, aged seven to two. On board, they only spoke French and Maureen, a French teacher, home-schooled her kids. They asked where we'd come from and seemed impressed with our long trip.

"We haven't done much cruising yet I'm afraid," said Jeff. "We're here waiting for our repairs to get done. For some reason, they're taking longer than we expected." He dragged his fingers through his sandy hair. Paul and I raised our eyebrows. *Quel surprise*, I thought, what a surprise. Not.

One of their smaller engines, an electric bow thruster, shorted out right after they bought the barge. I looked at Paul with the tiniest hint of a smile. Bow thrusters were a source of controversy among *bargées.* The small engines moved the front of the boat side to side and would certainly come in handy entering locks from Hell or parallel parking. Purists, however, thought them unconventional, unnecessary and just one more thing to break. *Imagine* didn't come equipped with one and Paul didn't mind. I threatened to have a t-shirt made for him that read, "Real men don't need bow thrusters."

The short ruined the rest of their electrical systems. They'd been weeks without lights. No microwave cooking, no washer, no dryer. No blow dryer. I shuddered. For every story you tell, there's always a worse one.

"How can a young couple like this afford such an expensive boat and take a year off from work?" I asked Paul later that night.

"Maybe they're trust funders."

The port rumor mill filled us in – they were "dot commers" who'd sold their shares at the height of the price bubble. Good for them.

When we said we were in the software industry, often people asked if we had anything to do with dot coms. We'd shake our heads. We were the generation before, not Information Technology, but Data Processing. My first job had been in "The Tab Equipment Department," where 80 column cards were punched with keypunch machines. This antiquated technology was now found only in data processing museums and voting booths. The amount of memory in the first computers Paul and I programmed was about what a microwave or cell phone contains today. No, we were not dot commers.

We were dinosaurs.

Paul and I strolled across the road near our mooring. A tiny Peugeot pulled up, with a woman passenger frantically waving at us.

We shook our heads at each other and shrugged. I couldn't imagine whom we might know in this French village, population 180. We walked toward the car and peered in.

"Fred! Shirley!" I stuck my head into the open windows to kiss our former shipmates on *Vertrouwen.*

"You didn't forget us?" Shirley said.

"How could we? It's only been a few months, last September." And a lifetime, I thought.

"What are you doing here?" Fred asked. Of course, they didn't know about us, I realized.

Paul said, "We did what we planned. We bought a barge, refitted her, and brought her down from Holland. That's our boat, *Imagine*, over there." I thought about how easily he'd summarized our last 11 months. "And you?"

"We're still thinking about a boat. We came by to port just to see what might be for sale here." Fred looked the row of boats up and down.

"We're still not sure if we really want to buy a barge," said Shirley. "Even though I'm feeling much, much better. My hip is almost normal." She beamed. Her hair was in a longer pageboy – I thought she bore a faint resemblance to Dr. Joyce Brothers.

"Would you like to come aboard?" I asked.

"Are you kidding? You bet," Shirley said. They stepped on board, and I noticed how much more limber Shirley seemed than when we trained. Fred stood at the wheel with a slight frown as he stared down the long deck.

Shirley climbed the steep stairs to the salon. She was so elegant, had such refined taste, I couldn't wait to get the reaction from this classy lady in her late sixties. She stopped, stared and said, "Holy shit, Michelle. Holy shit. This is *great.* This is fantastic! You did it, you talked about it, planned it and you really did it!"

We showed them around, glowed with pride as they admired everything from her lines, the antique pine floor, to the layout. Paul and Fred disappeared into the engine room while I demonstrated our microwave/convection to Shirley. Then, I demoed the *piece de résistance.* Fred and Shirley stood by while I put a piece of toilet paper into the toilet bowl and stepped on the pedal. It whisked away to the purr of the electric motor.

"*Voilà,*" I said with a bow as they applauded.

All the compliments were great. But we savored one above all the others.

"You did it."

Holy shit indeed.

The Klaxon horn sounded. I grabbed a few coins and climbed over the three neighboring barges, scurried over the gangplank and waited on the towpath. I spotted The Bread Truck Lady and felt a sense of dread. Just stay calm, I told myself as I walked up to the immaculate white Renault truck.

"*Bonjour, Madame,*" I said. "*Je voudrais une baguette, s-il vous plait.*" I would like a loaf of bread please.

"*Bonjour, Madame.*" She smiled, wrapped a crusty still-warm loaf of bread in floral-printed paper, and handed it to me.

Now for the tough part for both of us. I asked for an additional two croissants. I fiddled with my coins. Madame scrunched her face, stared into the air, and I swear I could almost hear grinding gears. I wished she carried either a cash register or at least a calculator. It would help both of us. She would come up with the same amounts for the same items; I could cheat and peek at the numbers instead of trying to understand them verbally.

After an awkward pause she said, "Quatre-vingt-deux-trois-blah-blah."

In my head I counted *un, deux, trois*, and so on to try to find a number that seemed to fit. Obviously, this sequential approach took a while. I tried to add up the price of a *baguette* and two croissants in my head. The total didn't sound anything like what she told me. It never did. I'd memorized the price of a loaf of bread and conscientiously brought out the exact four francs and twenty centimes – if I had them. From day to day, the price of anything other than a single *baguette* remained a situation for discussion between us. I felt the line form behind me comprised of port mates who all spoke better French than I. Madame looked at me with raised brows.

I'd already tried the wimpy approach of giving her a large note, knowing it would cover the cost, no matter what number either of us came up with. This wouldn't do – she coveted change as a precious commodity. I resorted to bringing out a large of variety of coins that looked like they might do the job. This seemed to please her more than my shotgun approach, but didn't eliminate the humiliation on my end as she took each coin out of my open palm, said its denomination aloud to teach me, and then "*Voilà!*" when she arrived at the "correct" amount.

They suppressed their giggles behind me, but I could feel the smirks. I couldn't wait for the Euro – at least with the numbers seven times smaller I may have time to count to the number she proposed. Except four francs and twenty centimes would be, let's see, divided by seven, seven goes into forty....

13 - *Beaune Est Bon*

The way to develop self-confidence is to do the thing you fear.
- William Jennings Bryan

The rehearsal over, we were going to cruise with paying guests for our last few weeks of the season. *Imagine* rumbled to life with the first turn of the key.

"So long guys," I said to Maureen and Jeff as we pivoted off their bow. "And good luck."

"When will you be back?" Jeff asked, looking wistful.

"In about a month."

"Well, I hope we're not still here." He sighed.

We planned to go up the *Canal de Bourgogne*, the Burgundy Canal, past Dijon and up to the tunnel near Vandenesse. This was as far as we could go up the canal because the tunnel was "not up to code," built long before the rest of the canal standards. *Imagine*'s pilothouse would either scrape the roof of the tunnel – or jam or shear off. None of these prospects appealed to us.

"How do other barges get through?" I'd asked Paul.

"They take their wheelhouse off. See here?" He'd pointed to hinges covered in almost a hundred years of paint. "No way can we take this apart anymore."

It must be an old tunnel as our chart warned us in red letters, "Attention. The tunnel is not lit. Have a good spot light, a life-jacket for each person aboard, bucket, bailer, fire extinguisher, boat-hook oars, warning hooter (in case of break-down)."

Some day when we had more time and money we might invest in a new pilothouse that could be disassembled. It didn't matter to me – I'd had enough of tunnels.

Our romance-reading lockkeeper was nowhere in sight. Instead, her male counterpart, who looked like John Belushi, let us out of the lock onto the

Saône. *Imagine* glided down the river toward nearby St. Jean de Losne, the closest shopping town to St. Symphorien, about ten minutes away by car. I'd had to ask Roger how to pronounce "Losne." "It rhymes with 'Bone'," he'd said.

St Jean sat on the Saône, at the intersection of six main waterway routes including the Burgundy Canal and the Canal du Rhône au Rhin. Further south were larger cities like Chalon-sur-Saône and Lyon, and another canal, the Canal du Centre. If we kept heading south, we'd get to the Mediterranean in a couple of weeks. Our chart described St. Jean as the largest inland boat harbor in France. A huge marina dominated the middle of town filled with hundreds of boats, mostly pleasure craft and rent-a-racers.

Originally, St. Jean had been a hub of commercial barging. We floated by the shipyard with its evidence of the commercial's decline. Three or four *péniches* were on the shore, ready for transformation into restaurants, bars, discos, hotels, or clubhouses. One rusty hull was being cut in two down its mid-section, morphing into a private houseboat like ours. Others sat in ruin; covered in rust, wooden trim weathered, one with a burned-out wheelhouse, waiting for the right visionary person to restore them. Two barges were suspended in dry dock. One of them was being power washed as a preparation for repainting. The other *péniche* had workmen swarming over it with welding sparks flying.

Through my field glasses, I spotted three cruisers, Jim and Ellen's smaller barge and Eammon and Pat's narrow boat, moored at the public quay. Some small speedboats for hire were also next to the public mooring. At the end of the quay was an area reserved for a single boat – *Beatrice*.

I surveyed the quay while *Imagine* circled. The smaller boats had as much space as possible between them, so no one else could fit. Great. Our next guests had been given detailed instructions how to find us so we had to find room here. Jim and Ellen had the last spot on the actual quay. Eammon and Pat were nowhere to be seen.

We circled near Jim and Ellen. Jim spotted us and shouted he'd move forward as far as he could. We'd tie behind them until a better space with mooring rings opened up. Jim caught my lines and Paul lined *Imagine* up behind our European friends.

We went ashore and studied our options. Since it is bad form to touch anyone else's mooring lines and reposition them without their consent, even those of our friends, we decided to wait for Eammon to reappear.

In the meantime, we needed lunch. As we walked down the street from our mooring, Eammon emerged from a small café. "Hey there! Come and join us for lunch."

We explained the quay quandary. "Not a problem that can't wait until after a proper *dejeuner,"* Eammon said with a wink.

Our proper *dejeuner* consisted of *coq au vin,* accompanied by the Burgundy specialty *Jambon persillé*, a ham, parsley and garlic pâté, and some local Burgundy wine by the carafe.

"Have you tried the local white *Aligoté* for anything other than as a base for a *kir*?" Eammon asked. "Don't bother if you haven't. It tastes like *pipi de chèvre."* Goat's pee. The man could really turn a phrase.

We saved money by ordering tap water *"une carafe d'eau"* as opposed to a *"bouteille d'eau."* While we finished our crème brûlée, we watched a fierce-looking Boxer, complete with a studded collar, sweetly kiss his master on the cheek.

We all headed back to the quay and eventually a French middle-aged couple returned to their rental *pénichette.* With gestures we explained if they pulled forward just a bit, Jim would go back, Eammon would pull out and *"le bateau Imagine"* would fill the empty space. We thought they understood. The man decided to have the woman pilot while he worked the lines. He started shouting at her. She looked worried and gunned the engine. He shouted some more. She threw the boat into reverse and banged loudly into the quay wall. Now she was obviously frazzled. The man grabbed the controls from her and pulled the boat out into the river. The boat disappeared down the Saône. We waited a while but they didn't return.

"I thought he'd understood he only needed to move forward a little," Paul said with a shake of his head.

Instead, we may have been a catalyst to a broken relationship.

After some repositioning we moored securely and checked out the town. We walked to market, past the church of St. Jean the Baptist. Next to it was *L'Amiral* where Paul and I ate when we'd barge shopped. We'd asked the grizzly-looking man what the *plat du jour* was. In a gravely voice he'd said "*pizza avec,*" and a word we didn't know. Okay, it was pizza with something. He'd spoken some English but was obviously at a loss for the word for the pizza topping. He'd tapped on his forehead with his fingers.

"Knuckles?" we'd guessed, feeling like we were playing a game of Charades.

"No, no." He shook his head and then tapped both sides of his head.

"Sausage? Ham? Headcheese?"

"No, no, no." He grew more frustrated by the minute. We wished we could help him but we were at a loss. Then an English woman chimed in.

"He's saying 'brains,'" she'd said.

We'd ordered the pizza with cheese.

Our friends, Holly, Doug, Greg and Julie, crawled out of a taxi in St. Jean late the next morning. They'd flown in directly from Minneapolis and were experiencing mega-jet-lag.

"I hope you guys are ready to be guinea pigs," I said as I hugged Holly.

"You betcha," Holly said. She stepped back and took a long look. "You two look great. This life must be agreeing with you."

"It's the barge diet," I said grabbing some of their luggage.

"Watch out, Paul, that's a heavy one," she said, pointing to one of the suitcases. Below, when she unzipped it, piles of paperbacks and magazines spilled out on the salon's antique pine floor. I fell on them with a sigh.

"Oh thank you, thank you, thank you. You really understand what it takes to make a girl happy when she lives overseas."

"You bet. English books were better than gold to me in China." She grinned at me with her slightly gap-tooth grin and I hugged my redheaded friend again.

"Thanks girlfriend." And it felt good to say "girlfriend" for the first time in months.

Paul and I exchanged glances. Our friends' eyes were all at half-mast. We showed them to their staterooms and within a few minutes, heard four distinct octaves of snores.

"I thought we'd take them out for lunch, but now…" I said to Paul.

"Let 'em nap. Let's walk over to Eammon's new mooring at the *port de plaisance*."

Amid the Tupperware cruisers, we spotted the narrow boat at the end of a pontoon. Eammon and Pat were on their aft deck reading the International Herald Tribune.

"And how's the crew of the *QEII* today?" Eammon asked with a mischievous grin.

"We're fine, thank you. And the *QEII* has her first passenger foursome," I said. "They're resting in their spacious quarters."

"Well, you must see the most beautiful cat we've come across lately," he said as he grabbed my arm and escorted me down the dock.

They'd met our cats and had petted the friendlier Sundae while Bear had cautiously walked up and sniffed Eammon's shoes. He couldn't mean this cat was better looking than ours could he? Sure Sundae suffered from hyperthyroidism, which caused her fur to come off like orange tumbleweeds, but I'd had radioactive iodine therapy done on her and she'd actually gained some weight.

The cat in question was sprawled on the deck of a cruiser, with golden hair and chocolate-colored paws and tail, probably a pedigreed-la-de-da-kitty, but nice-looking, I had to admit. Still I would've matched my Bear's domestic shorthaired black velvet fur and yellow-green eyes against any cat in a beauty contest. If I could drag him out of his hiding place long enough to show him.

His British owner, George, raved about his pet. The young cat sensed the attention and obliged us with a few spry jumps from the top deck down to the dock. Then he leapt back up to stretch out in the sun.

George rubbed the varnished mahogany trim of his meticulously maintained fifty-foot boat. I felt a slight case of cruiser-envy as I stared at the pristine white fiberglass finish. *Imagine*'s old steel hull was pockmarked with dents from our mistakes and those of her former owners over the past ninety-six years. Every sunny day in port, Paul painted the most recent scrapes, wiping out the sins of the previous week. He called it "going to confession."

"How have you found the commercial barges?" George asked Paul.

"Well, for the most part we think they're professional. Except for one who gunned his engine and drove us aground, we haven't had any trouble with them. Why?"

George gave us a dour look. "I've had a very bad experience with a local barge. Very bad." He shook his head.

"Our boat was moored for lunch along the bank of the canal when I saw a fully-loaded *péniche* heading toward us. I didn't think much of it, as there was plenty of room for him to pass. While my wife and I sat at the table I looked up and saw the barge bearing down with no let up in speed."

He took a deep breath. "He rammed the stern of my boat. I was using mooring pins about a meter long, and they were yanked out of the ground as my boat was sucked into him. Then my bow caught on the deck of his boat and he dragged me downstream perhaps a hundred meters."

"It must've been an accident, maybe the pilot hadn't seen you or he lost control somehow," Paul said.

George shook his head. "While we were hanging on the deck of the *péniche,* I saw the pilot's face quite clearly. He had a big handlebar mustache and beneath it, the bastard was smiling." He paused and cleared his throat.

"Worse yet, he is apparently well-known to the authorities as he's done this before. They gave me the universal sign for crazy when I told them who it was." George demonstrated, rotating his finger around his ear. "They told me he believes the canals are for working barges only. Pleasure boats don't belong in 'his' waterways. He's out there trying to run all of us off."

I wondered what he would consider *Imagine* – a pleasure boat or an old working barge? I hoped we didn't find out. The thought of a fully loaded commercial barge out there gunning for us was a chilling thought.

"What does it look like?" I asked.

"I remember a big light blue bow coming at me with a bright yellow name plate."

OK, so we knew we were looking for a blue barge with yellow on the front, driven by a man with a large handlebar mustache.

"But what's the name of the boat?" That was really the way to tell which barge to avoid. When George told us, it took all my willpower not laugh out loud.

"*Cutie Pie,*" he said gravely.

We had lunch with Eammon and Pat at the café near the quay. We took turns petting the Boxer, feeling the ripple of his muscular build beneath is silky fur. Our outdoor table overlooked wide cobblestone steps that lead to the boats moored below. The lower afternoon sunlight tinted the Saône silver blue. A few plane tree leaves, large as my hand, fluttered down.

"We're going home to England next week," Eammon said sipping his wine.

"It's only early September," I said.

"But it's been enough for us," Pat said. She caught my look of concern. "Oh don't worry, everything's fine Michelle." She pronounced my first name in the French way – Mee-shell – and patted my arm.

"But we have been talking about what this first year has meant for us," Eammon added.

"And…?" I asked.

"Well number one, we're relieved our thirty-six year marriage is still intact and survived our trip. And in very close quarters to boot," Eammon said. "In our minds, this was the real triumph." He smiled and squeezed Pat's hand.

Paul and I nodded. We understood. How many people dread retirement? The thought of spending unending days and nights together probably frightens more couples than any financial fear. Mix in assorted adventures people go through in a foreign country, then put a couple on a boat, which requires skill and cooperation. It was a recipe for disaster. I thought about how I felt like calling off the trip and our marriage when we broke down back near Monthermé.

I squeezed Paul's hand and said, "Yeah that's the real triumph. Just to have a marriage survive." And even thrive.

"Wake up sleepyheads." I banged on the stateroom doors. "Let's get this road on the show."

The six of us trooped to the Maritime Museum, which housed a small collection of barge memorabilia: old photos from the turn of the century, tools, models of barges and locks, and barge-related newspaper articles. I'd saved the best for last. We climbed to the second story and I pointed. "Look at her. Can you believe it?"

A mannequin wore a turn of the century dress, representing a woman about five feet tall and at most a hundred pounds. Around her neck and upper torso she wore a leather harness.

I said, "Before diesel engines, if a barge family couldn't afford a mule for towing, the woman of the family pulled the barge." Holly and Julie's eyes bugged out.

We studied the sepia photographs surrounding the exhibit. Harnessed women – and sometimes children – were pictured tugging barges on muddy towpaths while the men sat inside the warm, dry wheelhouse.

"I think this is symbolic of the lengths women will go to keep their relationships intact. What do you think?" I said to Holly and Julie. I noticed our men studying a barge model in the corner. We grinned and nodded.

"You remember John in the Midwest office?" Holly asked.

I shook my head. "Hired after I left I guess." Holly tried to update me on the latest office gossip as we put together our meal of *poulet en rôti*, rotisserie free-range chicken, with new potatoes and *haricots verts.*

"Hmmm," I murmured as I snapped the ends off the green beans. I'd always emotionally detached from former jobs. Now I'd detached from a career. I'd worried about my self-esteem when we'd started barging, so much of my identity had been formed at work. My favorite aunt, Vera, had warned me for years, "You are not your job, Michelle."

We talked about a co-worker who'd been found dead of a heart attack slumped over his computer at home with an office email on the screen. I hadn't much cared for the guy – he'd been a member of the chauvinist school of good old boys. But when I'd heard of the way he died, it had been one more reason to do what I did. I'd be dammed if I would go while replying to someone's interoffice memo with a hundred "cc:s".

I felt a shiver run down my spine. I'd been hoodwinking myself, telling myself I had a safety net. I could never go back to the computer industry again. "I read once, 'Dream as if you'll never die and live like you might tomorrow.'"

Holly grinned, patted me on the arm. "Looks to me like you took the platitude to heart, my friend."

The next day we decided to cruise to Auxonne, a short trip back up the Saône River, to give our guests a taste of easy river cruising and to visit the historical city where Napoleon's military genius was first recognized. After we moored, we all climbed out to explore the museum housed in a castle built during the reign of Louis XI. Inside the low-ceiling rooms collections of memorabilia were displayed, including a set of dinnerware with hand-painted portraits of Josephine, an assortment of cannons and smaller weapons and a full military uniform of Napoleon's. It looked like a Halloween costume for a child, yet it fit the man who ruled Europe during the early 1800's.

Outside we wandered to the nearby park where a few men played *boules.* Each man had his own technique of throwing the ball; one was hard and fast with the release, another was gentle. Both clunked into their targets. There was much discussion between the players with kibitzing from the sidelines. We didn't know the rules but we guessed it to be a cross between croquet and shuffleboard. The object seemed to get close to a target and at the same time whack your opponent's ball as far away from the target as possible. Interesting that in many competitive games it's not good enough to do well yourself - you must inflict damage to your opponent's position.

That evening while on deck we snacked on cheese and sipped wine. Young twenty-something men, probably from the nearby military academy, sat on the quay and drank beer. After dinner we heard occasional loud talking punctuated by laughter. It continued late into the night. The next morning, Holly and Julie were quick to point out the same young men were running. Jogging by, dressed in shorts and matching tee shirts they provided us with some fine "Beautiful Mens" scenery. We women forgave them their noisiness of the night before.

On the way to the Burgundy Canal, barreling downstream on the Saône at the breakneck speed of ten kilometers an hour, I smelled a familiar odor. In the same instant, Paul did too. Wordlessly, I took the wheel and Paul ran below.

"The engine's overheating again," he said. "At least we're not far from homeport and I can get some help there."

I sighed. That was the good news. The bad news was now we had someone else's vacation at stake. I nodded at our friends sitting up on the deck in the sun. Plan A had been to go to Beaune at some point. Plan B would be to go tomorrow – without Paul while he worked on the boat. I felt guilty about going without him but not guilty enough not to go.

I walked out on deck and explained the problem and our solution for the time being. Paul limped *Imagine* into port and we tied up to Maureen and Jeff's barge.

As soon as we moored, Paul crawled down to the engine room. Sweating and covered with grease he emerged from the ship's nether region and said,

"We've lost another impeller but at least I have a backup. Roger's told me where to look for little bits of impeller lodged in the cooling system. I just have to get all of those tiny pieces so the parts don't block the flow again."

Greg, an engineer, said to Paul, "Could I stay here tomorrow and help?" He raised his dark eyebrows over his glasses.

Paul shook his head. "God no, Greg. It's going to be backbreaking, hot as hell, and just plain miserable."

"But it's a diesel engine. I love to work on diesel engines."

His wife Julie gave him The Look wives give husbands after they've been married for a very long time.

"I guess I'll go to Beaune for the day," he said. Not too many people would think twice about spending the day in the wine capital of Burgundy versus a hot dirty job in a confined engine room. I love engineers.

The taxi arrived in St. Symphorien on time. I'd cheated and asked Maureen to call them. The telephone was my nemesis, I still worried my message wouldn't get across without the accompanying pantomimes and body language.

Our cab drove into Beaune, past medieval walls, and rumbled down the cobblestone streets. The temporary help agency advertised jobs for the v*endange,* the wine harvest. Beaune reminded me of Boulder as they both nestled against the foothills. There was a big difference, however, between the Flatirons and the Côte d'Or. These hills were covered in golden vines that produced grapes as valuable as gold.

The taxi dropped us off at the center of town where it was market day. Vendors sold Provençal fabrics, lavender-scented artisan soaps, hand-painted Alsatian pottery, Dijon mustard in several different flavors, unblemished new potatoes, pristine artichokes, and sausages dusted in flour. As we roamed the stalls, I heard something I hadn't heard in a long time – lots of people speaking other languages than French, including American accents.

"If you want to buy anything, get it now. The market closes around noon," I said. My friends took me at my word and loaded the men like pack mules. Maybe Greg had the right idea to stay at the boat, I thought, as he grimaced when Julie handed him another sack.

When we'd had enough shopping, we trooped across the street to the Hotel Dieu de Beaune, built as a hospital for the poor in 1443, now a museum. We picked up our self-guided tour English pamphlets and read that Nicolas Rolin, Chancellor to the Dukes of Burgundy, funded the hospital at his own expense. His enemies claimed his motivation was to win forgiveness for his many sins, rather than generosity.

Rounding the corner from the office we stopped open-mouthed in the courtyard. Geometric patterns of glazed ceramic roof tiles glistened in shades of amethyst, emerald and onyx. Set against the lapis sky, filigrees of fanciful ironwork topped each roof peak.

"It looks like a cloisonné jewel box," Holly said, snapping pictures.

"Unbelievable," her husband Doug agreed. "You'd never guess this from the outside." Our pamphlet explained the drab exterior had been designed to discourage robbers and brigands from plundering the hospital during the Hundred Years War.

We wandered into The Great Hall of the Needy, the *Grand Salle des Pauvres,* lined with small hospital beds draped in crimson velvet curtains. During busy times two people might occupy a single bed. Still, with its lofty ceilings, clean bedding, and view of the chapel for daily Mass, it must have been a much better place to be sick than the alternatives of the day. Every room was adorned with wrought iron, gold, woven tapestries, paintings and frescos.

All of this decoration was paid for from the surrounding hills and the real gold of the region – its wine. To provide continually for the hospital, Rolin donated vineyards to the Hotel Dieu and the inheritance grew to 60 hectares of the most prestigious Burgundy wines. For over 140 years a charity auction of the Hospice de Beaune wine is held annually and the proceeds equivalent to millions of dollars support the maintenance of this medieval building, other hospitals for the poor, two homes for the aged and a modern hospital built in 1971 when this hospital had its last patients. The gift that kept on giving.

State-of-the-art medieval medicine was demonstrated by a display of dull-looking surgical instruments and gruesome drawings. The pharmacy collection of medication pots included "Opium," "Cannabis" and "Cocaine." I wonder what people five hundred years from now will think of our methods. Barbaric, probably.

A separate dark room held the most important art piece in the hospice's collection, the "Last Judgment." It was a polyptych consisting of seven wooden panels designed to fold inward. Our printed guide read that Rolin commissioned Roger Van der Wyden to paint the altarpiece "to hang above the altar of the great hall in order to help the patients bear their suffering." How Catholic, I thought.

A woman attendant operated a hefty mechanical magnifying glass. When she pushed a button, a machine whirred, the two-foot magnifying glass slid on rails, then clunked into position to give us a closer view of different parts of the beautifully rendered, vividly colored ancient artwork.

But the subject matter was eerie. A larger-than-life austere Jesus sat in judgment while angels blew trumpets. A few lucky haloed-saints were depicted but most of the people on earth were naked, sinking in quicksand or running for cover. It was the stuff that made for nightmares rather than solace for the sick.

It reminded me of art reproduced on small devotional cards given to us as rewards in parochial schools during the 1950's. We called them Holy Cards and they usually pictured terrifying scenes of saints with exposed bleeding hearts and stigmata wounds resembling Christ's, holding various body parts in their hands. An occasional St. Francis of Assisi surrounded by birds and bunnies would break up the macabre monotony.

I remembered qualifying for several cards in a contest similar to a spelling bee. Instead of spelling words, however, we were asked detailed questions about Christ's suffering before he died. The master of ceremonies priest drilled us with questions, "Exactly how many wounds did He suffer? Where were they located? When His side was pierced, what precisely flowed from the wound?" A correct answer allowed you to remain standing. I'd stayed against the wall for a long time. Unfortunately, sometimes I have too good a memory.

A tapestry hung on the other wall depicting St. Eloi. I studied it hoping for more pleasant subject matter. But St. Eloi was standing next to a horse with a detached leg while blood flowed from the wound. I read the sign next to the tapestry. Eloi had tried to shoe the horse the quick way – by cutting off its leg to make it easier. Of course, it would've been a miracle if he had put the leg back on the horse. But he hadn't. It seemed to me while Eloi may have been a holy man, he was a man who lacked brainpower. Nonetheless, St. Eloi had been named the patron saint of blacksmiths and ferriers.

We sat at an outdoor café under the warm autumnal sun. Most of us ordered the local specialty *Bœuf Bourguignon*, beef stewed in the regional Burgundy wine, served on mashed potatoes, accompanied by a hot goat cheese salad and a couple of carafes of burgundy house wine. Greg alone ordered the *plat du jour* for the main course.

"This is the best salmon I've ever had," Greg said as he dug in. "I thought the food in France would be frou-frou. This is food for real people."

I agreed. We ate what the locals ate. It was not only easier on the budget, it was a more authentic everyday experience than three-star Michelin restaurants.

"Yep. If this is 'peasant food' then I'm a peasant through and through," I said after I swallowed some of my beef stew. Busloads of tourists walked by, dutifully following their tour guides who held umbrellas in the air. We heard German, Chinese, Japanese, British and American voices. "How about we order some dessert?" I said.

"And some coffee," Holly said.

"*After* dessert," I said.

Fortified, we walked to the Marche aux Vins for a wine tasting smorgasbord – eighteen different wines to sample in a candlelit cave. The woman behind the counter handed us tasting cups and told us we may pour as much as we like of the wines. We strolled through the cave, and pressed the button for English on the information kiosk. A French-accented recorded voice described the wines and some of the history of the caves, including a display of some of the ancient artifacts that were unearthed including an early Christian sarcophagus

I eyed the spittoon next to the first keg. Uh, uh. I wasn't about to use it. First we had *vins blancs*: Bourgogne Chardonnay, Pouilly-Fuissé, Savigny les Beaune, and Puligny Montrachet. Julie, a professional cook, made notes and critiqued each wine demonstrating her educated palate.

Following were the vins rouges: Bourgogne Pinot Noir, Marsannay, Côte de Beaune Village, Auxey- Duresses, Givry, Saint-Romain, Santenay, Savigny les Beaune, Pommard, Nuits Saint Georges, Gevrey-Chambertin, Vosne-Romanée, Beaune Premier Cru, and Volnay Premier Cru. Julie tasted and declared the Beaune Premier Cru, "festive, great for a holiday."

"At this point, I can't tell much difference between the fourteen reds," I said. They all tasted like forms of liquid velvet to me. "I wouldn't kick any of them out of my wine rack."

We purchased a few bottles and strolled out into a tiny vineyard outside, maintained, no doubt, for tourists like us to see what a real vineyard looked like. The green grapes were much smaller than the ones we ate as fruit. It seemed impossible so many flavors could be found in such diminutive bunches.

The last tour was the *Musée du Vin*, the museum of wine. Housed in the former house of the Dukes of Burgundy, it contained a collection of wine-related goodies. We studied the how grapes were grown, harvested, pressed and fermented. Modern tapestries displayed included one with a catchy name – "*Le vin, source de vie*"– Wine, the source of life.

There were some interesting old photographs. One depicted a unique way of stomping grapes – instead of being barefoot, the men in the picture had gone one better and were naked. The women in our group were fascinated by this display, but our men were missing. We found them outside in the barn studying the huge fourteenth-century wine press and speculating about how it worked.

I'd arranged for our taxi to come and pick us up and our same driver arrived right on time. He spoke no English and we'd conversed in simple phrases and gestures up until now.   He took a different way out of town. Vineyards surrounded us and I realized he was taking us on an impromptu tour.   The vines grew in every available square inch.   There was a hotel covered in ivy with grape vines growing right up to the door. I wanted to stay there surrounded by the golden vines in the warm autumn light. We continued up to Nuits St. George, then turned from the hills past fields with neat rows of bushes.   "Cassis," our driver said as he pointed to rows of black current berries.

That evening, Julie made spaghetti Carbonara with rich French pancetta-like bacon.   Our CD player blasted out oldies but goodies.   Chuck Berry's classic filled the salon, "It was a teenage wedding and the old folks wished them well. You could see that Pierre did truly love the *mademoiselle*."   We'd had quite a bit of Nuits Saint Georges and Côtes du Rhône. Paul rolled his eyes and said, "I apologize in advance. She can't sit down when this plays." I stood up and began a slow twist a la John Travolta in "Pulp Fiction."

Greg and Julie couldn't listen to Meatloaf's "Paradise by the Dashboard Light" without acting the parts.   They knew all the words and appropriate gestures – it was a good show.

Later, I crawled up to the pilothouse to hear if we'd made too much noise for our neighbors. There's nothing worse than a bunch of middle-aged Baby Boomers when we get raucous.   I decided the music wasn't too loud – thank God for steel hulls – and saw Maureen and Jeff eating by candlelight with their own guests in their pilothouse. Mist rose over the canal, the Little Dipper glowed against the night sky and the moon rose behind the big poplar studded with mistletoe.   I sang, "*C'est la vie* say the old folks which goes to show you never can tell."

14 - Dijon: More than Mustard

I have found out that there ain't no surer way to find out whether you like people or hate them than to travel with them.

-Mark Twain

Paul crawled out of the engine room. "I think I've fixed it for good this time." He held out a handful of black rubber bits in his greasy hand. "Just in case I've ordered two more impellors for back up."

"So it's safe to go on the Burgundy Canal?" I said.

"Well as safe as it ever will be." He grinned and wiped some sweat from his forehead with his handkerchief. I smiled back and hugged him.

"I would never ever do this with someone who wasn't mechanically inclined."

"Like Eammon?" He'd told us he carried only one tool – a cell phone.

"Only with you...or Greg." I grinned and gave him a peck on the cheek.

The smile left his face. "You know I can't do this without you."

I took in his salt and pepper hair curling in wet ringlets around his hairline, the red t-shirt smeared with grease and his grubby jeans. But I also studied his caramel eyes, his smooth hairless sun-bronzed arms, his corded forearms. I'd already observed a few of the women lockkeepers noticing him.

"Just keep that in mind," I said giving him a real kiss, grease and all.

The next morning we chugged out of homeport, down the Saône, past St. Jean to the entrance of the Burgundy Canal. Our friends munched croissants and pastries at the table on deck.

"We're not going in there are we?" Holly said wincing as she pointed to the first lock. "We can't possibly fit."

"Oh we will. But remember to sit down as we come in. After we stop, you're free to move about the cabin." I grinned and walked up the side deck to my position. I knew Paul would nail the entrance perfectly and he did.

Imagine slid in to the empty lock with inches to spare on each side. I stole a look at my guests and saw them nodding with raised eyebrows. A young *mademoiselle* with pretty legs in short-shorts grabbed our lines and wrapped them around the lock bollards for us. All of the men exchanged the We've Noticed The Good Looking Woman But Wives Are Around look.

"I think they've chosen the lockkeepers for the tourist's enjoyment, rather than tenure," I said. The men in our group didn't seem to care about the rationale. They just enjoyed the scenery.

The young lockkeeper cranked the large wheel and the doors clanged shut. Then she cranked a lever around and around and a waterfall poured in. I studied the plants growing out of the wall, infinitesimal ferns and tiny tree-like growths. Algae covered the rest of the granite block wall, creating "lock scum." I breathed in the fishy scent while my friends clicked photo after photo.

Just before noon, we pulled into a lock and told the lockkeeper we would eat *déjeuner* inside it. "It's lunchtime," I said to my friends. "The lockkeepers all get an hour off. So, let's eat."

We formed a human chain and passed food up the stairs to the deck. Our picnic lunch consisted of a tender mesclun salad dressed in Dijon vinaigrette, shredded carrot salad, tabouli, and celeriac salad in a creamy mayo-based dressing. I'd made a meat platter with sliced ham, chicken, spicy chorizo sausage and two pâtés, pâté de campagne made with ground veal, pork and pistachio nuts, and mousse de canard of duck liver.

Paul sawed two *baguettes* and placed the pieces into our Provençal fabric breadbasket. Our cheese tray held Abbey de Citeaux, a ripe Brie, a block of Emmental, and a pot of fresh chèvre.

We sat at the table under our umbrella and dug in. "This is fantastic," Julie said. I basked in her compliments as she sampled every bit. "The Emmental is great." She picked up a chunk of pale yellow cheese with large, scattered holes. "Wonderful nice nutty flavor. The Brie is good, aged a bit. But this artisan one is heavenly." She savored the Citeaux.

"Heavenly is a good description – it's made by monks," I said. She knew her flavors. It was the most expensive cheese we had.

"You have this much fun," Holly said looking at Paul and me. "And people pay you to do this."

We nodded and grinned. "It's a dirty job, but someone's gotta do it," Paul said as he rose up to grab the box of *petit fours* for dessert.

The six of us shopped for provisions in Longecourt en Plaine, a tiny village along the canal. Europeans believed in daily market shopping. I would too if there were stores available in every port. With six people on board, my tiny refrigerator and freezer emptied in two days. Our guidebooks had been less than accurate about the location of shops; so many of them had been closed especially along the Ditch. We hoped the tourist industry would keep some markets open along this canal. Julie wanted to make au gratin potatoes and needed nutmeg. We scoured the spice section in a local *épicerie*, looking for what might be "nutmeg." Torn between two possibilities, we decided to purchase both. When we opened the spice cans, one turned out to be nutmeg, the other cumin.

Greg and Doug took over my deckhand duty. Paul still called me if he needed "the expert." I took advantage of downtime and dropped below to chat with Holly and Julie. Holly smirked over her cup of coffee. "Sundae has you hoodwinked. I found her on the table eating croissants."

My cat blinked innocently at me probably thinking, "Tattletale!" I hadn't bothered to put pastries away so people could snack on them all morning.

"She never goes on the dining table."

"Not when you're around," she said grinning.

I remembered scraps I'd found in unusual places. I shook my head. "You might be right. She may have fooled me for fourteen years." I'd thought she had a sensitive stomach and I had called her "my bulimic kitty." I suspected some of the people food she'd been sampling didn't agree with her cat digestive system.

"Bad kitty. From now on, no more food out once we're underway." I shook my finger at her. She gave me the cat equivalent of a shrug – she licked her shoulder three times, circled around and curled up on the chair for a nap.

We speculated on the best way to handle the situation if we encountered the maniac pilot determined to reclaim the canals for commercial barges. All of us liked the approach of fighting fire with fire and being intimidating ourselves. I proposed capitalizing on the fear Americans are armed and ready to shoot. A toy cannon installed on the foredeck might be a deterrent.

The canal bordered a large military airfield. French fighter jets, Mirages, with afterburners aflame roared down the runway. I thought about the incongruity of a thirteenth century church on the left horizon while on our right was a state-of-the-art military airstrip. *Imagine* moved at her sedate four mile-an-hour pace while Mirage jets zoomed by at a hundred times our speed.

The only "automatic" lock in this section of the canal didn't work. Paul crawled up the slimy ladder in the lock and used the emergency telephone. The lockkeeper from the next lock came by, flashed us a buck-toothed grin, worked some controls on the panel, and the lock doors banged shut behind us. He hopped on his scooter and drove home to meet us.

At his lock house a small sign read, "*Exposition Les Tresors de l'ecuse,*" treasures of the lock. We disembarked and followed him into his lush backyard with a small pond filled with ducks. Occasionally a jet roared overhead killing all attempts at conversation. His cellar overflowed with canal memorabilia: vintage photographs of the canal, coins from around the world, wine labels, and old family portraits. Photographs pictured barges frozen in ice and trucks fished out of the canal. The most dramatic photos were from the Second World War. The nearby airfield had been occupied by the Nazis. An airman had taken a photo of a U.S. Liberator bomber dropping its bomb load directly on this lock.

As we neared Dijon, the rutted gravel towpath had been paved. Instead of VNF workers roaring by on their *mobylette* scooters, the primary traffic consisted of bicyclers in spandex outfits, joggers in nylon shorts, and rollerbladers skating in pairs. Then we passed the inevitable industrial area, which had sprung up near the canal when barges were the main way to ship. Now most of the moorings for commercial barges remained empty.

Nearing the port of Dijon, we passed a silo labeled "Maille," a major brand of mustard in Dijon. People may not know where Dijon was located – about 200 miles southeast of Paris – but they did know Dijon mustard. The best Dijon mustard recipe was simple: black or brown seeds were ground, passed through a sieve, white wine vinegar added and the mixture packed into jars. No additives whatsoever, no coloring, no fillers, no unpronounceable chemicals. It was hotter than the mustard we get in the States labeled "Dijon," more like the kind in Chinese restaurants with a kick that sent a rush through your nose.

I grew up with a tradition of French's classic yellow used liberally on ham sandwiches, polish sausage and hamburgers. Gene and Jude's drive-in stand in River Grove sold a Chicago specialty – Vienna hot dogs. I'd order two hot dogs slathered in thick yellow mustard embedded with chunks of raw onions. The hot dog and bun were topped with fries and then wrapped in brown paper that would immediately start to breakout in grease spots. I'd burn my mouth on the hot oily fries covered in mustard and ecstasy would follow. A few years later ads aired for "Gray Poupon." We knew this was classy mustard because people in chauffer-driven Rolls Royces would ask each other politely if they had any.

We rose up in the deep lock and spotted the harbor. An oasis in the middle of city, it was surrounded by a park studded with calla lilies, mums, and marigolds. I stepped off the boat to find the Harbor Master. I stopped at the *capitainerie* and read the office hours posted on the locked door. He should be here but he wasn't. I walked around to find a mooring. There was *a port de plaisance* area with small pontoon docks for the Tupperware, unsuitable for us. I spotted an English narrow boat with a woman aboard.

"Do you know where the *capitaine* might be?" I shouted.

She shrugged and yelled, "He'll probably show up when he feels like it."

I noted the book she was reading and said, "I love P.D. James. She's a great writer!" She smiled and nodded.

Around a tree-covered island was a quay with large bollards, water and electricity. This will be heaven, I thought. Several hotel boats were moored nearby. Most of the hotel boats were purpose-built or converted *péniches* designed to be as big as possible and still fit in the standard French canal lock, 38 by 5 meters or about 120 by 16 feet.

The top deck of this boat had a small outdoor seating area, and an interior dining room and salon. The aft galley held a full-time chef. The staterooms were below. Depending on the hotel barge, there were rooms from six passengers up to twenty. Most of the crews spoke English since the majority of passengers were Americans. We'd heard crewmembers converse with other hotel barges and ground support staff on the VHF radio. Some were owned by the same company and traveled in pairs. Usually the conversations regarded provisioning, "I think we have enough white wine–about twenty cases remain."

I walked up to a twenty-something tanned, shirtless guy and introduced myself.

"Ah yes I remember *Imagine.* You let us by yesterday. Sorry about cutting in front of you but I'm on a timetable," he said in a delicious Australian accent.

"No problem. We know hotel barges have schedules." I felt extremely understanding as I studied his pecs. Hotel barge companies must have a hiring policy skewed toward good-looking Beautiful Mens, I thought. He pointed where he thought we could moor.

I signaled Paul who slowly brought *Imagine* around. This would be easy – if it weren't for a fisherman. He sat with four poles in the water where we wanted to moor. I explained I was desolate but he must move. He pointed at the sign in French, "No docking," but I shrugged. *Imagine* continued to bear down. He collected his poles, shot me a look of disgust and walked away.

As soon as we moored, the Harbor Master arrived, introducing himself as "Ludwig." He was G.Q. handsome with dark hair and blue-green eyes framed by eyelashes every woman covets. Dressed in a white uniform with gold braiding he looked very official.

He started to speak to us in French, and then switched to English when he heard our accents. "I am very sorry, you must move. You see the sign, yes? Have you not noticed the bollards here broken out of the concrete?"

Paul nodded. Ludwig asked us to moor across the canal out of the harbor for the night with no services.

"A spot will open up tomorrow I am sure," Ludwig said.

We did as we were told. The fisherman I'd displaced fished near the pontoons, silently regarding the commotion.

He didn't need to speak. I knew he'd told me so.

The mooring on the canal was adjacent to a park next to a series of nice-looking high-rise apartments. The park bench near us was lined with elderly Mesdames, wearing similar dresses, cardigans and low comfortable shoes. The appointed spokesperson approached Paul. He understood they were interested in the bateau *Imagine,* pronouncing it in the French fashion, "Ee-ma-gene".

"Is it yours?" she asked in French.

When Paul answered in the affirmative, she conversed a while with her friends, then conveyed they were impressed with our large private boat. It was a most beautiful boat. All of the ladies nodded and smiled. "Where are you from?" she asked.

This wasn't an easy question. You must declare a state of residence, pay their taxes, and get car insurance and registration somewhere. So, we'd chosen Paul III's address.

"Chicago, America. Where are your from?" he asked. The joke was understood. They all laughed. Dijon, France of course.

Holly pointed to the wobbly satellite dish. "There's a lot of broken stuff around. If I didn't know you guys better I'd be worried we could sink."

She was right.   Not about sinking or anything unsafe, but the list of broken items had grown longer as our season progressed: our vacuum cleaner hose had cracked and had to be nursed along or it fell off; the freezer door of my little refrigerator was cracked so it had to be carefully placed back on whenever it was opened; the satellite antenna had fallen over so many times its protruding arm was held together with a piece of rope.   And of course she'd noticed the engine repair the day we'd gone to Beaune.

"Next year. We have a long list of work to do."   Some of the poplar leaves had turned gold and there was a strong hint of autumn in the cool evening breezes.   In little over a month we'd return to the States.   I tried to remain in the present and enjoy the moment. But it was hard not to realize the season was drawing to a close.

"Let's go out and eat," Holly said.

"Yeah it's about dinnertime isn't it?" Doug said.

Paul checked his watch. "Restaurants don't open until at least seven. And at that hour we'll be the only ones there."

My friends raised their eyebrows. In the Midwest people arrived at work before dawn and ate at six.

At the restaurant Holly scanned the menu looking for *cassoulet*.

"You won't find it on the menu. *Cassoulet* is from the southwest region of Languedoc and so I've rarely seen it on the menu. Especially not in ones that specialize in Burgundian cuisine like this one," I said.

"But the Hotel Sofitel in Minneapolis serves all the Burgundy specials along with *cassoulet*," she said.

I didn't have a response. I exchanged looks with Paul. We shrugged.

"Could you ask the waiter for some ice water?" Greg asked. "And while you're at it some butter for this bread?"

Drinking ice water or using butter on bread hadn't occurred to me. We were so used to the French style of dining we didn't question it or ask for things the American way anymore. I wondered how much of me was American and how much of me was French.

"OK," I said, "but I refuse to order coffee until after the dessert."

The next morning a taxi appeared on time to pick up our friends. It's a miracle, I thought. I had called the cab on the telephone using my French the day before and given them directions to the port. Anxiety woke me at 5:30 a.m. and I'd had a nervous half hour as we waited in the darkness for the cab. As the sun rose, we waved goodbye in true Minnesota fashion waving and saying goodbye several times over.

Then I crawled back into bed. I wasn't on a Midwestern time schedule anymore.

Later that morning, I heard a gentle knock on our pilothouse door. I crawled up the stairs and recognized the woman from the narrow boat. In her hand she carried precious books in English including the P.D. James paperback she'd just finished.

"Oh thank you," I said, wanting to kiss her. "Please come aboard." She introduced herself as Joyce.

"That's a nice narrow boat you have," I said feeling nautically knowledgeable.

"Thank you, but it's not that kind of boat. It's wider than a narrow boat's six-feet." She noticed my crest fallen expression. "Lots of people make that error. My husband is on a crusade to explain the difference to the world. Do you enjoy humorous reads?"

"Of course. I love a good laugh."

"The second book is rather different, but funny. My husband begged me not to give it to you. You might find it...offensive."

That did it. I couldn't wait to read the innocently titled "Blott on the Landscape."

"Oh and look at the kitty," she said. "I love cats." She reached over to pet Sundae. My normally friendly feline took one look at this grandmotherly lady and ran away. I retrieved my cat and tried to get her to stand still so she could get the attention she usually craved. No way. She wouldn't have anything to do with the nice lady with the gray hair. Sundae hissed, growled and galloped down the stairs. I felt my face flush with embarrassment.

The next day I scrutinized my library for a suitable book for Joyce. I walked to her mooring, a book about barging in my hand. Too late. Her boat was gone. I'd try to repay her by giving books to someone thirsting for a good read. I dug into the Blott book and discovered a satire on English society. One of the central characters, the Lord of the Manor, hadn't performed his marital duties. The only way he could get excited involved spanking, bondage, and infantilism. It was hilarious and witty but I remembered the very sweet grandmotherly lady tentatively offering it to me. No wonder her husband had been worried about my sense of humor. Or perhaps, Sundae with her animal wisdom had spotted a true dominatrix underneath a grandmotherly disguise.

We had nearly a two-week gap before the next guests arrived.

"If we cruise hard, we could make it back to homeport in two days ...wait a minute." Paul shook his head. "What am I thinking?"

We nodded at each other. "The lesson of Château Regnault. What's the rush?"

Ludwig made us a "good price" for the longer stay and we settled in for ten days in one of the most beautiful cities in France.

The Romans built a wall around Dijon in the third century. It contained the heart of the current city, now the capital of Burgundy. Some of the half-timbered structures still stood. In one of these ancient buildings we discovered the restaurant *Le Sauvage,* a French grill. We sat in the sunny courtyard enclosed by the ancient half-timbered inn, listened to the muffled sounds of the city and inhaled the scent of geraniums.

"This is an incredible morel sauce," Paul said pointing at the cup of creamed wild mushrooms with one of his brochettes of beef.

"Hmm. And my duck is great but the *gratin dauphinois* is phenomenal." I chewed the firm potato casserole baked with loads of cream, hints of garlic and nutmeg, all under a crunchy crust. "I want to know how they figured out how to do this on the grill."

Researching restaurants was a dirty job, but someone had to do it.

We hiked to the *Musée des Beaux-Arts in the Palais des Ducs*, the former palace of the Dukes of Burgundy. The elaborately carved limestone building housed one of the finest art collections in France. Paintings and furniture from the 15th to 19th century decorated the vast palace. I stood at the courtyard entrance and imagined life 500 years ago and pretended I heard the clop of horse's hooves instead of the roar of Renaults.

The galleries contained old masterpieces and contemporary minimalist paintings. The highlight of the museum was the tombs of the dukes. For nearly one hundred years the Dukes of Burgundy were the most powerful royalty in all Western Europe. Their territory stretched from the North Sea to the Loire and from the Loire to the Rhine.

There'd been four dukes: Philip the Rash, who established them as a power, John the Fearless, who engaged in feuds that almost destroyed their fortunes, Philip the Good, who sold Joan of Arc to the English, and Charles the Bold, the richest of them all.

The museum was a good visit but it was also a tremendous value with free admission on Sunday.

Along with the museum, botanical garden, and gorgeous architecture, Dijon had another big draw – great shopping. We hunted for things we hadn't been able to find in smaller villages. We found a nice pair of black trolleys for carting groceries. I was a little disappointed in the sedate color – I'd wanted something snazzier like a leopard print.

Paul needed new eyeglass frames. I didn't need them but I wanted them. Sporting new glasses we left the optical store feeling *très chic*, with the added benefit of being able to see. I located a fantastic shoe store near the Maille mustard store downtown. I indulged my shoe obsession and splurged on three pairs of shoes – all flats.

We made a point of strolling into the heart of the city every day. We'd pass the Hospital, cross the road under the busy train tracks overhead, go past the botanical gardens, into the downtown shopping area. Nearby squares were outlined with cafés. On the Square Emil Zola, we ordered the best *moules and frites* we've had since Reims. Redolent of the sea, the tender mussels were combined with cream, wine, garlic and onion. Accompanied by crunchy fries and white Burgundy wine, we feasted under the shade of plane trees. We were lucky to get a table – most of the time reservations were required.

When we tried to return on a Sunday, the maitre d' shook his head at my request for seating and turned away, the closest thing to rudeness I'd encountered. Abrupt and harried came to mind. I must get over my phone phobia, I thought. Learning how to make reservations here might be the catalyst.

The Dijon Market on Tuesday, Thursday, Friday and Saturday filled the streets for several blocks. The permanent market building had stalls for fifty vendors crammed with food for sale. Vendors artfully displayed delicate endives, firm artichokes, and the slimmest of green beans, *haricot verts.* Cheese stalls carried *chèvre,* Brie in varying flavors, and stronger Camembert.

Butchers boasted white, brown and black sausages, whole ducks, *fois gras*, organ meats like tongue, livers and brains, chicken from the Bresse region, the *Poulet de Bresse*, with one or two blue feet left on for proof of their species. Sometimes the heads were left on for good measure.

The outdoor market sported clothes, shoes, music, furniture, bedding, and crafts. Ladies' lingerie, a favorite, ranged from delicate lace underwire bras and matching thongs to booths specializing in the *madame* of a certain age: sturdy bras with seven or eight hooks, girdles and long-line bras, white nylon and cotton underpants the size of small continents.

After so much sensory overload, we chose a *crêperie*, sat outside and settled in for some good people watching. I tried a buckwheat *crêpe* with corn, chicken, tomatoes and chèvre. Paul had "*Crêpe* Burgundy" with *escargot* in a garlic cream sauce. The house beverage of choice was hard cider but we had a carafe of light rosé. For dessert, we munched *crêpes* filled with whipped cream and strawberries and covered in chocolate. We didn't ask for ice in our water and had a café at the conclusion of our lunch, not during dessert. Restaurateurs might know we were foreigners once we spoke, but not by the way we ate and drank.

15 - C'est la Vie

Let us celebrate the occasion with wine and sweet words.
-Plautus

Eight months earlier I'd told Paul, "I want something really special for my fiftieth birthday."

He'd looked dumbfounded. "I'm taking you to France for the summer – what more do you want?"

He'd had me there.

But for my birthday week I did get something really special after all. I hummed while we waited on the Dijon station platform for the TGV train from Paris.

"Nervous?" Paul said. I gave him half a smile. My hum was an audible indication of my anticipation. A recording announced the arrival and a train shaped like a bullet screeched to a halt at our platform, the *voie*. My dear friend Jo Ann, her boyfriend Richard, my cousin Renee and her husband Gary stepped off the TGV in a flurry of luggage.

"God, you guys look great," Jo said. "You are slim, my friends."

"It's the barge diet," I said as I hugged her.

She gave me a quizzical look. "You'll have to tell me all about it."

"Like you need it." She was still the same size two – or was it zero ? – she'd been thirteen years ago. We'd become friends when newly wed Paul and I had rented her house in Boulder. It seemed a lifetime ago. Several lifetimes.

We hiked back to the port and rolled suitcases along, turned past the gardens studded with mums and asters, past the obelisk commemorating the canal completion in 1833, and stopped at an iron bird-like sculpture dedicated to Eiffel.

"Gustave Eiffel was born in Dijon," Paul said pointing at the iron sculpture. "He built much more than the famous tower, like the canal aqueduct in Briare." We rounded the corner to where *Imagine* hugged the wall. The four of our friends stopped short.

"Wow," said Renee. "It's huge. Much bigger than the pictures. They don't do it justice." Her big brown eyes widened. I put my arm around her shoulders, felt her long luxuriant hair against my arm. She was shorter and darker, but side-by-side, we had a family resemblance. I studied her high cheekbones and her dimpled chin, so much like mine.

"Thanks. And it's 'she' not 'it.' Boating talk and all."

"She's fantastic," said Richard. "And just great being here with you guys. I can't believe it." I gave him a kiss and his beard tickled my cheek.

"Far out man," said Gary grinning. I hugged his considerable girth and thought he could use a diet a lot more than Jo Ann. As if he'd read my mind he said, "I've put on a little weight. But my doctor says I eat perfectly – for a sumo wrestler."

"Let's get you settled in," I said. "And I'll fill you all in on the barge diet."

Perfect weather of sunny days and cool nights created an ideal backdrop for exploring Dijon together. On my birthday we went out to dinner to the Cave at the Hotel Sofitel featuring local fare and sing-alongs in French. We didn't know exactly what we sang but we had the chorus (*"Oui, oui, oui."*) and the hand gestures down well enough to participate. Later I discovered the tune was a famous Burgundian wine lover's song, which asked the question, "Tell me is the wine good?" A table of burgundy-faced businessmen took the song seriously and one showcased his baritone with emphatic *"Ouis."*

The accordion then played a familiar tune – "Happy Birthday." I felt my face blush as the waiter sat a cassis sorbet and vanilla ice cream dessert in front of me. A single candle burned in its center. "Happy Birthday" in English was scrolled in chocolate. Apparently everyone in the restaurant knew the English words to the song too, I thought, as I endured two verses with a reddened face.

I unwrapped my gifts at the table. Jo Ann and Richard gave me a watercolor of *Imagine* painted by a local Dijon artist. I loved the way the he'd captured her Klipper lines, especially the bow. She looked jaunty with our multicolor pennants flying on her mast, all set against the trees of the island in the Dijon harbor.

"I went out one day for my jog," Jo said, "and there was this guy doing a painting of your boat. I loved what he'd done so I asked him if it was for sale. He said if it turned out he would sell it to me. I hope you don't mind knowing but he only charged me 100 francs." That was about $14 U.S. I knew she'd done the entire transaction in French and I envied her student years in Paris.

"Thank you, it's perfect. I'll treasure it always," I said running my finger around the edge of the paper. I thought of the new sketchbooks Renee and I had bought together, the 4H, B2 and B4 pencils and travel watercolor set. I felt the urge to start drawing and painting again.

I opened the present from Renee and Gary. I already wore the crystal necklace and earrings Renee had given me earlier after she assured me they were the latest craze. I'd always relied on my artistic cousin to help keep me fashionably current.

"Wow. A pair of walkie-talkies. How did you know I could use these?"

"It made sense," Gary said. "I'm a boater and with one as big as yours we figured you could use them."

"Yeah, we use them when we're at the mall with the kids. It's a great way to keep in touch while you're shopping," Renee said.

I wouldn't need to use our problematic intercom system when I'm on the foredeck. And we could communicate from ship to shore without hand signals or shouting. Maybe someday we'd even need them in a mall.

"This is a great gift, life-changing even. Thank you so much."

I opened Paul's presents. The first was a sleek ebony Rado watch perfect for my small wrist. I tore open the second package and spotted something bright yellow.

"Hey – the bottom half to my foul weather gear. How romantic," I said kissing him. The shiny pants weren't what I'd had in mind when I'd asked for "something special" just eight months before but I couldn't think of a more thoughtful gift.

That night Bear hopped into bed and curled next to me. It had been a year to the day when Paul told me I'd surprised him by how I'd taken to barging. Fifty wasn't really mid-life, I realized, as I had little chance and no desire to live to be a hundred.

I think most people who fear birthdays aren't living their life the way they want and the date highlights another wasted year. Time didn't seem to flit through my fingertips any more in a haze of working at an unfulfilling job. I'd had time to think, to recharge, and to just "be."

Bear put his paw on my shoulder. Turning fifty wasn't bad at all, I thought as I stroked his velvet fur. I reached over and grabbed Paul's hand and soon two sets of snores lulled me to sleep.

.

"We want to get married on board and we want Captain Paul to perform the ceremony," Jo Ann said. Richard beamed and nodded.

"Ah…I'd love to do it but it won't be legal," Paul said.

Jo Ann waved her hand. "We'll go to the Justice of the Peace when we get home but we want to get married here."

"Oh Jo Jo." I wrapped my arms around her. "Really?" She nodded and grabbed Richard's hand.

"We've been planning it for a long time. We're both ready to take the plunge again," Richard said.

And Jo Ann added, "I can't imagine a life without Richard so why not?"

"No better reason to me," I said hugging Richard. "Besides I like him."

"Everybody likes Richard," Jo Ann said. "My friends, my family, my parents, my kids. In fact, I think my boys like him more than me." She grinned her dimpled smile and her blue eyes twinkled.

"Nah. But you know that's really a good sign."

Jo and Richard found gold bands at a jeweler in Dijon. We took off for a day's cruise up the Burgundy as it wound its way out of the city through a recreational zone. We glided by a skateboard park, where kids were clad in the same skateboarding gear as in the States as they swooped and turned. More bicyclists whirred by and through the golden poplars we spotted Lake Kir below limestone cliffs. The lake had been named for the mayor of Dijon, Monsieur Kir, now famous for his clever use of local ingredients. To promote the use of the abundant but inferior white wine, Aligoté, he'd mixed it with crème de cassis and *voilà* – the *"Kir"* had been created.

Gary sat with me on the foredeck as I taught him to work the lines through locks. He learned quickly enough but any lapse in conversation was anathema to him. I realized how much silence I'd been used to riding on the bow listening only to birdsong punctuated by an occasional *gronk* of a heron. And worse still, his and Renee's confidences convinced me I was witnessing the beginning of one marriage and the end of another.

"Hey give Renee a break. Her dad just died, it's a tough time." My mom had died four years earlier and the initial sting had changed into a dull pain whenever I thought about her.

"I'll try." He looked away.

We moored along a grass bank near the tiny village of Velars-sur-Ouche. The Ouche River was little more than a creek gurgling by the side of the canal framed by steep forested hills. The highest hill was crowned with a cross-shaped monument identified as "Crucifix" on our chart.

Richard put George Winston's "Prairie" CD on our player and set it on deck. Jo and I refashioned my birthday spray of stargazer lilies into a bridal bouquet. Renee set up her video camera to record the event. Richard handed Paul his script. Paul raised his brows. This was going to be quite a ceremony. Richard held his reading material with steady hands. Gary fiddled with the ring for Jo Ann's hand while I rolled the other around in my pocket.

Jo Ann walked onto the deck as serene as a sunset. The scent of her stargazer lilies wafted behind her. Overhead, lacey cirrus clouds veiled the sky. Children's voices rose as they played in nearby yards, bicyclists zoomed by on the towpath, dogs barked in the distance, but we only heard Richard read how he first fell in love with Jo Ann on a hilltop above Boulder, recognizing she was the Beloved, the person he'd been looking for all of his life, for now and for eternity.

Jo Ann's speech was shorter and more succinct. "I love you Richard and I want to be with you forever."

Paul followed his script verbatim up to a point. I realized he'd adlibbed a bit when he said, "By any powers vested in me by the US Coast Guard and the *Voie Navigable de France* I now proclaim you eternally committed to each other."

We popped open a chilled bottle of Bourgogne Crément, Burgundy's sparkling answer to Champagne, added a little crème de cassis and produced *Kir Royales*.

"*A votre santé*." We clinked our glasses together. To your health.

We settled at Pont de Pany, a small town described as "a pleasant stop with essential supplies" by our guidebook. Paul fussed with the mooring lines on the bank to ensure *Imagine* would stay put when we left her for a day trip to Beaune. Even with a cell phone I had no idea where to find a local taxi, so Jo Ann and I went on a mission to the Le Pont de Pany Hotel and Restaurant. The man behind the front desk graciously telephoned a taxicab to pick us up the next day.

After dinner on deck, Paul and I walked along the towpath. He held my right hand in his and said, "Your hand feels different." He squeezed it and rubbed his thumb across the calluses on my small palm. "It's... strong."

I flushed. "It's from hanging onto lines in abject terror."

"I think it's great you're so fit," he said bending over and kissing me. Jo and Richard rode up on their bikes.

"Hey you two. Leave that stuff for the newlyweds," Jo said. Paul and Richard walked ahead to load the bikes on deck. She leaned toward me and said, "I've never seen you two so affectionate."

I told her about Suzanne's question about marriage. "But for now, we are so happy."

" 'For now' is all we ever have."

The cab arrived on schedule and took us on a now familiar trip to Beaune. But when he told us the fare, Jo Ann and Paul were surprised. As usual, I hadn't a clue to the amount he'd quoted. We all dug for francs and handed him a wad of cash. He frowned, peeled off a bunch of bills and returned them to us. They'd misunderstood to the tune of a thousand francs.

"Wow that was honest of him," Jo said.

"And not uncommon," I said and told them the story of Joel the cab driver and rescuer extraordinaire in Château Regnault.

The Hotel Dieu was a must for our friends even though Paul and I had recently been there. I'd better get used to it, I thought. All of our guests should see Beaune if they never had.

"Look at this." Jo Ann, a Physician's Assistant, pointed to a particularly gruesome large syringe. "I think it's used for self-enemas."

"Good thing there are people like you because I'd never make it in the medical world," I said with a grimace. Around us were portraits of agonized patients under the scalpel. "What's this, a facelift?"

Gary, who owned a masonry company, busied himself photographing the building techniques from hundreds of years ago. "This is so cool. It's so sophisticated I can't believe it," he said pointing to an archway. "Do you know how much it would cost to do something like this today?" He shook his head.

Renee stood transfixed in front of the Van Der Wyden. "Look at those details, the skin tones, the folds in the fabrics. We used to call them 'head-banging' in art school."

Across the street from the Hotel Dieu we perused the Athenaeum wine store. It went on and on, starting with beautiful postcards, art glassware, and cookbooks. The heart of the store held wine gadgets of all kinds: carafes, corkscrews, temperature collars, cellar notebooks, classification aids like a scent kit to help a budding oenophile identify wine aromas. Jo and Richard admired the cellar rat candleholders with "rat's tails" to hang on a wine barrel in a cellar.   They didn't have a wine cellar per se but decided they'd look great on a table.

At the Marche aux Vins, we discovered the secret to enjoying the experience to its fullest. After tasting the "regular" eighteen wines, Gary told the cashier he wanted to buy a few cases of wine and have them shipped to Chicago. Two salespeople appeared and escorted him into a gated room filled with comfortable chairs.   The fashionably thin woman dressed in Chanel, brought out bottles hidden in the cellars. We all joined them and tasted and tasted…and tasted.

We drank from bottles of Burgundy retailing in the hundreds of dollars – Pommard Premier Cru, Santenay Premier Cru, Corton Grand Cru. Gary kept ordering more cases and his salesman kept upping the ante. Dressed in an exquisitely tailored gray suit, he'd pour some in a tasting glass, sniff though his Gallic nose, swirl the wine around and savor the sip. We chugged it down.

"This is fantastic," Richard kept repeating, as his face grew ruddier. I remembered he normally didn't drink much.

"We'd better go. The taxicab will be wanting us. Er… I mean waiting for us." I stood up a bit unsteadily.   The salespeople escorted us to the door and with the faintest traces of smiles, shook our hands goodbye. I envisioned them calculating their commissions. And I thought I had a good job.

As they loaded into the taxi the next morning, Jo Ann's eyes overflowed with tears, Renee wiped her eyes, and then my eyes brimmed. We waved goodbye until the cab drove out of sight. I'm notoriously bad at saying goodbye, barely able to croak out the words between tears.

I felt sad but not too sad to walk over with Paul and try the Hotel Pont de Pany Restaurant for lunch. Fresh daisies and roses adorned tables covered in starched white linen. I marveled at my *amuse-bouche* – literally translated 'amuse the mouth'– a tiny tidbit of salmon mousse served in an endive leaf. We feasted on a fish course of pink trout followed by a breast of chicken, both served with delicate sauces, as we sipped chilled Bourgogne Blanc After a *crème brûlée* and coffee I felt much less sad.

Two days later on our way to Vandenesse we arrived at the port of Pont D'Ouche. "Houston we have a problem," I said to Paul. "We're out of fresh food and dangerously low on wine. Tonight's meal is from my emergency rations unless we find something."

The chart had shown shopping and *boulangeries* at Bussiere and La Forge where we'd toured the towns on our bicycles to make sure we weren't missing the obvious.

"Here's the Abbey pictured in our guidebook. We must have the right town," Paul had said as he shook his head. But nothing resembled a food store.

In Pont D'Ouche, we spotted a Hotel restaurant, ran across the street and read the sign posted on the door. "It says it's closed for holiday for the month," I said. We walked around the few square blocks to no avail. No food here.

When the *capitaine* returned from his hour and a half lunch we explained our plight to him. "No," he said. "There are no shops here."

"We are out of bread," I said.

A look of pure compassion crossed his face. He held up a finger. "One moment." He grabbed the telephone and spoke urgently into the receiver. "One of my friends, a lockkeeper, has a car and will drive you to a *Supermarché.* In exchange, all he asks is you pay for his fuel."

Our driver, a round-faced man with a handlebar mustache, pulled up in our Peugeot chariot. In French, we told him we needed cheese, vegetables, meats and wine. We zoomed off to the supermarket near Pouilly en Auxois further up the canal, past the low tunnel where we would not be able to go on *Imagine.* He followed us through the store as we loaded our shopping cart to the brim and then helped us pack everything into our two new trolleys.

When we reached for a bottle of Burgundy red, he frowned and told us he had better wine for us to buy at his lock house. On the way, he gave us an impromptu tour of his favorite church at Sainte Sabine. The walled village of

Chateauneuf-en-Auxois perched on a hill above us like a set design from a fairy tale production of Sleeping Beauty.

At the lockkeeper's cottage we hurried down into his dank cellar that proved to be a miniature *Marche de vins*. We tasted several wines and decided on a case of red Nuits St. Georges and a few bottles of white Côte de Beaune. He returned us to our boat, complimented us on it and then helped us unload.

"How much do we owe you?" Paul asked in French.

The lockkeeper shook his head. No money. Buying the wine from him was enough, he said.

At our first lock the next morning, a friendly face with a handlebar mustache greeted us. "*Bonjour mes amis*," he said.

After much waving and promises of our return, we continued on. There were locks every half a kilometer or so as we climbed toward the summit at Pouilly en Auxois. Through this stretch of the Burgundy Canal we were assigned the luxury of a traveling lockkeeper. Smaller pleasure boats were expected to operate the locks themselves. Few lockkeepers lived in cottages and most were leased to private parties.

At one of the cottages, a sign advertised an art exhibit. We went in and found a dark, quiet man surrounded by his paintings and drawings, which were as dark and somber as the artist. I suspected his favorite subject matter was figure drawing but he devoted a large part of his space to pen and ink drawings of the hotel barges that traveled this section of canal regularly. He introduced himself as Phillip Leroy.

"Can you can do a pen and ink of *Imagine*?" I asked. He nodded, snapped some photographs of our barge and quoted us a price. We would return this way in a few days to pick it up.

Further along the canal, another former lockkeeper's house also had art for sale. A friendly woman displayed handmade jewelry – pins, earrings, and necklaces, all made of wood. I picked up most of my Christmas gifts for the women on my list. When she understood these were gifts, she carefully boxed and wrapped each pin with flowered gift-wrap and ribbon, finishing each with a sticker carrying her name and the address of the lock, the *écluse*.

While she wrapped, I looked around the interior of the lock house. Once it had probably held a family. The interior walls had been torn down to make the studio, but I envisioned a tiny kitchen, bedroom and sitting/dining room in this 40 X 25 foot space. Above me, the roof peaked, held by ancient hand-hewn beams. The uneven ochre flagstone floor had probably been swept and scrubbed thousands of times from the millions of footsteps traipsing across it.

We made our way to Vandenesse. Above us for the last several kilometers loomed the hill town of Chateauneuf. After we secured a mooring, Paul said, "Does the barge moored behind us look familiar?"

"You always remember individual boats much better than I do." I turned around and squinted. "Nope. I don't recognize it."

"She's the *Lady A*," he prompted me.

I still drew a blank. Finally he grabbed the book from the ship's library, *The Insite Guide to Cruising the Waterways of Europe.*

"Ah," I said. The barge was on the cover. Moments later, a trim blonde woman appeared on the towpath walking her Bichon Frisé, a white puffball of a dog.

"Hello there. I'm your neighbor, Lisa. Welcome to port." I heard the lilt of a faint Dutch accent. She pointed to the *Lady A*. "Would you like to come aboard?" We accepted the invitation to her immaculate boat while she told us her story.

Like us, she and her husband had bought the barge to operate as a cruise boat but he'd caught a strong case of wanderlust and wanted to sail around the world. He was at sea and she ran the *Lady A* alone as a hotel, *chambre d'hôte*. For a reasonable price, she included breakfasts and dinners, along with accommodations for the evening.

She climbed aboard *Imagine* and paused in the pilothouse to sniff. "Ah, diesel," she said. "How I miss the smell of cruising." Spoken like a true Dutch person, I thought. We gave her the tour of our old boat.

"Your barge is charming, charming. And how long will you be here?" she asked.

"Only a couple of days till we pick up our next guests," Paul said.

"Oh that is good. I was afraid you might be opening a *chambre d'hôte* too."

I felt a rush of pleasure to think we might offer competition to cover girl *Lady A*. *Imagine* had come a long way from her Hippie days.

Tiny Vandenesse offered two restaurants and we set out to try the nearest café for lunch by the side of the canal in the autumn sun. We sampled the *coq au vin*. Only one other couple sat at another table. Their American accents drifted over. We introduced ourselves as barge owners.

"I'm Art and Mary here is an artist. We come to Europe every year to build up our inventory of stock photographs. We sell lots for web sites and we're big with the Silicon Valley crowd. Have you visited there yet?" He pointed to Chateauneuf up the long steep hill.

When we shook our heads no, they offered us a ride in their rental car. The engine strained as we made the almost vertical climb to the top. As we entered the town limits, a sign boasted an award: "*Un des Plus Beaux Villages de France*," one of the most beautiful villages in the country.

The four of us spent the afternoon ambling around the tiny medieval town surrounding an ancient château. I pictured peasants working in the fields below running for cover from invading barbarians in this steep hill fortress. We combed the cobblestone streets looking for photographic material. It wasn't difficult to find suitable subjects – bright daisies, old stone walls covered in ivy turning autumn red, and lace-curtained windows framed by trails of red-orange geraniums beside purple-blue lobelia. Paul and I posed in front of a spray of yellow asters framed against the gray stone wall of an ancient building while Art took our photograph.

"It's a town of cats," I said to Paul as one gray and white kitty sunned in a garden. There were felines scattered about the center of the town studiously ignoring pigeons only a few feet away. A sign on a store read *Le Chat Qui*

Dorm with a painting of a sleeping calico, while a black and white kitty strutted by us on the road.

"There's a cat house," Paul said pointing at a stone house with four cats lounging in the front yard. An iron wind vane shaped like a cat crowned the top gable.

We stood by the crumbling stone wall surrounding the town and stared at the expansive view. Directly below us sloping green fields of hay were sectioned off by hedges and dotted with grazing white Charolais cattle. In the distance, *Imagine* was moored in front of the *Lady A.* They both looked like toys. Tall sycamores bordered the other side of the canal and beyond them more patchwork fields covered the gentle hills.

"It wasn't always this peaceful and pastoral," Art said. "In the fifteenth century, Catherine de Chateauneuf poisoned her husband and the Duke of Burgundy, Philip the Good, took the château away from her as punishment."

"It could have been worse," I said.

"It was. Later he had her put to death."

16 - September Songs

After a final wrestle with the duvet covers, I finished making the guest beds. I took one more swipe at polishing the chrome bathroom fixtures. Then I spotted a smudge on the port bedroom mirror. Paul clomped on the top deck as he finished washing it down. The outside windows were next for me, first the eight side windows, then the two hatches, and finally the pilothouse. I tunelessly whistled while I rubbed on the glass. Paul walked by and said, "Nervous?"

"Yep." Our first guests to have found us via our website were due to arrive in minutes. They'd be with us for six nights and seven days. Up until now we'd had forgiving friends and family aboard. How would strangers react? "Aren't you?"

He smiled. "Excited but not worried. I figure if another impellor goes, I can change it out in less than fifteen minutes. I could enter an impellor-changing contest and win."

I took a deep breath and decided to get dressed for company, putting on my best boat attire – my LL Bean perfect fit pants and my striped red French sailor shirt. I studied myself in the cabin mirror. I was a far cry from the businesswoman of a few months ago. Gone were the suits and silk blouses, all donated to the battered women's shelter. I applied some more Dior lip-gloss and a spritz of *J'adore* perfume.

On deck Paul and I sipped Perrier and waited. We'd turned the boat around and pointed *Imagine* in the direction of Dijon. A taxi pulled up on the small gravel drive. "It's show time," Paul said as he hopped off the deck to help with the luggage.

"Welcome aboard," I said as I shook their hands. The retirees introduced themselves as Nicky and Dan, and Pat and Jerry, (she-Pat, he-Jerry). "Any problem finding us?"

"Not at all," said Nicky. She wore a hand painted jacket and arty hammered earrings. "Your email was perfect. My, this boat is big. Bigger than it looked on the website."

"Let me lead the way down," I said as I grabbed some of the carryon luggage. "You keep a free hand so you can hold on to the railing. The stairs are a bit steep."

"No problem for us," Dan said. "We're boaters." That's a good start, I thought. He clambered down the stairs ducking his head. He was long and lanky as a gray heron.

When we crawled down to the salon I waited for their reactions. They beamed. I tried to see the salon through their eyes – the antique pine floor gleamed, the throws covered the worst of our furniture, and a Provençal tablecloth draped the dining table surrounded by rattan chairs. Fresh mums sat in the middle of the table, giving off an undeniable autumn scent.

"Nice and homey," Nicky said. I caught a note of relief in her voice. It had been she who'd done the actual web search to find us. I'd thought of her and Dan as the "lead couple," the ones who'd made the original decision to find a barge trip. "This is beautiful," she said pointing to my framed seed packets displayed over the sink. Next to it hung two copper pots and a wreath of wheat.

"And the staterooms are huge," said Pat. "Plenty of room for our luggage." With her red pixie haircut and mischievous grin, she reminded me of an elf.

I stayed with Nicky and Dan to give them a tour of their bathroom. "Here's how the shower works. You turn this knob here to the desired temperature and it maintains it. No mixing on your own and risk scalding yourself. And the water pressure's great too. Three showers can run at once, no problem. And here's how the electric toilets works." I stepped on the pedal, listened to its whir. "You can even put toilet paper down it." I beamed, expecting them to be as excited as I was. Instead, I encountered polite but slightly puzzled looks.

"I'm sure this will be fine, dear," Nicky said patting my arm.

Paul poured the bubbly Champagne–like Crément into the glasses with a bit of crème de cassis as we sat at the table on deck. Chateauneuf dominated the horizon and a light breeze fluttered the poplars. A golden carpet of leaves covered the surface of the canal.

"Welcome aboard," we toasted as we clinked our glasses. We talked about our backgrounds and our geographic roots while we munched on our peanuts and Belin pizza-flavored crackers. We answered the difficult question of where we lived by explaining we toured the States in our motor home.

"Basically, we're homeless," Paul said with a grin.

"You're vagabonds, not homeless. How did you ever decide to do this?" Nicky asked as she sipped her *Kir Royale*. "This is such a fantastic life." She waved her hand at the scenery and canal.

Paul and I exchanged glances. I let him answer that one. "It goes all the way back to a program we saw on PBS, *Barging through France*," he began.

Below deck I put together the "welcome aboard dinner." I plunked the tiny new potatoes into my enamel pot labeled "*Soep van de dag*," a souvenir of our Dutch life. I took *jambon persillé* from the tiny fridge and sliced the jellied ham and parsley pâté into strips. The pungent aroma of garlic filled the air as I placed the meat on top of delicate mesclun salad. I drizzled Dijon vinaigrette over the salads and added some sliced *cornichons*, small French pickles, for garnish.

I poured the *coq au vin* into another pot to reheat it. Yesterday, I'd asked the woman at the café for take out. I tasted it – the smooth wine sauce was studded with pearl onions, mushrooms and tender chicken falling off the bones. But most importantly, I thought, would my guests like it?

I lit the candelabra, then the cellar rat candles, a gift from Jo Ann and Richard. I hollered through the hatch, "Dinner is served." Paul led our guests to the table and opened the red Nuits St. Georges and white Côte de Beaune wines we'd bought from our lockkeeper-driver.

"*Bon appétit*," we wished our guests as we dug into our entrée, the first course. I anxiously watched their appetites as the meal progressed. Everyone seemed to savor the Burgundian specialties. I'd entertained a lot in my life and loved to cook, but this was the first time in my life strangers had paid me to feed them.

I was so distracted watching my guests that a small chicken bone stuck in my throat. I coughed. Tears brimmed in my eyes. I coughed again. This is great, I thought, I'm going to choke to death at my first "welcome aboard dinner." Finally a piece of bread dislodged it. I could feel the sharp bone going all the way down my esophagus and briefly wondered if instead of choking, I would end up with a punctured stomach and bleed to death internally. Would it help that Dan was a retired surgeon? Probably not, I decided as I wiped a few tears from my eyes.

Following the cheese course, we devoured my purchased apple *tarte a la mode*. I noted who ate more cheese and who loved the sweets. After desert we had fresh French decaffeinated café. Pat and Nicky jumped up and helped me clear the table and do the dishes. The men were enlisted to dry them. I felt the knot in my neck and shoulders begin to loosen. This was going to be all right, I thought. "Come up top," I said. "You need to see something."

It was full night. A few streetlights couldn't dim the spectacle. Illuminated by spotlights, Chateauneuf glowed like a diamond tiara against the dark sky.

Nicky reached over and hugged me. "We are so lucky we found you."

Paul jumped up early and biked over to the local shop for fresh pastries and bread. I staggered out of bed, threw on my robe and went to galley where the aroma of fresh café welcomed me. Paul had already made the coffee, bless him. As I sipped at the warm brew I set out breakfast: *confiture* of strawberries, Muesli, pots of creamy yogurt, butter from Normandy, milk, orange juice, sugar, pastries and a *baguette.* A bowl held bananas, Pink Lady apples and Williams pears.

"Good morning," I said as our guests stumbled out of their rooms for their coffee. "I hope we didn't make too much noise and wake you."

"Nope. The smell of this coffee did though," Jerry said smiling. "Hmm. What's this?" He picked up a flakey *pain au chocolat* and took a bite. "Wow," he said shaking his head.

After breakfast Paul climbed down the stairs. "Can we all meet on deck in a few minutes?"

I took a quick shower and joined the group on deck where Paul earnestly lectured them on the hazards of barging. As I listened to him, I realized all of the stuff we'd had to think about: the deck could be slippery, especially in the morning dew, watch out for the lines coiled on the deck, they could be like marbles if you step on them, don't try to stop the boat with your hands, and never at any time put your hands between the barge and the lock wall.

I suppressed a yawn and took a swipe at a spider web glistening in the morning dew. The spiders seemed more industrious later in the season. Honeybees were autumn visitors when we picnicked. They particularly seemed to like the meat pâtés of all things. I tuned back in.

"Most importantly, I need to see when we're entering a lock so whatever you do, please don't block my view." He walked around demonstrating where it was okay to sit and where it wasn't.

They all nodded, grabbed their cameras from below and sat on deck. Paul squeezed our good-luck Buddha and with the help of his squeaky chant, we took off at our usual leisurely four miles an hour. We arrived at our first lock for Paul's date with the lockkeeper right on time at 9:00. I sat on the foredeck while Paul approached the lock. I knew he'd want to do it perfectly and impress our guests with his prowess.

About a hundred feet from the entry the engine slowed and I glanced back and shook my head. All four guests stood with their cameras raised and blocked his view like a stone wall. Paul banged on the pilothouse window and motioned them to sit down. They plunked down like a bunch of guilty schoolchildren until the barge stopped.

Imagine lowered down in the lock and more of the algae-covered stone wall came into view. Cameras flashed and clicked. I worked my line and saw Paul talking to the guests. I heard him explain how the locks operated. The manual locks were good teachers. The system worked on gravity and didn't need pumps. The downstream lock doors had sluice gates in the bottom and the lockkeepers cranked them open with handles. The water rushed out and went into the next downstream pond between the locks. Locks were filled when an upstream boat approached by cranking open the upstream sluice gates. The water's source was a reservoir at the top of the canal and it flowed all the way down to the Saône.

We stopped for lunch at a lock and I put together my usual picnic of various local cheeses, bread, salads, sliced ham and pâtés. I explained all of the items and watched the guests devour what I thought of as a "standard" lunch. I poured a carafe of water, took a Perrier for myself and offered wine to the others. Paul sipped his water.

"Aren't you having wine?" Jerry asked. We both shook our heads. We'd agreed not to drink alcohol while operating the boat. I'd tried a little wine at lunch once and figured I didn't feel different. Then I'd missed simple tosses. The gruesome stories of maimed women came to mind. It wasn't worth it.

"This is fabulous," Pat said with a grin on her face. "It's wonderful to sit outside and enjoy the view and fresh air while we eat." The others nodded, too busy chewing the crusty French bread to comment.

We cruised on. I watched our guests' heads turn first to the right then to the left as they took in the sights, pointing first at the heron standing on the shore, then at the perfectly matched pair of chestnut Comtoise draft horses who shook their flaxen manes at us. Pat and Nicky settled in on our chaise lounges in the sun and sipped glasses of *vin blanc*. Jerry and Dan came up and sat with me on the foredeck where I showed them how to work the lines. They were boaters and weren't intimidated. A good thing, I thought. Unfortunately

Dan wasn't intimidated enough. When I demonstrated how to wrap the lines around the bollard as I'd been taught, he insisted on doing it his way.

"Just don't get it jammed in something like that," I said pointing to a nasty crack in the top of the lock wall. "You might see Paul running out with our hatchet." He gave me a nonchalant shrug. I went back into the pilothouse and told Paul I was having trouble getting Dan to do as told.

He looked at me and said, "He's a retired surgeon and head of surgery to boot. He's used to giving orders, not taking them."

I kept a close eye on Dan as we neared our evening mooring at Bussiere-sur-Ouche. I gathered a line to toss over a bollard by the side of the canal when he leapt off the bow to the ground, six feet below. "I'll catch the line for you." That move was identical to the one where I'd ended up in a heap. Thirty-something Suzanne could do it, but could sixty-something Dan? I glanced back at Paul, who tossed his line to Dan on shore. "Hey, be careful jumping off, huh Dan?"

We sent our guests to explore the remains of an 11th century Cistercian abbey. They walked down the towpath past red-roofed cottages toward a cross on the hill.

"Why didn't you stop him?" Paul asked me. I felt the heat rise in my face.

"He was too fast. I wasn't expecting it."

He frowned. "It's a tricky situation. He's a paying customer but all I can see is the lawsuit if he hurts himself." We had boat insurance with a Dutch company. It included liability –but would it be enough?

The thought of dealing with an international legal situation sent a shudder through me. "Well, you try to talk to him. He won't listen me."

When our guests returned from their exploration, Paul concocted *aperitifs* - *kirs*. First he poured Aligoté white wine and then poured the cassis slowly down one side of the glass. The reddish liqueur stayed at the bottom, blended a bit in the middle, while the top of the drink remained pure white wine.

Pat said, "It reminds me of a sunset."

Nicky nodded and sipped. "Hmmm. It's pretty and delicious."

Paul and I cooked dinner in our galley, which starred *Magret de Canard du Cassis*, Breast of Duck with Cassis. The liqueur lent a subtle fruit flavor to the wine sauce. Paul crosscut the fat side of duck breast on the diagonal, just exposing the flesh below it. In a sauté pan over high heat, he cooked the duck four minutes on the fat side, drained the grease, then he cooked it for two minutes on the other side, poured off any fat and reduced the temperature.

He took the breasts out, and I tented them with aluminum foil. In a tablespoon of butter, he sautéed a shallot until tender. Then he added about ¼ cup of Burgundy Haute Côte du Beaune, and reduced it for 3 minutes. After it thickened, he poured in 2 Tablespoons of cassis, simmered the sauce until it reduced by a third. As a final touch, he whisked in two more tablespoons of butter.

He thinly sliced the breast on a bias, placed it on a platter surrounded by rosemary and thyme I'd picked from the herb pot on deck. I dished up fresh gnocchi and steamed artichokes.

"What a meal. This is the best duck I've ever had," Jerry said

Our guests nodded in assent and raised their glasses. "To our hosts."

The next day we continued down the Burgundy Canal. The locks were about a kilometer apart, an easy walk or bike ride on the towpath to rejoin us. Each guest had a turn at helping the lockkeepers. I got out and helped Nicky with a heavy handle. We grunted and pushed together at the large lever. "How do these slim little lockkeepers do it? She asked me, panting. "Or the old ones with cigarettes hanging out of their mouths?"

"They make it look easy, don't they?" I huffed as my feet slid on the gravel. "Hey, don't take a picture of my rear." Pat grinned and her camera clicked. With renewed appreciation for their efforts, I gave each lockkeeper icy cans of Coke and Perrier as tips.

On deck I hummed a song I'd learned in grade school about the Erie Canal. Even though I'm musically challenged Dan recognized the tune and we sang appropriate lyrics about locks and low bridges. I visualized straining mules on the towpath pulling barges like ours. Or a tiny *bargée* treading along wearing her custom-designed yoke.

At the lock where we'd commissioned our artwork, I stepped ashore and tried the studio door. Locked. I remembered Phillip had a second studio address in Paris. I frowned, sure we'd told him we'd be by today and stuck one of our business cards in his mailbox.

I used our cell phone to arrange a taxi for Wednesday, one of the market days in Beaune. Nicky and Pat were on deck and overhead me. "You really speak French well," Nicky said as Pat nodded.

"I try but it's still hard to use the phone." I carried my small French dictionary with me in my purse, picked up flyers from the supermarkets and practiced translating, listened to my French language CD. I made a point of speaking whenever I could to lockkeepers and store clerks, even simple pleasantries. "If I would've spent more time studying in language lab instead of staring at cute guys…" I sighed.

Beaune's Wednesday small market catered to tourists – Provençal fabrics, pottery, honey and handmade soaps. I stood admiring the Alsacien pottery hand painted with ducks and geese. A small, elderly lady sidled up next to me. "Do you like it?" she asked in a British accent.

I nodded. I half expected her to open her camelhair coat to display her own assortment on sale. She leaned up to me and said in a voice just above in whisper, "Don't buy it here," she said. "If you go up to the Alsace it's much cheaper there."

"We plan to cruise there next year. Thanks for the advice." We could continue up the Canal du Rhône au Rhine from homeport all the way to the Rhine River on the German border. I went in search of my guests and found them laden with souvenirs they'd have to lug around for the rest of the day.

At the Hotel Dieu, I passed Dan staring at nasty looking medieval surgical implements and joined the women in the kitchen. A sound and light show progressed as we sat on benches and listened to the recorded French voice explain the kitchen's features periodically highlighted by spotlights: immense copper pots and pans, an enormous stove and oven, a copper sink with gooseneck-shaped faucets, and a huge fireplace with a rotisserie tirelessly turned by a jester automaton. Two mannequins dressed in starched habits with Flying Nun *cornettes* posed as if at work on piles of plastic vegetables and skinned chickens.

"A beautiful kitchen," Nicky said as we trooped out. "But it goes to show you all the real work was done by women."

Pat and I exchanged surprised looks. All this week Nicky had been waiting on Dan hand-and-foot. We dropped back a few feet and Pat whispered, "She's dreading retirement with him."

"Just hope they don't try living together on a boat."

Fortified by a four course lunch at an outdoor café, our guests shopped for more souvenirs. At our appointed meeting time, we crammed everything into our taxi. Our driver drove north along the N74 wine route marked with historical interest signs "Route de Grand Cru." Vineyards rolled up hills crowned with limestone cliffs. Tiled-roofed churches and châteaux glittered above stone houses and wineries. Golden rows of grapevines trimmed low to the ground snaked by. Red rose bushes stood like sentinels at the end of each row. Clusters of people hunched over the vines, handpicking ruby and peridot grapes. The signs for the villages read like an expensive wine list: Aloxe-Corton, Savigny Les Beaune, and Nuits St. Georges.

Paul narrated the tour as our guests swung their heads from left to right. "The best wine comes from grapes grown on the slopes. You see the limestone cliffs up there? The soil is rocky with limestone, which is fantastic for drainage. The vintners only use two types of grapes, Pinot Noir for the red and Chardonnay for the white, and there's no blending. Not like in the States, or even other regions of France. Instead, they claim it's the combination of the soil and the microclimate that gives the wine its unique flavor. They call it '*terroir*'."

"The vines look much shorter here than in Napa," Jerry said.

Paul nodded. We studied the wide gnarled roots with almost stubby offshoots. "That's because they're pruned to concentrate the flavor in the grapes, not the leaves. There's even a green harvest where they'll cut grapes off the vines mid-season to control production. They're growing for quality not quantity. They don't need much rain either, as the roots in the older vines go down 15 meters or more to the water table."

"What are the roses for?" Nicky asked.

I knew the answer and said, "It's like the canary in the mine. If there's any fungus or mold around, the theory is the roses are more fragile and will catch the disease before the grapes. Then they get busy spraying the vines." We'd done enough presentations together in our software careers to know when and when not to step on each other. Okay, Paul, I thought, I'll be quiet.

Paul cleared his throat and continued. "Burgundy doesn't use château names on the label like in Bordeaux. And since the grape varietals don't vary, the type of wine usually isn't listed."

"That would be Pinot Noir and Chardonnay," I added ignoring Paul's side-glance.

"The wines are rated in order of the best to the most common: Grand Cru, Premier Cru, Village, or just Burgundy. Only two percent of all the wines in Burgundy get the Grand Cru appellation. The rating is based only on the location of the vineyard and its *terroir*. And one of the vineyards is right up there." He pointed at Aloxe-Corton with its cadmium yellow and black Burgundian tiled château glistening in the sun.

"But if it's based on location, not the actual wine itself, is that fair?" Nicky asked.

"A vintner could lose the designation if he consistently made some lower grade wine. But that's not likely with his reputation at stake on land worth a million dollars an acre – if you could buy it. Prestigious vineyards like these usually stay in the same family for generations.

"There's a joke about a prominent vintner who interviewed a potential suitor for his homely daughter. The suitor took a look at her picture, set it down and said, 'Now about the vineyard...'"

"You've learned a lot," Dan said.

"It's easy when it's a labor of love," Paul said with a wink.

The next day we continued our cruise past flocks of ducks and pastures of huge white Charolais cattle. I sat on deck with the women. At one point I felt *Imagine* snaking back and forth. Paul was giving Jerry and Dan each a turn at the helm. As we approached a lock, Paul took the wheel.

"What did you think of piloting?" I asked the men. I knew it was more difficult to steer *Imagine* on a canal than a river. Our propeller sucked the shallow water and continually drew the barge toward the bank. The wheel constantly had to be adjusted and the tendency was to overcorrect.

"She doesn't respond like a cruiser," Dan said. "Everything seems to happen in slow motion. And the flat bottom makes the sideslip extra tricky."

Paul aimed the barge at the lock and the boat nosed in perfectly. "I have a new appreciation for our captain's skill," Jerry said as he moved forward to work the bowline.

Paul walked up to us and said, "Did you notice someone coming at us?" I nodded. "I'm going to need you up front," he said to me. "A hotel boat is going to pass us going the other direction," he said to the others.

Nicky said, "I'd looked at those on the Internet. I didn't at all like the idea of their structured cruises compared to this. Besides, we have the barge to ourselves."

"Well you'll get to see one up close and personal," I said.

The lock gates swung open. Ahead loomed a one hundred and twenty-foot long hotel barge motoring toward us in the middle of the narrow canal where the water was deepest. Paul steered *Imagine* to the side; he knew the other barge drew the full six feet and was probably plowing the bottom. I stood at the bow with my fender in my hand ready to fend off the other boat. I glanced down – the water level seemed low. I winced as I heard our hull scrape on the rocks below.

The hotel boat chugged within a couple of yards. We had a good view of their foredeck and salon where several of their passengers waved at us and took our picture. I was too intense to wave back as their powerful engine pulled our bow toward them like we were magnetized. We were so close I could shake hands with their deckhand. The galley came by and I caught the aroma of roast chicken and then their huge aft engine rumbled past and shoved our stern against the bank. I let my breath out. I waited for forward motion. I read the now familiar signs of trouble – our prop threw up mud, blue engine smoke billowed, *Imagine* didn't budge. We'd run aground.

It had happened before but not with paying guests. What would they think? And we seemed to be more aground than usual. Was the water lower later in the season? Paul shoved the gearshift back and forward and gunned the engine. A cloud of diesel smoke engulfed us. He got out and grabbed a boathook and shoved at the bank. Nothing.

"I have a plan," Paul said to us. "It may help if you all go ashore and hold the bow in." Dan leapt ashore and snatched a line. Paul lifted the gangplank down for the rest of us. We lined up like a tug-of-war and pulled. Paul pushed on the bank with his bargepole.

As we tugged and strained Jerry remembered one of the phrases on our website: "You can do as much or as little as you like." We'd meant leisure activities, but now the slogan took on new meaning as we giggled with every yank on the rope until *Imagine* broke free.

Just as we are arrived in Dijon someone waved from the towpath. It was Phillip carrying our drawing. He'd probably asked the lockkeepers who knew exactly where we were. He scowled at me as I tried to explain we had come to pick up our artwork, hadn't he seen the business card? He took the francs I offered and walked off. I studied the pen and ink drawing depicting a sinister black *Imagine* plowing through churning ebony water. The first bright and cheerful watercolor of our barge contrasted with this moody, dark abstract expressionist drawing. I wasn't sure I liked Phillip's version until I studied it a while. Then it struck me: our paintings represented the two sides of barging, the yin-yang of life with its mix of good and bad. I would hang them directly across from each other in the main salon as a reminder.

We pulled into Dijon harbor and I breathed a sigh of relief. We'd done it, cruised for six days... and no one got hurt.

"Where's the main shopping?" Nicky asked. I pointed to the old town center on the Dijon city map. I shook my head. They would have a time of it carrying all of their stuff up and down the stairs of the train stations. "We'll be back in time for *aperitifs* and then we want to treat you to dinner," she said.

"Thanks. I'll phone for a reservation. I know just the place," I said as my mouth watered at the thought of the *dauphinois* potatoes at *Le Sauvage*.

I scrubbed the guest toilet and reflected on the past week. If I hadn't worked in a manufacturing company, if I hadn't learned computers, programmed in Fortran, taken one job or another, then I wouldn't have worked at a fast track company, had the promotion, won the awards. Now I knew I was finished with that career and that part of my life.

I thought of all the "what ifs"– if Paul and I hadn't met, if we hadn't come to France for our tenth anniversary, if we hadn't run our own businesses before, if we hadn't lived overseas in Asia all strung together like the pearls on my necklace each connected and leading to the other.

This week had been the real test of our Barge and Breakfast. I'd needed to answer my biggest concern –could I tolerate strangers living in our home? After all the kidding about the *QEII, Imagine*'s layout and size proved we'd picked the right barge for us and had planned the rebuild well. We couldn't hear a thing from the guests once we were cozily ensconced in our cabin.

I snapped off my yellow rubber gloves. My knees ached and my back hurt. I fondly remembered my cleaning help over the last twenty years. Then I snickered and wondered what my ex-managers, my past Fortune 500 customers, and my former employees would make of my glamorous new cleaning occupation. I smiled and thought, Vera, you were right. I'm not my job.

The upside to the week had been what we'd expected – we loved to share what we'd learned. It'd been a joy to give others a glimpse of our watery life in this gorgeous country. It was a good thing we enjoyed it – the stock market was plummeting, our savings were shrinking and retirement moved further away every day.

Barge and Breakfast had to provide us with a living.

17 - Full Circle

Success is not the key to happiness. Happiness is the key to success. If you love what you are doing, you will be successful.

-Albert Schweitzer

Svetlana and her daughter Masha gaped at *Imagine* in Dijon harbor. "It's so nice to meet you. I saw your pictures on the website but this is something else," said Svetlana. Her green eyes sparkled above high cheekbones. She sighed. "When your friend Irene told me about this I couldn't resist. My life's dream has always been barging through Europe. I had to find out more." Her voice still held the lilt of her heritage. She turned to her daughter and said something in Russian.

Masha was a hip twenty-something American girl with her baseball cap and trendy thick-soled sneakers I'd spotted on young *Mademoiselles.* "Oh yeah," she said. "This is way cool."

We crawled down to the salon and Svetlana clasped her hands to her bosom. "Oh my God, this is…your home. I don't know what I expected, more of a business I guess." Then she smiled and ranted in Russian for a while.

"Yeah Mom, this is beautiful." Masha cast me a wide smile. "We'll try to speak more English."

Over our *rôti* chicken that evening, I asked them more about their heritage.

"We emigrated to the United States from Moscow when Masha was a baby over twenty years ago," Svetlana said.

"She was a physician in Russia but can only be a nurse here," Masha said. Her mom cast her a warning look, but Masha ignored it. "They take advantage of immigrants in the States and it pisses me off."

I explained my grandfather emigrated from Russia when he was seventeen and met my grandmother on the sea voyage over. They were both from villages near Vilnius, which is now the capital of Lithuania. "My maiden name is Amelianovich."

"You know," Svetlana said, "you are a real Russian – a White Russian." I didn't know. My grandpa Joe didn't talk about the old country very often. He refused to speak Russian at home, saying to his family, "We are in American now. We only speak English."

Fluent in Russian, Polish, Lithuanian and English, Grandpa had been a handsome man who'd outlived two wives and continued to search for a third mate well into his eighties. He flirted with the Polish waitresses in restaurants in Berwyn and Cicero over our dinners of sauerkraut soup, roasted duck, cabbage, rye bread, and boiled potatoes. "What did you just say to her?" I'd ask, seeing the telltale red blush up the waitress's crepey, beefy neck. He'd only smiled at me and shrugged. No wonder he hadn't wanted me to learn the language.

"I wish I'd inherited his linguistic ability," I said with a sigh.

"It looks like you've inherited some of his wanderlust though," Svetlana said with a smile. "And your mother?"

"She was third-generation German."

"Quite a combination," Svetlana said. I nodded. My mom's stubbornness and my father's passionate Russian nature made for some interesting fights. My dad had an intellect and a sardonic wit, but my mother had the advantage of always being sober. Frustrated when he was losing a particular skirmish my dad would finally shout, "Who won World War II, huh? Who won the War?"

Svetlana was determined to use her new video camera to document the entire cruise. She filmed so often Masha nicknamed her mother "Spielberg" after the director. Svet shot a good close-up of *Imagine*, party pennants flying, framed by the wildlife refuge island in Dijon harbor. She narrated in a combination of Russian and English since the resulting tape was for her husband and other Russian relatives.

Against a backdrop of October cumulous clouds tinged autumn-gray, we wore long-sleeved shirts, baseball caps and jackets. We waved and smiled a little self-consciously at the camera. An unleashed spaniel pooped on the gravel path next to the boat, I cleaned out the cat box, Paul carried the garbage bag to the dumpster, and we cast off. *Imagine*'s engine throbbed in the background as Svet continued to film and narrate.

Masha joined me working the lines. She told me that she was a writing student, a veteran of the publishing industry, and an avid reader.

"I notice you're not reading that," I said pointing to *The Three Musketeers* unopened on deck.

"There's either work to do or scenery I can't miss," she said grinning.

"Don't feel bad. I can't read either when we're cruising. There's just too much to see if you look around – even that." I pointed to the petroleum storage tanks decorated in day glow orange, lime and black-sprayed graffiti.

"It's cool. I really like the stuff 'Enjoy' does."

We'd nicknamed the lockkeeper at the next lock "Sailor Hat" based on her attempt at nautical attire. Thirty-something and scrawny, she kept her Marlboro between her lips as she cranked the lock doors open for us, the clouds thickened, the rain poured. Sailor Hat looked miserable as the water streamed off her headgear and was probably contemplating another career as Masha and I hurried back to the warm and steamy pilothouse. Masha studied the labels on the dash. "Those are the 'whipers' I assume," she said as the windshield wipers clacked.

A few locks later a hotel barge ran us aground. Svetlana filmed while we tried a new method. I piloted while Paul shoved at the bank with a boat hook. Forward is back and back is forward, I chanted to myself as I shoved the long gear pipe with my hip and two hands. Paul strained against the bargepole and I thought, no wonder he'd lost weight. After a half an hour of work, *Imagine* broke loose. The rain stopped, the plane trees were a mottled green and gold, a few golden leaves floated down to the canal. One of us sneezed in the background – both Paul and I had colds.

The next morning Masha videotaped an interview with her mother. "What do you plan to film today?" Masha asked Svetlana.

Svetlana remained silent. Masha said, "Like all great directors Spielberg is shy in front of the camera."

As we continued down the Burgundy Canal, Masha worked the front lines. "You don't sound good," she said after I coughed and hacked through a few locks.

"I'm losing my voice. I'm not feeling very well at all." That was an understatement. My head hurt, the chill of the cold wet lines went right through my work gloves.

"Why don't you go inside and stay warm? I can do this."

I wanted to kiss her but I didn't want to give her my cold.

At night, we talked about books and writing. I'd been sending out stories for the last two years and had several in print. I brought out my story "How Cliché" published in the literary magazine "Happy." I held my breath while Masha read it. Fortunately it was a very short story.

Masha nodded. "Good, clever, and funny. Have anything else?"

I handed her my second accepted story, "North Star" and finally the latest one I'd written this summer, "Here's What's Happening in Your Neck of the Woods."

I've had critiques before in my artwork and in writing workshops. Waiting drove me crazy. I liked to watch for the tiniest facial expressions. I wanted to stand behind her, reading with her. She was a writer too. "I'll read these later."

Her critiques were favorable. "I think you might have the beginning of a novel in this one." She pointed at "North Star."

"I have this idea for a book about this first year. I'm thinking of calling it *Just Imagine: A New Life on an Old Boat.*"

"Write it," she said. "You have a great plot already. Just do some kick-ass story telling." She grinned down at Bear who scooted by. "Speaking of asses, get your cute little black ass over here," she said reaching for him.

The next day we cruised past an eclectic collection of boats moored along the bank: tired-looking cruisers in need of some varnish, a workboat, another cruiser painted in paisley. Past the mistletoe-wreathed poplars lining the banks, the recently plowed fields sprouted a cover crop of winter wheat. We'd soon be in St. Jean and then homeport.

I looked ahead to the harbor of St. Usage. *Péniches* in various stages of transformation lined the banks. A group of live-aboard 1920 Luxemotor barges clustered together in another spot. Homemade-looking craft moored alongside sleek cruisers. Through our field glasses, I spotted a New Zealand flag on a familiar boat.

"Hey there's *Déesse* anchored in the harbor." I ran out on deck shouting and waving at Val and Rolly. Val waved and pointed to her hand – she still had all of her digits. I wiggled my fingers in return. Rolly ran below and came back holding something large in his arms – bagpipes. The bittersweet music reverberated around the harbor. Dockworkers paused from their painting and welding and listened. When the song ended Paul answered with a blast of our air horn that echoed off the other steel boats. I knew we were making a scene, but I didn't care. We had reason to celebrate.

We were almost home.

I stepped off the boat at the lock and hiked toward to the St. Jean de Losne quay, past the war memorial decorated as always with red, white and blue flowers. I passed the fuel barge where we loaded up with diesel.

"Walkie-talkie *noir*, this is walkie-talkie *bleu*, come in." I'd always wanted one of these things ever since I read Dick Tracey.

"I hear you loud and clear," Paul said. "Remember to press the button before you start talking."

"I'm crossing the bridge right now. Looks like we have space on the quay, I'll go pace it. Over and out." I stood on the geranium-bedecked bridge over the Saône and watched for *Imagine*'s bow coming out of the last lock of the Burgundy. The flags on the bridge welcoming international boaters fluttered beside me: French, Dutch, the Union Jack, the Stars and Stripes, Italian, German, and Norwegian.

Imagine steamed toward the quay. I cast a glance at the boat. I always loved looking at her from a different perspective. I hurried over to the graduated stairway and paced out the space I'd learned we needed. Twenty-five good-sized steps were enough.

"We have plenty of space, walkie-talkie *noir*. Come to Mama."

Paul didn't bother to answer and just pointed *Imagine*'s Reubenesque black bow at me. Masha lobbed the bowline to me. I grabbed it and walked it to an eight-inch iron ring on the steps. I pulled a clevis from my pocket and secured the eye of the line to the heavy clip, then to the ring. Paul pulled the stern in and I caught his line. Voilà, we were moored.

"That was good work crew," Paul said high-fiving Masha, then me.

"My God... we're looking...competent," I said.

The four of us walked up the quay stairs to tour St. Jean de Losne. We passed the cafés with their view of the Saône, turned right at the only stoplight in town on the main street, the *Rue de la Liberté*. St. Jean the Baptiste church, with its chocolate brick façade and gold and green Burgundian tiled roof, hugged the road. I caught the scent of the artisan *boulangerie* across the street. Their bread was so good that Paul and I always had to bite the ends off as soon as we walked out of the store. We stopped in the *Tabac* and picked out a few postcards, then walked the cobblestone streets to the modern post office, *La Poste*, to mail them. A stained-glass window adorned the exterior depicting St. Jean's church and a *péniche*.

"Want to come to the Casino with me?" I asked Masha and Svet. They frowned. "Don't worry; it's a grocery chain, not a gambling enterprise." The small store had the seasonal items up front: schools supplies, fall clothes and

Halloween candy. The produce display featured autumn's bounty of acorn squash, pumpkins and fresh fennel. I picked up some pre-made quiches and salads from the deli and replenished our cheese supply with some Regal de Bourgogne, cheese flavored with raisins soaked in Marc de Bourgogne. We ambled along the river back to the boat along the *quai Lafayette*.

"There's a nice place you can go to eat tonight," I said pointing at the *Auberge de la Marine* just across the bridge.

"Aren't you coming with us?" Svet asked. I shook my head. It hurt to talk.

"Not going out to a restaurant?" Paul frowned and put his hand on my forehead. "You must really be sick."

The next day our St. Jean taxi took us to Beaune. At the Hotel Dieu, I stood in front of the intricate tapestries lining the walls. I thought of all the work involved in something so complex, some tiny nuns sitting for hours weaving. Any textile surviving hundreds of years was a miracle. I thought of my small needlepoint sunflower I'd just managed to complete. Someone told me once 'Amelianovich' meant 'weaver of great tapestries.' If it did, I certainly hadn't inherited the talent. Or the patience.

We all paused in the apothecary. The earthenware containers bore labels of the latest in medieval medicines: woodlouse powder, fish glue, burnt sponge, chamomile, and ether. "How about these?" Masha said. We laughed as she pointed to jars marked "opium" and "cocaine."

We sat at the outdoor café in Beaune, sipping our coffees. Spielberg continued filming. Masha said to the camera, "I like this town – it reminds me of Spain."

"As usual," Svetlana teased. "Everyplace reminds you of Spain."

Masha gave her mom a look. "What I mean is, I've traveled to most of Europe's major cities, but the only time I spent in smaller towns was in Spain. I loved the glimpse into the small village life. You know, people shopping together, walking their children to school, couples socializing in the restaurants. Like this." She pointed around at the people ambling by.

"Yes, I do know," I said.

The next day we planned to make a final cruise up the Saône to Auxonne and then to homeport. I tossed some day-old *baguette* to the swans. The dark low-level clouds threatened rain. Masha's breath steamed as she cast off the bowline. I stood at the helm and piloted us out. I drove up the river a while.

"Care to pilot?" I said to Svetlana.

"Are you kidding?" She grabbed the wheel. Paul had been giving her driving lessons all week.

"Spielberg's driving the boat," Masha said into the microphone, "and Michelle is copiloting. Look at her new barge shoes that don't slip on deck." I displayed my brown rubber clogs to the camera. My foul weather gear finally complete, I wore my full outfit today: yellow slicker with hood, matching pants, and my barge clogs. Sweet.

Paul climbed up from our cabin and stood next to Svet. A tight bridge loomed ahead. "Here Paul, you take the wheel," Svet said.

He shook his head. "You can do it. Now look at the chart and look at the signs on the bridge." The chart showed one thing but the bridge signs clearly indicated we must choose either the far left span or the far right. The middle was reserved for the traffic coming the opposite way. "Always believe the actual signs over the charts," Paul said stating just one of the invaluable lessons we'd learned in a few months.

I sat on the bench behind them while Paul assumed the position Roger Van Dyken had taken with me only a year before. Masha stood in the pilothouse doorway filming.

"Take the right span," Paul said.

"The boat won't fit," Svet said. "You take the wheel back."

"Don't worry. I know we have plenty of room. I'll be here for you." He patted her shoulder.

Svet took a deep breath and wiped her palms on her jeans. I listened to Paul and thought how much he mimicked our teacher's calm attitude.

"To the left, to the left. Keep the flags on the front of the boat in line with the two yellow markers on the bridge. Now to the right, to the right. Faster, faster. Now, a little bit left, back to the right, to the right. More, more more. Hold it there. Now, to the left, to the left. Very good."

Imagine glided through the bridge span and Svet let out her breath. "You make what's hard look easy Paul," she said.

"We only have three locks to go through today. But we have three dicey maneuvers for our 'final exam,'" I said to Masha. "We're going to pull alongside the fuel barge and fill up with diesel, go through the most difficult lock we've been through together, and finally parallel park alongside another barge in our homeport." She nodded. She was as much into doing deck work as her mom was piloting. "I'll be up front with you." I glanced out at the foredeck. Fat raindrops bounced off the steel. My sore throat tightened at the thought of handling wet lines in the cold rain, even in my foul weather gear.

After the short cruise to Auxonne, we turned around and steamed back toward St. Jean de Losne for our third tank of fuel for the year. Just below the bridge, I spotted the permanently moored *péniche*. Paul swung *Imagine* in a wide turn as graceful as a swan. "We always moor upstream so the current helps us stop," Paul said to Svetlana.

Masha and I cushioned the two hulls with bumpers as Paul slowly pulled *Imagine* alongside the fuel barge, reminding me of airplanes refueling in mid-flight. We wrapped our soggy lines around the other barge's bollards. The attendant came out carrying a hose, Paul opened the fuel cap by the engine room window, and the pungent smell of diesel filled the pilothouse for a half an hour.

"How much did that cost?" I asked Paul when he climbed back on board from the fuel barge "office" – their pilothouse.

"3,315 francs about $ 470 US," he said, doing the math for me. "That makes our season's fuel bill around $1200."

"Not bad. And I think I'll give us an 'A minus' for this maneuver, since we had one small bump." Masha and I went back to our post on the foredeck and cast off.

We huddled in the pilothouse as we headed upstream toward our homeport in St. Symphorien, about five miles away. Paul said, "It's nice to get away from the hustle and bustle of St. Jean de Losne."

Masha and I gaped at each other – he was serious. This was a man who grew up with a view of Manhattan and regularly visited New York City. St. Jean had a population of about two thousand souls, one traffic light, and a handful of shops. "Oh yeah," I said, "That's some hustle and bustle all right."

"Sheer craziness," Masha agreed, who lived in downtown Chicago. "I could hardly stand all that activity."

Paul shook his head. He knew when he'd said something he'll never live down. Besides, we had it on tape.

"Ready for part two of the final exam?" I asked Masha. She nodded. The entrance lock to the Canal de Rhône au Rhin loomed ahead. Despite my foul weather gear, rivulets of rain found their way down my neck. Waiting for *Beatrice's* "lock experience" our first day in homeport seemed a long time ago. Waves lapped at the hull and the ochre Saône sported whitecaps. "La Saône" was a feminine noun, and the recent rain had her riled up, just short of flooding – "in spate" our charts described it.

I felt Paul use more speed than usual and glanced back. The current shoved *Imagine* over the side. The boat looked catiwhompus to me. I gulped. Paul spun the wheel so hard it blurred. Then back again. We're doing fine, I thought. The approach was perfect. *Imagine* slid into the lock without a bump.

I put my line on my boathook and waited for the lockkeeper to come and take it. Masha and I stared at the bollard ten feet above. Cold rain stung my face and I wondered if it was turning to sleet. After a few minutes, the door clanged shut and I realized the lockkeeper wasn't going to help. With a curse, I gave the line on my boathook as much slack as possible, stood on the highest part of the foredeck and stretched, stretched, stretched and reached the line around the bollard. Masha cheered as we tied off.

The water cascaded in spraying us like a waterfall and the boat rose in the lock a few inches at a time. Finally, I could see who was operating the lock from inside the dry lock station. It was the bodice-ripper fan who'd operated the lock on our eventful first entry. "I give both the pilot and crew an 'A,'" I said to Masha. "But our lockkeeper over there gets a 'D.'" The blonde looked away, staring at the Saône.

"I think you're being generous to her," she said.

There wasn't time to brood. The doors banged open and I stared at homeport. We were cruising late. Most of the forty or so barges were moored for the winter and tied several deep along the shore. Paul walked forward and he counted the rows to where Roger had told us to moor. "There's the spot. Fifth row ahead. See where we're going?" he asked me.

I nodded and studied the location. "Oh boy. There're barges in front and behind our space." We'd be surrounded on three sides, no room for error, our closest mooring yet.

Paul inched our barge forward. I held up my fingers to give him the distance between *Imagine*'s bow and the boat we'd tie to. It could be catastrophic if I made an error judging this distance. Five... four.... three... two... one. I made a fist to signal him to stop. He shoved the boat into neutral, then reverse.

I nodded and Masha threw the line to catch the bollard on the other barge...and missed. She tossed again. The line hung on the bollard's ear.... then fell off. We were already starting to float backwards from our reversing stop, getting further away from our target and uncomfortably close to the barge behind us. We have to do it now, I thought.

I snatched the line, knew this was my only chance, reached out, reached out, flipped the rope.... "Got it!" Masha applauded. I tied off just as Paul walked forward. "Any problems?" he asked.

"Nope." We'd aced our final exam.

I let out my breath and looked around. Moored directly in front was *Sea Lion*, our first barge lock mate. Behind us was *Vertrouwen,* on which we'd trained so many months ago. We'd come full circle.

That night we watched the video of the cruise. We'd taken turns interviewing each other after we'd arrived in homeport. "What was your favorite food on the trip?" I'd asked.

Svet had thought for a few seconds and said, "There were lots of good things, but I loved the quiche." I'd raised my eyebrows. She'd loved an easy meal, pre-made cheese tarts from the Casino.

"What was your favorite story about our adventure?" I'd asked her.

"Barry not being able to relax was a good one. But my favorite was the crazy commercial boat, *Cutie Pie*."

"What was your biggest surprise Spielberg?" Masha asked her.

Svetlana grinned. "That's easy. I expected to be living in a hotel, not someone's house. I'm sure those hotel barges would never let me drive." She'd looked long and hard into the camera. "My real life-long dream was not just to be on a barge but to *drive* one."

Now it was Spielberg's turn to ask the questions. "Tell me captain, what was this first year like for you?"

"The learning curve was second only to when I was five years old," Paul had said. "I'm still finding new things every day."

She'd asked Paul if he minded all the responsibility of piloting and handling the mechanical aspects. "No...just the opposite. I love France, the waterways and the people. And I enjoy sharing the experience with others."

She'd asked me if this summer was what I'd expected. I'd thought about it for a few seconds, adjusted my French glasses. "I had so much to learn about this barge. I had no idea how much, even with our training course." I rolled my eyes. "And never underestimate the value of foul weather gear."

"Would you do it again?"

"Oh yes," I'd said while a grin spread across my face. "Oh yes. I really wouldn't trade this past year for anything."

"Do you have any regrets?" she'd asked.

Paul had answered for both of us. "Only that we didn't do this years ago."

18 - *Dulce et Decorum Est*

Peace is more than the absence of war.
-Rick Steves

I sat cross-legged on the galley floor, surrounded by plastic bags and piles of food boxes. I picked up an open box of rotini pasta and threw it in the garbage bag. We didn't need mice or worse – rats – on board looking for tidbits over the next six months. The washer and dryer chugged and hummed as more loads of bed linens washed and dried. I moved Evian water bottles to a staging area. If we didn't finish them before we left, they'd go to Roger. The refrigerator dripped next to me as it defrosted. Tonight's dinner and tomorrow's breakfast were in my cooler bag. I stacked the canned tuna, the unopened jars of olives and canned lentils in the cupboard I'd just scoured.

I looked around and shivered at how lifeless *Imagine* already looked. We'd covered the furniture with drape cloths, including the chairs and couch from Desirée. Paul was busy outside taking everything off the deck and stowing it away. Most of it went in the forepeak – the bicycles, the table and chairs. Some things we'd lower down the hatch and store in the salon, like chair cushions and pads. Other outdoor work had been minimal. We'd touched up as many scrapes as possible with Owatrol, the rust stopping paint, but the weather hadn't cooperated for us to do much other painting.

I crawled to the deck, grabbed my flowerpots and lugged them across five other slippery and unevenly matched barges. I held on to a rail and hauled myself up then stepped down a foot or two, picking my way over coiled lines. A few months ago I would have shuddered at the thought of this feat of balance. Now I hardly gave it a thought. On shore I dumped the last remaining petunias and geraniums from Holland in the ravine to compost. The lobelia had fried long ago in the warm French weather.

To take a break from work, I walked toward tiny St. Symphorien, past the mill and made a right at the farm closest to port. The drizzle had stopped although the sky was charcoal gray. Golden poplar leaves floated down around me. I passed huge Charolais, ghostlike hulks of cattle breathing out white steam clouds, observing me with pink-rimmed eyes. I smiled at our Dutch waitress's prophetic words – we had indeed seen many cows over the last months.

A few blackberries remained by the side of the road. I plucked a couple and bit into the bittersweet essence of late summer turned autumn. The tang of wood smoke hung in the air, replacing the odor of mown hay that had permeated this farm only a few short weeks ago. The fields lay fallow ready for spring planting. Hardy Queen Anne's Lace still bloomed by the side of the road, untouched as yet by the frost, as did the yarrow and cow's parsley, three flowers all variations on the same filigreed theme.

I made my way to the *Mairie*, the tiny town hall where a French tricolor flag hung above the door. The window contained a list of every family in St. Symphorien. I counted the surnames and calculated about 180 souls in the village. Our harbormaster, Roger, was listed separately as a renter of property at the bottom of the list, an outsider after twenty years.

The war memorial across the street was inscribed "A NOS ENFANTS MORTS POUR LA PATRIE 1914-1919" and listed fourteen men who gave their lives for their country. For World War II, 1939-1945, only one name was engraved. The Algerian conflict of 1957 had claimed one casualty. On the other side of the monument, "DULCE ET DECORUM EST PRO PATRIA MORI"– It is sweet and fitting to die for your country. All of these men dead in such a little town, I thought.

Across the street in the cemetery next to the church, I matched names on the monument to names on the graves. I located the second name listed on the monument also engraved on a large tomb, "Familles Mitaine – Vachet" and below carved "Lucien Mitaine" who died in 1916 at 20 years of age. Affixed to the tombstone under a glass plate was a faded black-and-white photograph of a young man in uniform. Blossoms blanketed the grave: living trumpet flowers, plastic roses, and silk lilies. I watched a bee climb into one of the roses to get some pollen, fooled by the fake flowers. He shouldn't be wasting his time with winter so close, I thought.

The rest of the graves were in varying stages of maintenance. Well-tended mini-gardens decorated the gravesites of those whose ancestors were nearby. I noticed a convenient water spigot in the cemetery for tending plants. Ceramic bunnies and seashells decorated children's headstones. Others had plaques displaying the deceased's interests and occupations: farmers, hunters, *boules* players, fishermen, and *bargées*. A few abandoned gravesites had no legible inscription.

My life this past year would've measured an astronomical number on a "Stress Scale": a move to a foreign country, a career change, my house sold along with most of my things, a fiftieth birthday, and the loss of daily contact with friends. The only things missing were a divorce and the death of a child. I studied a caved-in grave covered with moss and realized my former life was dead. Most of this year had been overlaid with grief: denial then anger at the shipyard, sadness and homesickness in Fumay, and finally a growing acceptance. Like climbing monkey bars, I'd had to let go to move forward.

I wandered into the unlocked church, a mute statement to the French way of life. In Chicago, Paul's daughter's purse had been stolen from a pew the night of her wedding rehearsal. The church of St. Symphorien was made of unadorned stone. The sturdy clock tower chimed out the hour as many French churches do – twice in case you missed it the first time. Twenty pews lined the interior, with a gap around the coal stove that warmed parishioners in colder weather. The floor was ocher flagstone, the cream-colored walls were trimmed a soft spring green.

Six statues of saints stood sentinel in front of stained glass windows, which depicted more saints against a lace-curtain-design of grape vines. I recognized some of them: Mary, of course, Joseph, Jesus with his sacred heart and St. Joan of Arc, the patron saint of France. The tiny stained glass windows let in a green and gold-tinged light, illuminating St. Symphorien's only altar adornments: asters, hedge clippings, and a few African violets.

Seated in a pew, I closed my eyes and felt an overwhelming peace. The lingering smell of incense reminded me of my first communion, my confirmation, and my first marriage in St. Gertrude's church, a huge cold 1950's modern monstrosity, built to accommodate the Baby Boom. Its main crucifix loomed thirty feet into the air, blood poured down Christ's body against a backdrop of gold leaf curled out from the wall like the head of a cobra. I'd long ago lost my faith in the dogmatic religion it represented.

I recalled the lyrics of John Lennon's song for which we'd named our barge. Could we imagine a world without war, without countries or religion to die for? Penang had been a perfect microcosm of three different nationalities with three major religions – Buddhist Chinese, Hindu Indians and Islamic Malays. They'd managed to live in peace and tolerance of each other. Could there ever be a world where we learned to allow people their own beliefs and not try to impose our own?

I pondered the conviction of the men listed on the memorial, the belief of their families who worshipped in this small church while their sons, brothers, uncles and fathers were fighting somewhere. I wondered if the person who chose the quote for the war memorial had read the poem "Dulce et decorum est" written by Wilfred Owen, the soldier. He'd been killed at age twenty-five just five days before the armistice. After watching a comrade die hideously of gas he'd written these last four lines:

My friend, you would not tell with such high zest
To children ardent for some desperate glory,
The old Lie: Dulce et decorum est
Pro patria mori.

The last morning on board I took a final look at *Imagine's* empty deck and closed curtains. With a throat tight with tears I said goodbye. We climbed into our taxi from St. Symphorien for one last racecar-speed drive to Dijon, took the TGV fast train to Paris, stayed overnight at the airport Hotel Ibis, had a *kir* at the Novotel bar, and dinner in the Ibis dining room. I had a final taste of potatoes d*dauphinois* and *crème brûlée* for desert. The waiters and waitresses all spoke good English, but I tried to speak French as long as I could. I heard American accents around me as people asked for Diet Coke and ice in their drinks.

At De Gaulle airport, we waited in our long line for check in. A redheaded middle-aged man stood behind us. "Hey," he said in a loud voice to the security person pointing at us, "What about them? What about those bags or animals or whatever they are? How come you didn't open them, huh? I want more security here."

As if I wasn't there right next to him, I thought. At another security stop, we'd take our cats out of their carriers and hold our pets in our arms through metal detection, while the bags were x-rayed. I knew this and could explain it to him, but he wouldn't look at me. I felt like an invisible middle-aged woman – too old to be a sex object, too young for respect for the elderly.

He cut in front of us at baggage check in, bumped into me without so much as a *"Pardon, Madame."* He talked loudly and brashly to the young woman behind the counter demanding a better seat than he'd been assigned. I cringed at the volume and the arrogant tone. "I love it when Americans tell me the French are rude," I whispered to Paul. "This is the rudest guy we've seen in six months."

Shortly after takeoff, we lost sight of Paris and climbed up over the French countryside. Somewhere to the south, *Imagine* sat in the harbor, while the canal was closed for the *chômage* and much needed maintenance on the locks.

I had nine hours to think about this season and how it had changed us. I studied the cumulous cloud tops below us, and remembered a time when I was six years old. I'd been perched on the back stoop of our white ranch house with my dad. Our diminutive yard bordered a dusty alley alongside five pairs of railroad tracks. Across them were the backsides of ragged shops lining "uptown" Franklin Park, Illinois. Cicadas chanted in the stifling heat and a cumulonimbus bloomed over the cottonwood in the corner of our yard.

I'd sported a red bandana tied roguishly to my head, a leftover from a game of pirates. "Look, Daddy," I'd said pointing to the south. "That cloud looks like a ship. I want to fly there and sail away in it like a pirate."

He'd dragged on his unfiltered Camel, looked up and shook his head. A puff of acrid smoke hung over us. "No, Pookie, you wouldn't. Even a twin engine prop would have its wings torn off if it got anywhere near that thunderhead."

I'd flinched with this new knowledge. There was danger in something so beautiful. Danger when storms blew through and bent our Lombardy poplars to the ground like a row of peasants bowing before royalty. I became deathly afraid of storms, especially tornadoes. "A Wizard of Oz" complex, one of my friends called it.

Later, I'd better understand my dad. An amateur radio operator, he'd yearned to sail the seas on a merchant vessel as a ship's radio operator. Instead, saddled with a mundane factory job, he'd never traveled further than New York. He deadened his feelings of failure with shots of Jim Beam followed by Hamm's beer chasers and was fond of saying, "Others look at the world through rose-colored glasses. Mine are tinted brown."

I'd vowed I'd tour the globe, especially Europe, and planned to become a flight attendant after college. Instead, I married my high school sweetheart, then fell out of love and divorced. My fantasies of traveling the world were for vacations. The rest was reality, what I expected from life and what society expected from me.

Then I'd met Paul at a computer software company where we both worked. His conservative preppy exterior belied the adventure-seeker inside. In one of our first conversations, Paul told me his hero was Charles Kuralt.

"Wouldn't you like to travel all the time and just see what's around the bend in the road?" I'd agreed, but thought Paul was thinking about retirement, years away.

I looked over at my co-conspirator who metamorphosized in my eyes from a middle-aged man into a trim swashbuckler, determined to rescue us from convention and boredom. I reached over and grabbed his hand. He lifted his headset from his ears with raised brows.

"Nothing," I said. "Just… I love you."

He flashed me a roughish grin, squeezed my hand and went back to his movie.

An anvil-shaped cloud spread over the distant horizon. I'd seen firsthand the worst storms could bring when a tornado once snaked out of the southwest and leveled the building behind me. I'd survived my worst fear come to life. I thought of my dad, who'd died an early death from his addictions, and felt he would've been proud of my vagabond plan. I considered the thunderhead an omen and dreamed of tomorrow, what might be, the endless possibilities derived from hope.

We flew up over the Atlantic following the sun. With the time difference of seven hours, we would arrive mid afternoon, gaining back the hours we'd lost six months ago. The weather was clear, the air October-calm, as we circled out over Lake Michigan, looked down at the Chicago skyline dominated by the Sears Tower and John Hancock Center. Our approach followed the Kennedy expressway to Cumberland Avenue and descended over Franklin Park, where I knew the little white ranch house still stood. I picked out the Tri-State Tollway as the 777 floated down over Mannheim Road. After the wheels touched and the plane shuddered to taxiing speed, the voice on the P.A. welcomed us to Chicago's O'Hare International Airport, announced the local time, first in English and then repeated the message in the last fluent French I'd hear for months.

I was home – or was I?

19 - Tripping over Angels

The world is a book, and those who do not travel read only a page.
-- St. Augustine (354-430)

Paul pulled our VW Bug in front of Smith's grocery store in Taos, New Mexico. A man walked by us, smiled, pointed at our old heap and said, 'Hey, I had one of those once."

I crawled out of the miniscule car, grabbed a shopping cart, reached into my pocket for a coin to release it – and then realized I didn't need one. I shook my head. I steered into the noisy crowd and perused a flyer of Thanksgiving specials. At least I could read it and know how much things cost, I thought. The pasteurized cheese collection was no *fromagerie*. I picked a fresh turkey shrink-wrapped in white plastic, its innards discretely hidden inside. I stopped at the bakery, selected a cellophane-encased loaf of bread and asked the woman behind the counter to slice it for me. I bit back the impulse to say *"Merci bien, Madame."* I glanced at my wristwatch. It felt odd to shop during the lunch hour, let alone on Sunday.

We'd stopped in Golden, Colorado on our tour of the Southwest in our Winnebago Adventurer. When we'd walked into our old office, the new receptionist didn't know us, so we'd waited in the lobby like any other visitors. Former colleagues greeted us with hugs and handshakes, but already I felt our common ground ebbing.

At our motor home dinette, I looked out over the campground sagebrush at the Sangre de Cristo Mountains and caught the smell of piñon pine in the air. Our good luck Buddha perched on the dashboard. Paul sat at his computer, working on the website, while Sundae and Bear slept at my feet. I picked up our emails on my VAIO.

One from Pat, our September cruiser said, "Thanks much for our trip–we have raved and repeated everything so much, people are tired of us! Now that you're back in the U.S, we can send you some pictures."

I made a note to buy a guestbook in my excel spreadsheet that listed all the things we needed next season. At the top of the sheet was a car. Then I opened the next email from Eammon congratulating us on our decision to go back to the States and the warm sun.

"France is rigid with cold. There's a savage sirocco blowing up from the Sahara: the Pope has not had a cup of tea without sand for the last four days," he wrote. "Throughout October, we did our walk in glorious sunshine, but after All Souls, the cloud base dropped and we are in danger of tripping over angels."

If the clouds lowered we too could trip over angels who hovered 7000 feet above the plains. I missed my fellow boaters, and thought about my two different barge depictions, the yin and yang of traveling around the country or the world, always something to miss and something to look forward to. Jo Ann and I'd noticed when people were about to move from Boulder they picked the city apart: too Yuppie, too insulated, the restaurants were expensive, even the windy weather. We'd called it "Boulder Bashing" and decided it was meant to soften the pain of leaving. It never worked. There was always the sadness of parting, a small death of a piece of me with each goodbye. But if part of me had to die so a new part could be reborn in its place, I'd live with the grief if that were the price I paid for joy.

I'd had more money, but I'd never been richer.

In April we'd return to France and *Imagine.* The canals would thaw and the *chômage* would end. Spring would be glorious; the rapeseed fields near St. Symphorien in golden bloom, the wisteria flowering in phosphorescent purple, and lilacs perfuming the air. We'd be back to the now familiar canals and the beautiful but moody Saône. The day we arrived in port, a double rainbow would appear after the rains, a sign of the future beyond the past storms.

But there were different kinds of storm clouds on the horizon, ones that would have the force of a tornado and threaten to destroy our life and livelihood.

The following year was 2001.

Appendix - Boat layout

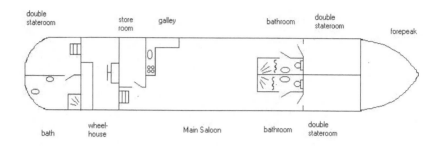

double
stateroom   store   galley   bathroom   double
            room   stateroom
                                                              forepeak

bath   wheel-   Main Saloon   bathroom   double
       house   stateroom

Overview of the boat

Imagine is a Dutch *Klipper* built in 1906 in Zwartsluis, Nederland. Originally equipped for sailing, she was used to haul cargo in Holland such as potatoes and grains. The superstructure, the part over the original hold, was added during the 1950's.

Imagine is:
24.85 meters long, or about 80 feet
4.60 meters wide, or about 15 feet
and weighs 70 tons. Some of this weight is her steel hull; the rest is in the concrete ballast that lies below the flooring so that she rides properly in the water as if she were carrying cargo.

Now a 6-cylinder Volvo Penta diesel engine with 112 horsepower and a 30-inch in diameter propeller move her through the inland waterways of Europe.

The floor in the salon and galley is of antique pine recycled from an old hospital in Holland when *Imagine* was converted to a houseboat.

Imagine carries 3,000 liters of drinkable city water, or approximately 800 gallons. Our electricity is a combination of batteries and inverter, a generator and shore power.

Glossary of Terms

Anchoring – *Imagine* has a large anchor on the front, but we've only used it a couple of times. It's heavy and hard to use. Instead, we moor at quays or by the side of canals.

Bollards - There are several uses of the word in the book:
1) They are metal posts on the boat itself, usually with two metal perpendicular pegs called "ears." When tying up the boat, the lines are crisscross around the ears.
2) On the side of locks, they're for holding boats steady with ropes against the turbulence during lock operation. Boats should never be tied up in a lock. Instead, the linesman works the line by letting it out or taking it in.
3) There are bollards for mooring along walls or the side of canals. They can be metal, wooden or concrete.

Bumpers – I used the term to describe the rubber inflatable balloons which vary anywhere in shape and diameter around 10"across, to my big ball 18"across. They're used to provide a cushion the boat from walls, other boats, or piers.

Eye – The loop at the end of a line.

Fenders - Our first year, we used pieces of wood hung on the side of the boat to protect it from bumps. Now we use a more modern moulded rubber version.

Francs – French currency in 2000, with the approximate exchange rate of 6.5 francs to 1 US Dollar.

Guilders – Dutch currency in 2000. At the time, the exchange rate was about 2 Guilders to 1 US Dollar.

Lines - Ropes used on boats. "Break away" lines do just that and come in handy for items that might get caught, like our fenders.

Locks - A granite enclosure in canals or canalized rivers, with gates at each end. Locks raise or lower boats as they pass from level to level. The number of locks depends on topography, the hillier it is, the more locks there are. Without locks, canals or rivers would be un-navigable water rapids.

Metric system – Throughout the book, I reference both the metric system and our American system of measurement.

- Kilometers are about .6 of a mile.
- Meters are shade over a yard, and about 39 inches

Mooring – I used the term to mean tying the boat up to shore, usually for the night.

Mooring rings –metal rings attached to walls for mooring.

Plane trees – The English name for sycamores.

Quai/Quay - A wall for mooring boats, usually equipped with either bollards or mooring rings.

VNF – *Voies Navigables des France* The French government organization for whom lockkeepers work.

Resources

Barge and Breakfast, LLC
Find out more about our successful chartering business at
www.bargeandbreakfast.com
Contact us at info@bargeandbreakfast.com

You can also check out my personal website at
www.MichelleCaffrey.com
E-mail Michelle@MichelleCaffrey.com

Bourgogne Marine - Our homeport. Roger Walster also sells boats and
barges.
BOURGOGNE MARINE, Le port, 21170 St.Symphorien-sur-Saone, France
Tél: 03 80 39 25 63
Fax: 03 80 29 11 49
E-mail: bourgogne-marine@wanadoo.fr
web: http://bourgogne-marine.com

Dutch Barge Association (DBA)
http://www.barges.org

3 Norfolk Court, Norfolk Road, Rickmansworth, Herts, WD3 1LT, U.K.

DBA (previously known as the Dutch Barge Association), is generally but by
no means exclusively concerned with Big Old Boats from any origin
converted for living afloat and pleasure cruising in Europe. Typically these are
ex-commercial cargo vessels, often from the Netherlands or UK because those
are the best sources of craft of a suitable size.

Richard Goodwin's wonderful series *Barging Through France*, I is now
available on DVD at www.RichardGoodwin.org
See for yourself the show that aired on PBS and inspired our life-change. This
exclusive DVD collection tells the story of a slow voyage through the
legendary Provence region of France aboard an old tug boat, the Regina. At
the helm Richard Goodwin has collected an array of fascinating meetings with
beekeepers, cooks, horse breeders, chocolate makers etc. These are everyday
people living near Provance's canals and rivers whose professions, or metiers,
are extraordinary. Beautifully filmed over the seasons, Richard shares the
festivals and traditions of the villagers and townspeople he meets on his
journey. This is a collection for boat people and everyone else with an interest
in France and her rich way of life

Roger Van Dyken – our instructor and author of "Barging in Europe," now in its second edition.

http://www.bargingineurope.com

Welcome to the one stop service site for barging on the waterways of Europe. If you have questions, we have answers. Explore with us the wonderful world of cruising ancient locks, medieval villages, and great cities as you experience this unique slice of European life.

Telephone and FAX

360-354-5770

Postal address

145 East Cedar Drive
Lynden, WA 98264

General Information: info@bargingineurope.com
Webmaster: webmaster@bargingineurope.com

Information on France

The Burgundy Canal The very best information on the canals of Burgundy
http://www.burgundy-canal.com

FranceKeys.com - http//www.Europe-france.com.. France is the most-visited country in the world, and FranceKeys.com is a place where you can organize *your* visit. If you're planning a picturesque tour, a romantic getaway, or a cultural adventure, we can help.

Our information about France comes from years of work and a lifetime of experience, assembled with care for your use and enjoyment. It includes everything we can think of that might be of interest to a future traveler. You can also refresh your French with our improved **French lessons**, featuring more than 250 expressions. Whether you're a casual visitor, a student of French, or a dedicated Francophile, we have something for you, so take a trip through our web site and discover the many faces of France. ***Bon voyage!***

FranceWay.com – A wonderful travel site to arrange your trip to France, information on culture, history, facts and figures and French items for sale.
http://www.franceway.com

Travel With a Challenge – a site designed for mature travellers.

About the Author

MICHELLE CAFFREY is an owner/operator of Barge and Breakfast, one of the most successful barge chartering operations in Burgundy, France. She and her husband, Paul, travel the European Waterways from April to October on their 1906 Barge *Imagine*. The rest of the year, they wander the United States in their motor home.

Visit my website at www.MichelleCaffrey.com

I would love to hear from you at Michelle@MichelleCaffrey.com

Travel with a Challenge features richly illustrated articles on family vacation cultures and countries, cruise and train travel, nature and wildlife holidays suitable for mature travelers.

To read an excellent article on barging, click on:
http://www.travelwithachallenge.com/Barging-In-Europe.htm

Made in the USA
San Bernardino, CA
29 April 2015